JEWISH VOICES

Inspiring & Empowering Quotes from Global Thought Leaders

DANA RUBIN

wellfleet
press

Contents

artist | **Leah Bar Shalom,** *Love*

INTRODUCTION

Words and language have always occupied a place of special reverence in Jewish life. From the beginning of recorded history, the wisdom and culture of the Jewish people have been communicated through the written and spoken word. Centuries before the printing press, Jews cherished and preserved the language of their ancestors. Ancient scholars and scribes lovingly hand-lettered their books in elegant calligraphy, taught the *aleph bet*, the Hebrew alphabet, in classrooms, and debated the nuances of the sacred texts, with language analysis at the heart of religious practice, study, and prayer. High priests, rabbis, and scholars transmitted values and customs through language, and worshippers recited and repeated the ancient prayers as a communal act, as they still do today.

Nomads for centuries, the Jewish people have absorbed words and language from every place they have made their home. Like cultural magpies, they borrowed from their environment, collecting and developing new ideas and concepts but retaining a special reverence for their ancient language as an immutable fact of their identity.

In modern times, the Jewish love of language flourished in the Yiddish theaters on Second Avenue in New York City, in the resorts of the Catskill Mountains, in the lyrics of the Great American Songbook, and in London's West End. Beginning in the nineteenth century, the revival of sacred, ancestral Hebrew and its eventual adoption as a modern, breathing language in the new nation of Israel is one of the most remarkable achievements in linguistic history. This renascence of modern Hebrew has enriched the Jewish identity with a common language for connection, learning, and celebration.

In these pages you will find a mix of Hebraic quotes that incorporate Greek, Latin, and Aramaic teachings; Yiddish lore; and sayings inflected by Jewish migration to the Aegean, the Iberian Peninsula, Asia Minor, and the Russian steppes. All these are present in the Jewish voice in a rich multicultural feast.

Throughout their many journeys, Jews have also developed a distinctive mindset, a way of seeing the world that has emerged from the hardships and challenges they've faced. Waves of persecution, centuries of abuse, displacement, and upheaval have bred a certain wariness, a tendency toward fatalism, melancholy, and irony. On the flip side is the long and rich tradition of humor developed by the Jewish people to cope with the darkness; that distinctly Jewish mix of gloom and comic genius is also reflected in these pages.

In Judaism, language is intimately tied to the holidays and holy days, the worship services, life-cycle events, the Bible and religious commentaries, spiritual and cultural life, theological debate, political speech, anecdotes, proverbs, and poems—all these contribute to the diverse cornucopia of the Jewish experience. The quotations in this volume belong to poets and philosophers, artists and homemakers, scientists, scholars, and ordinary people who found themselves in extraordinary times and places. *Jewish Voices* puts a spotlight on them all.

Immersive and inspiring, this collection pays homage to the creative virtuosity, heroic endurance, and ultimate triumph of the Jewish people. Though the contributors in this book are Jewish, many of their sentiments will ring true for all, embracing everyone with the open arms and welcoming spirit of the Jewish people.

LAND OF MILK AND HONEY

The Jewish people have been bound to the Land of Israel for more than 3,700 years. In the Hebrew Bible, the land is described as "flowing with milk and honey." From the verdant highlands, snowcapped mountains, and fertile valleys of the north to the arid desert in the south, this narrow strip was the crossroads of the ancient world. At various times called Canaan, Palestine, and Eretz Yisrael, it is the birthplace of monotheism, the revolutionary belief in the oneness of God.

Two monumental Jewish temples were raised and then destroyed in Jerusalem, first by the Babylonians in 586 BCE, and then by the Romans seven hundred years later. Bereft, exiled, and dispersed, Jews turned toward Jerusalem as they prayed, seeking restoration and redemption.

But Jews also maintained a continuous presence in the Land of Israel. For centuries, religious pilgrims and holy men flocked to centers of learning like Jerusalem, Hebron, and Safed. In the late nineteenth century, thousands began fleeing persecution and poverty in Eastern Europe and settling in Palestine, then under Ottoman rule. Many thousands more sought refuge after the horrors of the Holocaust, and in 1948, the sovereign nation of Israel was born.

Israel today can mean many things—a place, a people, a nation, or a spiritual ideal. Religious Jews see the hand of God at work in the fulfillment of God's prophecy to Abraham in the Book of Genesis with the words "I will make you into a great nation." Others see the Zionist dream as the answer to thousands of years of displacement and suffering. Today, upwards of seven million Jews—more than in any other country, and nearly half the world's total Jewish population—make their home in one of the world's most advanced, technologically developed nations.

This section includes expressions of the profound ties of the Jewish people to their ancient homeland and the modern State of Israel.

artist | **Chavi Feldman,** *Star of David*

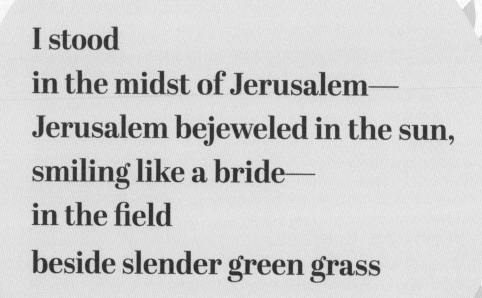

I stood
in the midst of Jerusalem—
Jerusalem bejeweled in the sun,
smiling like a bride—
in the field
beside slender green grass

ZELDA SCHNEURSON MISHKOVSKY, Israeli poet

8

Born in Chernigov, Czarist Russia, **Zelda Schneurson Mishkovsky (1914–1984)** was descended from a long line of illustrious Lubavitch Hasidic rabbis and grew up in a home steeped in Jewish tradition and mysticism. In 1926, her family settled in Jerusalem, then the capital of the British Mandate of Palestine, where she attended a religious girls' school and teacher's college. Zelda worked as a schoolteacher until her marriage in 1950, then, encouraged by her husband, she devoted herself to writing. In 1967, she published her first volume of poetry, *Penai* (meaning "Leisure"), to great acclaim. Five more bestsellers followed, all infused with vivid imagery drawn from Jewish rituals and mysticism, the religious ecstasy of Hasidism, and Russian fairy tales. Beloved in Israel and around the world, she is known to her readers simply as "Zelda."

If you will it, it is no dream.

THEODOR HERZL, playwright, novelist, and journalist

Theodor Herzl (1860–1904) was born to a secular German-speaking Jewish family in Budapest and became a playwright, novelist, and journalist. Despite his assimilation, he came to believe that Jews would never be fully accepted in Europe——a sentiment reinforced by the notorious Dreyfus affair, in which a French military officer was accused of treason because he was a Jew. In 1896, Herzl published the pamphlet *Der Judenstaat*, "The Jewish State," a proposal for a new sovereign Jewish state. The following year, he convened the First Zionist Congress in Basel, Switzerland. Herzl worked for the rest of his life to build support for the Jewish homeland but did not live to see his dream fulfilled. He died in 1904 at the age of forty-four. After the birth of the State of Israel, his remains were brought from Vienna to Jerusalem, where he was reinterred on Mount Herzl.

Melinda Strauss (b. 1983) is a Jewish educator and cookbook author who shares knowledge about her life as a Modern Orthodox Jew on Instagram and TikTok. She grew up in Seattle, where she loved helping her parents cook and bake, and she graduated from Yeshiva University. A diagnosis of type 1 diabetes led her to explore nutrition and the world of kosher food. She is passionate about pushing the boundaries of traditional kosher cuisine, and she infuses her traditional Jewish recipes with fresh and unexpected flavors. Strauss works as a health coach, motivational speaker, and author, and recently published her first kosher cookbook. She also runs a personal growth conference called Kavana—Hebrew for "intention"—where Jewish women come together for knowledge and inspiration.

I stand with Israel because when I walk around Jerusalem, every step I take is a part of my history.

MELINDA STRAUSS, Jewish content creator
and kosher cookbook author

We Jews only want that which is given naturally to all peoples of the world, to be masters of our own fate.

GOLDA MEIR, fourth prime minister of Israel

Golda Meir (1898–1978) was the first and only woman to serve as prime minister of Israel. Born in Kiev, in the Russian Empire, she immigrated to the United States as a young girl. Growing up in Milwaukee, Wisconsin, she became a passionate advocate for the Jewish homeland, and in 1921, she and her husband settled in Mandatory Palestine, where she became active in the Jewish Agency, which aided Jewish immigration. A signatory of Israel's Declaration of Independence in 1948, Meir was elected to the Knesset, Israel's parliament, and served as labor minister until 1956, when she was named foreign minister by then-prime minister David Ben-Gurion. Meir served as Israel's fourth prime minister from 1969 to 1974, when she resigned due to public outrage over the government's role in the Yom Kippur War. Meir died of lymphoma in 1978 and is buried on Mount Herzl in Jerusalem.

The trip is never too hard if you know you're going home.

CHOFETZ CHAIM (YISRAEL MEIR KAGAN),
Lithuanian rabbi, author, and ethicist

Yisrael Meir Kagan (1838–1933) was his given name, but the revered Eastern European rabbi and philosopher is more widely known today as "the Chofetz Chaim." That designation comes from his most famous book, the *Sefer Chofetz Chaim*— which, translated from Hebrew, means "seeker of life." He is most closely associated with the Jewish community in Raduń, an epicenter of Jewish cultural and spiritual life in the former Russian Empire (today Belarus), where he established a highly influential yeshiva. In 1925, the Chofetz Chaim expressed a wish to move to Eretz Yisrael. When his students and followers pushed back, saying the journey was too hard, he countered by simply saying he would be going "home." But he never made it. In 1933, the Chofetz Chaim died in Raduń at the age of ninety-five. His tomb has become a place of pilgrimage for orthodox Jews from around the world.

If I forget thee, O Jerusalem,
may my right hand forget its
cunning, may my tongue cleave
to the roof of my mouth,
if I do not remember you,
if I do not place Jerusalem
above my highest joy.

THE BIBLE, Psalms 137:5–6

In 586 BCE, the soldiers of Nebuchadnezzar II, king of Babylonia, demolished the holy temple of the Kingdom of Judah in Jerusalem. The Temple of Solomon, as it was called, had been built on the spot where God was said to have created Adam. Based on descriptions in the Bible, scholars say the temple walls and floors were lined with gold. Behind the altar of incense was the most sacred room, the Holy of Holies, entered only by the High Priest. With the Babylonian destruction, that temple and the entire city of Jerusalem were utterly destroyed. Those who weren't slain were captured and sent into exile in distant Babylonia. Psalm 137 is a foundational text of the Hebrew Bible for the Jewish people dispersed throughout the world, who remember Zion and yearn to return.

Known to her devoted social media followers by her handle @jewishlyliz, **Liz Rose (b. 1985)** shares content on kosher vegetarian cooking, Jewish living, and Israel. She grew up in Georgia with a strong Jewish identity, attended a Jewish summer camp, and graduated from Georgia State University. An active member of the Atlanta Jewish community, she served on the board of Hillels of Georgia, a regional Hillel system that provides students across twenty-four college campuses with connective strings to their Jewish lives. Rose has volunteered for the Jewish Women's Connection and PJ Library, a nonprofit that sends free Jewish books to families around the world.

Israel has a duty to protect and defend its citizens, citizens who are Jewish, who are Arab, who are Christian, who are Jews, and every other minority who is living there.

LIZ ROSE, Jewish lifestyle influencer

Enough of blood and tears! Enough!
We have no desire for revenge.
We harbor no hatred towards you.
We, like you, are people—people who want to
build a home, to plant a tree, to love, to live side
by side with you, in dignity, in empathy, as human
beings, as free men. We are today giving peace a
chance and saying to you, enough!

YITZHAK RABIN, Israeli politician, statesman, and general

Born in Jerusalem to Eastern European immigrants, **Yitzhak Rabin
(1922–1995)** studied agriculture before joining the underground Jewish
army in British Mandatory Palestine. Rising through the ranks, he served
as chief of operations during Israel's War of Independence, then joined
the nascent Israel Defense Forces, staying in the army for the next
twenty-seven years. As a politician and statesman, Rabin held many
senior positions, including two terms as prime minister. In September
1993, after secret negotiations with the Palestinians, he signed the
historic Oslo Accords, and in an emotional speech on the White House
lawn used the phrase "Enough of blood and tears!" He expanded upon
that language in a speech one week later before the Knesset, the Israeli
parliament. In 1994, Rabin was awarded the Nobel Peace Prize, along
with Foreign Minister Shimon Peres and PLO Chairperson Yasser Arafat. A
year later, Rabin was assassinated by a right-wing Jewish extremist.

DIASPORA

Nearly three thousand years ago, in 720 BCE, when Assyrians invaded and destroyed the Northern Kingdom of Israel—known as Samaria—the Israelite tribes began fleeing their ancestral homeland and became known as the Ten Lost Tribes of Israel. By the time of the Roman destruction of the Second Temple in 70 CE, more Jews were living abroad than in Palestine.

Since then, the Jewish people have continuously been uprooted and forced to abandon and rebuild their lives in a perpetual state of *galut*, or "exile." Centers of vibrant Jewish life arose and thrived in the Tigris-Euphrates valley, medieval Germany, on the Iberian Peninsula, and in Ladino-speaking communities in the Balkans, the Aegean Islands, Greece, and Turkey. But as the Jews would learn from bitter experience, periods of acceptance and good fortune were followed by persecution and repudiation. During the Spanish Inquisition in the fifteenth century, as many as three hundred thousand Jews were forced to make a horrific choice: convert to Catholicism, be killed, or flee. More than half of the population packed up and left. Nearly fifty years later, the Portuguese Inquisition sent thousands more to the Netherlands, Constantinople, and the New World.

Following the Israeli-Arab war of 1948, more than 850,000 Jews were expelled from their homes in Egypt, Iran, Lebanon, Syria, Iraq, Yemen, Libya, Morocco, and other Arab countries, where they had lived for centuries alongside their Muslim neighbors. From 1989 to 2006, more than a million Jews emigrated from the former Soviet Union after forty years of persecution. Russia's invasion of Ukraine in the winter of 2022 spurred yet another Jewish exodus from both countries.

This centuries-long wandering has shaped the unique nature of the Jewish identity. Some say the never-ending threats and constant adaptation under duress have forced Jews to be outsiders, even in the most hospitable of circumstances.

The quotations that follow explore the experience and meaning of diaspora and how it has transformed and shaped Jewish identity.

artist | **Leah Bar Shalom,** *Figs*

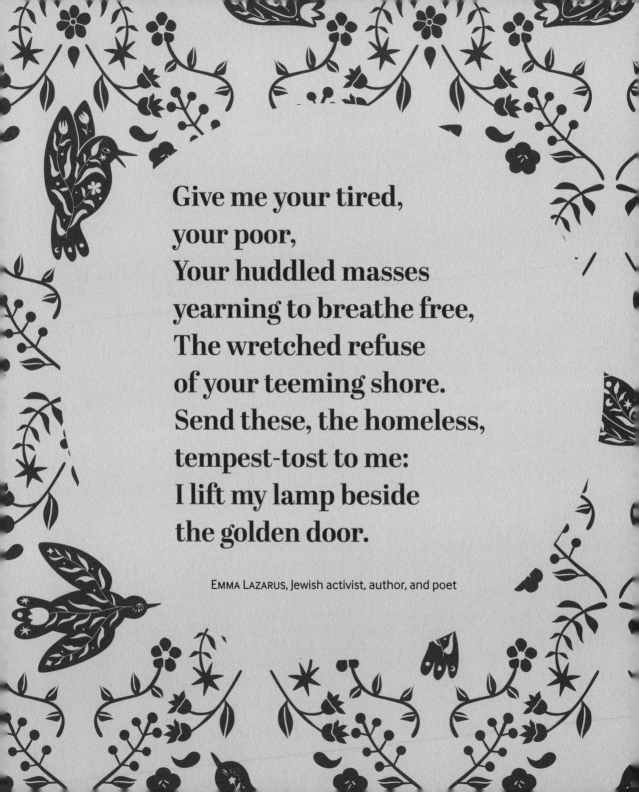

Give me your tired,
your poor,
Your huddled masses
yearning to breathe free,
The wretched refuse
of your teeming shore.
Send these, the homeless,
tempest-tost to me:
I lift my lamp beside
the golden door.

EMMA LAZARUS, Jewish activist, author, and poet

Emma Lazarus (1849–1887) grew up in the borough of Manhattan in New York City in an assimilated Sephardic Jewish family. Attracted to poetry, she penned her first verse at age eleven. In 1881, after the assassination of Tsar Alexander II, an outbreak of violent pogroms prompted thousands of Russian and Eastern European Jews to leave their homes and immigrate to the United States. Lazarus responded by writing poetry, essays, short stories, and reviews that protested the rise of antisemitism and argued for better conditions for the immigrants crowding into New York's Lower East Side. In 1883, she wrote the stirring poem "The New Colossus" for an auction raising money for the pedestal of the Statue of Liberty. Lazarus died in 1887 at age thirty-eight. Sixteen years later, her iconic words were engraved on a plaque at the base of the statue, greeting all those arriving in America in search of a new and better life.

The Jewish masses, though dispersed to the four winds of the world and mostly destitute of mere shelter—because tenacious of their creed, endure, true to themselves and to their past.

WALDEMAR HAFFKINE, Russian-French bacteriologist

A pioneer in the development of vaccines, **Waldemar Haffkine (1860–1930)** inoculated millions against cholera and bubonic plague, but his accomplishments remain little-known today. He studied in his hometown Odessa but in 1888 was barred from becoming a professor at Odessa University because he was a Jew. Working at the Louis Pasteur Institute in Paris, he risked his life by testing an experimental cholera vaccine on himself. Bolstered by his success, he relocated to India to conduct large-scale human trials. In the Calcutta slums, hundreds stood in line for hours to receive his vaccine. Haffkine was knighted by Queen Victoria and called "the savior of mankind." He spent his final years in France and Switzerland, where he rekindled his dedication to Jewish observance, and he founded a Jewish educational foundation.

The son of impoverished, Yiddish-speaking Russian immigrants in upstate New York, **Kirk Douglas (1916–2020)** was born Issur Danielovitch, known in boyhood as Izzy Demsky, and then adopted the stage name Kirk Douglas——a story lovingly told in his 1988 autobiography, *The Ragman's Son* (Simon & Schuster, 1988). Douglas supported himself through college and acting school and went on to become a major Hollywood leading man. In a long and illustrious career, he worked with several of the most renowned directors, starring in Vincente Minnelli's *Lust for Life* in 1956, and Stanley Kubrick's *Spartacus* in 1960. Douglas has been beloved by generations of Jewish audiences for his leading role in the 1966 *Cast a Giant Shadow*, portraying Colonel Mickey Marcus, a commander in the Israeli Defense Forces during the 1948 Arab–Israeli war. Among Douglas's four children is the well-known and loved actor, Michael Douglas. Kirk Douglas died in 2020 at the age of 103.

The more I studied Jewish history, the more it fascinated me. How did we survive? Lost in different parts of the world, among strange cultures—constantly persecuted. Yet, our tormentors rose and fell, and we still hung on.

KIRK DOUGLAS, American actor and filmmaker

The basis of our national idea consists in the fact that all the scattered parts of the Jewish Diaspora constitute one indivisible people, united by common interests.

Simon Dubnow, Jewish-Russian historian, writer, and activist

Despite a religious upbringing in the town of Mstislavl, in what was then Czarist Russia (today Belarus), **Simon Dubnow (1860–1941)** was drawn to the ideas of the Jewish Enlightenment. He embraced a secular, cosmopolitan lifestyle and, in the face of violent pogroms and anti-Jewish legislation, he began writing and campaigning for the political and legal rights of the Jews. In 1906, Dubnow helped found a Jewish political party, Di Folkspartei, to achieve national rights for the Jewish people. He became a historian, among the first to understand that the Jewish people could not just be defined by their religion but also by their cultural and sociological identity. He wrote many books, including a detailed history of Hasidism and the monumental ten-volume *World History of the Jewish People*. After Hitler's rise in Germany, Dubnow, then living in Berlin, fled to Riga, Latvia. When the Nazis invaded Riga in 1941, Dubnow was murdered alongside twenty-five thousand other Jews in a two-day rampage in the Rumbula Forest, known as the Rumbula Massacre.

Being Jewish means that you are part of a family that spans across the globe, through different races, ages, sexualities, political beliefs, and histories. Being Jewish means that no matter where you are in life, you have a home.

HEN MAZZIG, writer, educator, and activist

Hen Mazzig (b. 1997) is a proud Mizrachi Jew, a term applied to descendants of Jewish communities from the Middle East and North Africa. His grandparents were forced to flee Iraq and Tunisia in the early 1950s and immigrated to Israel, where he was born and raised. When he was twelve, he found himself blown out of an ice cream shop by a suicide bomb attack that killed two people, an experience that left an indelible mark. Today, he's a writer, educator, and openly homosexual man who speaks around the world about terrorism, antisemitism, his Mizrachi heritage, and LGBTQ+ rights. In 2019, he cofounded the Tel Aviv Institute, where he teaches social media strategies for activism and advocacy. He has also published a memoir, *The Wrong Kind of Jew: A Mizrahi Manifesto* (Wicked Son, 2022), which has been met with notable success.

As one of the dumb, voiceless ones I speak. One of the millions of immigrants beating, beating out their hearts at your gates for a breath of understanding.

Anzia Yezierska, Jewish-American novelist

Anzia Yezierska (1880–1970) emigrated from Czarist Russia to New York City in the early 1890s, where she and her family lived in a tenement slum on the Lower East Side of Manhattan. Her father was a Talmud scholar who did not earn a living, so Yezierska, her mother, and her sisters had to work domestic and factory jobs to bring in funds to support the family. Yezierska's literary breakthrough came with the 1920 publication of her short story collection, *Hungry Hearts*, which focused on the hardships and poverty faced by immigrants, especially women, children, and the elderly, and their bittersweet pursuit of the American Dream. The stories became the basis of an acclaimed silent film of the same name by Samuel Goldwyn in 1922. Yezierska went on to write many short stories and novels, including 1923's *Children of Loneliness*, depicting the challenges of immigrant life.

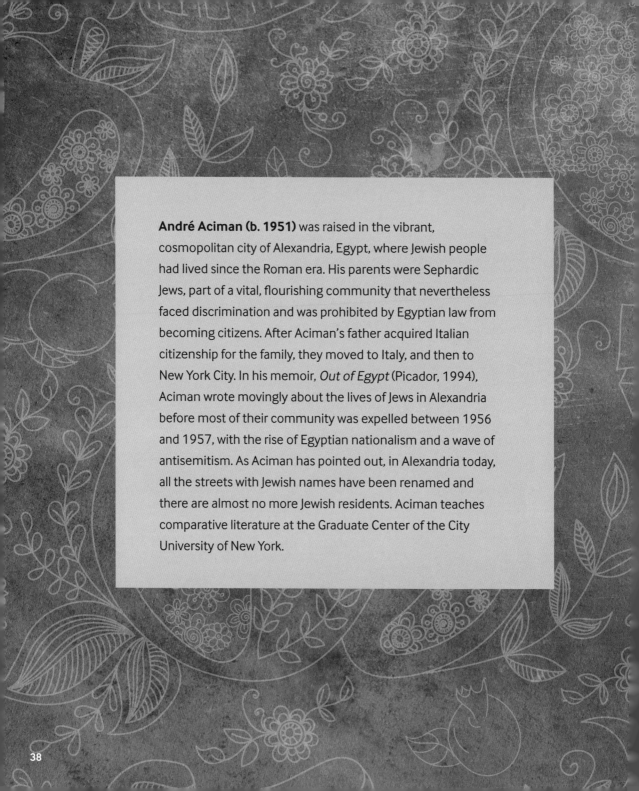

André Aciman (b. 1951) was raised in the vibrant, cosmopolitan city of Alexandria, Egypt, where Jewish people had lived since the Roman era. His parents were Sephardic Jews, part of a vital, flourishing community that nevertheless faced discrimination and was prohibited by Egyptian law from becoming citizens. After Aciman's father acquired Italian citizenship for the family, they moved to Italy, and then to New York City. In his memoir, *Out of Egypt* (Picador, 1994), Aciman wrote movingly about the lives of Jews in Alexandria before most of their community was expelled between 1956 and 1957, with the rise of Egyptian nationalism and a wave of antisemitism. As Aciman has pointed out, in Alexandria today, all the streets with Jewish names have been renamed and there are almost no more Jewish residents. Aciman teaches comparative literature at the Graduate Center of the City University of New York.

An exile is not just someone who has lost his home; it is someone who can't find another. Some no longer even know what home means. They reinvent the concept with what they've got, the way we reinvent love with what's left of it each time. Some people bring exile with them the way they bring it upon themselves wherever they go.

André Aciman, writer, teacher, and historian

ART AND CULTURE

The songs of Irving Berlin are often said to have captured the essence of the American dream and contributed to what's lovingly known as the Great American Songbook. But more than three decades before Berlin (born Israel Beilin) wrote the seasonal classic "White Christmas," he scribbled a little tune called "Yiddle, on Your Fiddle, Play Some Rag Time."

Berlin was just one of a multitude of musicians, artists, writers, actors, and entertainers around the world with Jewish roots who are disproportionately represented in creative realms. Historians have compared the achievements of the Jewish people in the arts to the Greeks in the Age of Pericles, the Italians during the Renaissance, the Dutch during the Golden Age. Their story is an unparalleled explosion of creativity amid oppression, joy amidst horror, and creation as an act of resistance and survival.

From 1941 to 1945, at the Theresienstadt concentration camp in Czechoslovakia—a transit stop for Auschwitz-Birkenau and other death camps—inmates produced an extraordinary outpouring of poetry readings, lectures, concerts, storytelling sessions, and theatrical performances. As the renowned theologian Rabbi Leo Baeck recalled, "In the sheltering darkness of the long evenings, they gathered in the cold and gloomy attic of a barrack, just under the roof. There they stood, pressed close to each other, to hear a talk about the Bible and the Talmud, about Plato, Aristotle, Maimonides, about Descartes and Spinoza, about Locke and Hume and Kant, or about days and problems of history, about poetry and art and music, about Palestine of old and of today, about the Commandments, the Prophets, and the Messianic idea. All those hours were hours in which a community arose out of the mass and the narrowness grew wide."

This section features quotes by Jewish artists whose reflections on the creative process reveal the large tapestry of the Jewish artistic experience.

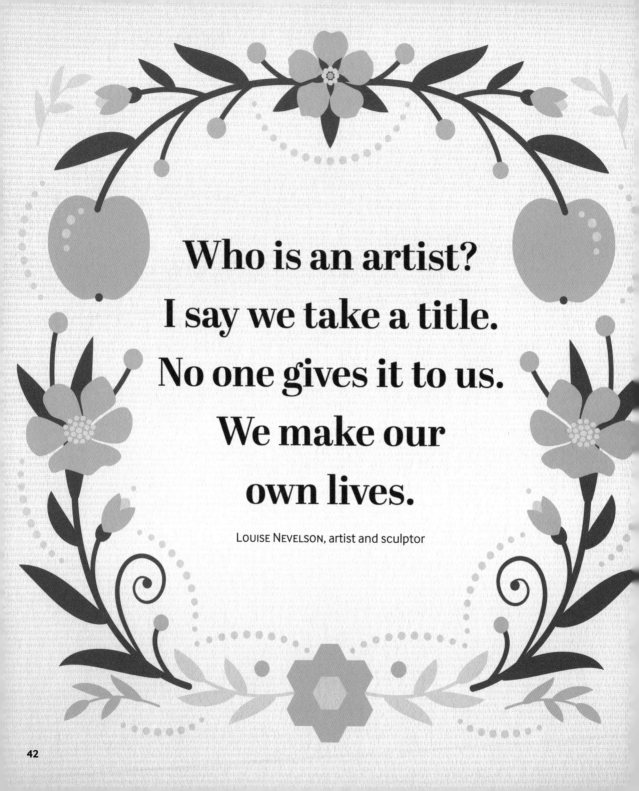

Who is an artist? I say we take a title. No one gives it to us. We make our own lives.

LOUISE NEVELSON, artist and sculptor

Louise Nevelson (1899–1998) emigrated as a child from Russia to Rockland, Maine. Her father worked in a lumber yard where Louise fell in love with the texture and warmth of wood and made her earliest sculptures. Yiddish was her first language, spoken at home, but she learned English in school. When she moved to Manhattan, Nevelson studied at the Art Students League, a nurturing ground for struggling artists, and she experimented with painting, printing, and small sculptures. Eventually, her scale enlarged as she began salvaging discarded objects and incorporating them into wall pieces and outdoor sculptures. Nevelson's later work is monochromatic and often monumental in size. Iconoclastic and imposing, Nevelson is considered a leading sculptor of the 20th century.

Art, in itself, is an attempt to bring order out of chaos.

Stephen Sondheim, Broadway composer and lyricist

Stephen Sondheim (1930–2021) learned the craft of writing lyrics for musical theater sitting at the feet—or on the piano bench—of the great Oscar Hammerstein II. Sondheim was just a teenager and by a stroke of fortune, a neighbor of Hammerstein's. The many side-by-side piano mentoring sessions that followed proved to be the lucky break that set Sondheim on his own path to greatness. He went on to find Broadway success with lyrics for the hits *West Side Story* and *Gypsy*, then began writing both lyrics and music for a string of warmly received and critically acclaimed works such as *A Funny Thing Happened on the Way to the Forum, Company, A Little Night Music*, and *Sunday in the Park with George*. Just as he was mentored, Sondheim returned the favor by encouraging other emerging talents such as Jonathan Larson and Adam Guettel. Sondheim passed away in 2021, but his work is now more popular than ever.

A native New Yorker and lifelong bookworm, **Zibby Owens (b. 1976)** transformed her love of literature into Zibby Media, her company that includes her own publishing house, Zibby Books; a literary lifestyle magazine, *Zibby Mag*; a book club; an independent bookstore in Santa Monica, Zibby Books; and an award-winning book review podcast called *Moms Don't Have Time to Read Books*. Owens is involved in the Jewish community and has served as a judge for the National Jewish Book Awards. In the spring of 2024, she published her debut novel, *Blank: A Novel* (Little A, 2024) about love, family, friendship, and her journey of self-discovery.

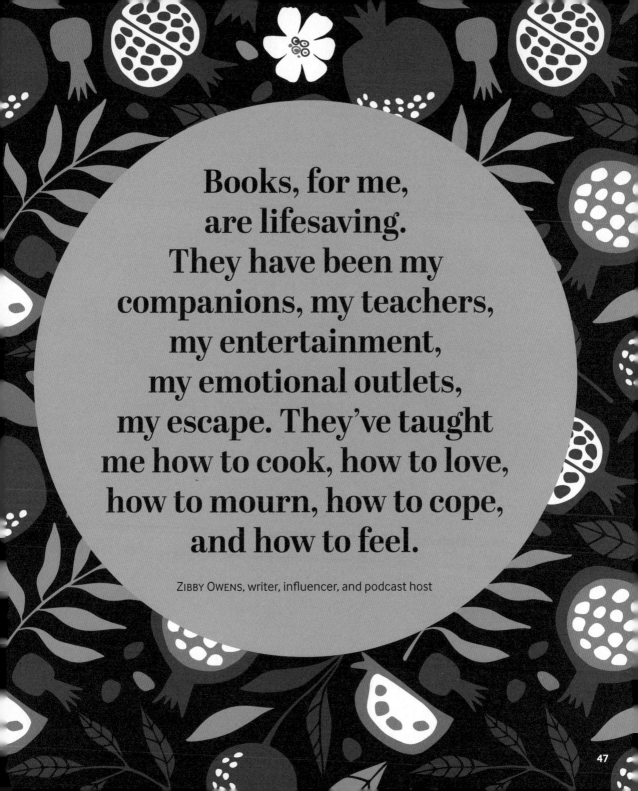

Books, for me, are lifesaving. They have been my companions, my teachers, my entertainment, my emotional outlets, my escape. They've taught me how to cook, how to love, how to mourn, how to cope, and how to feel.

ZIBBY OWENS, writer, influencer, and podcast host

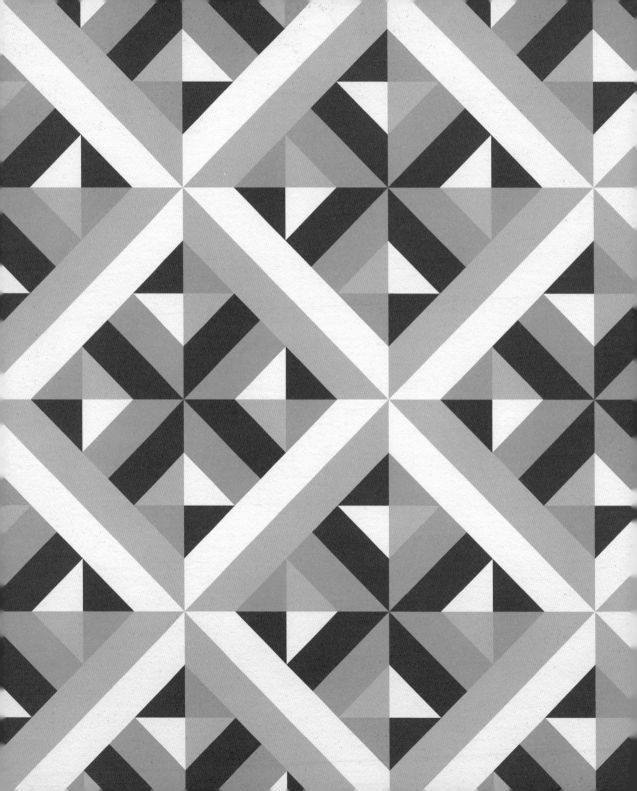

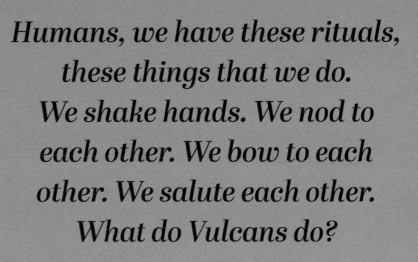

> *Humans, we have these rituals, these things that we do. We shake hands. We nod to each other. We bow to each other. We salute each other. What do Vulcans do?*

LEONARD NIMOY, American actor

Leonard Nimoy (1931–2015) developed his singing voice as a young man in his synagogue choir in the West End of Boston. At his bar mitzvah at age thirteen, he performed so well he was asked to repeat his Torah portion the following week at another synagogue. Nimoy's acting career took off in 1966 when he agreed to play the cool, logical Mr. Spock on a new science-fiction television series, *Star Trek*. He came up with the hand gesture that became the Vulcan Salute, and, together with writer Theodore Sturgeon, the greeting "Live long and prosper!"—both borrowed from the Hebrew priestly benediction from the ancient Temple. *Star Trek* lasted only three seasons, but the iconic franchise is still going strong thanks to legions of devoted science-fiction fans and "Trekkies." Despite many other roles and accomplishments, the Spock character remains Nimoy's most prized and enduring contribution to American culture.

I cannot and will not cut my conscience to fit this year's fashions.

LILLIAN HELLMAN, playwright, memoirist, and screenwriter

Lillian Hellman (1905–1984) was one of the most outspoken women on the cultural landscape of the 1940s, but she's widely remembered today for what she didn't say. A playwright, screenwriter, and author, she got caught up, like so many others, in Cold War politics. She was the writer of a string of popular film scripts and plays in the 1930s, including the Broadway hit *The Children's Hour* and the Academy Award-nominated *Little Foxes*. But in 1952, at the height of Senator Joe McCarthy's anti-Communist crusade, Hellman was called before the House Un-American Activities Committee. Asked about her Communist ties, she adamantly refused to "name names" and implicate her peers. Her indignant rejection of "this year's fashions," in a letter to HUAC Chairman John S. Wood has gone down in history as a principled stand during a time of rank cowardice and political acquiescence.

We meet aliens every day who have something to give us. They come in the form of people with different opinions.

WILLIAM SHATNER, Canadian actor

William Shatner (b. 1931) was only six years old when he had his first acting experience at a Jewish summer camp in the mountains north of Montreal. While attending McGill University, he performed in a variety of stage, film, and television roles, but it was the role of Captain James T. Kirk in NBC's science-fiction series *Star Trek* that changed his life. He occupied the captain's chair of the Starship Enterprise for three seasons before the show was canceled, but *Star Trek* developed a cult following that exploded into a pop cultural phenomenon. Seven movies followed, along with video games, novels, comic books, and conventions, cementing *Star Trek*'s status as one of America's most iconic media franchises. In almost every episode of *Star Trek*, the crew of the Starship Enterprise came into contact with a fictional alien race and were forced to navigate the cultural differences, exposing American audiences to important messages about empathy and inclusion.

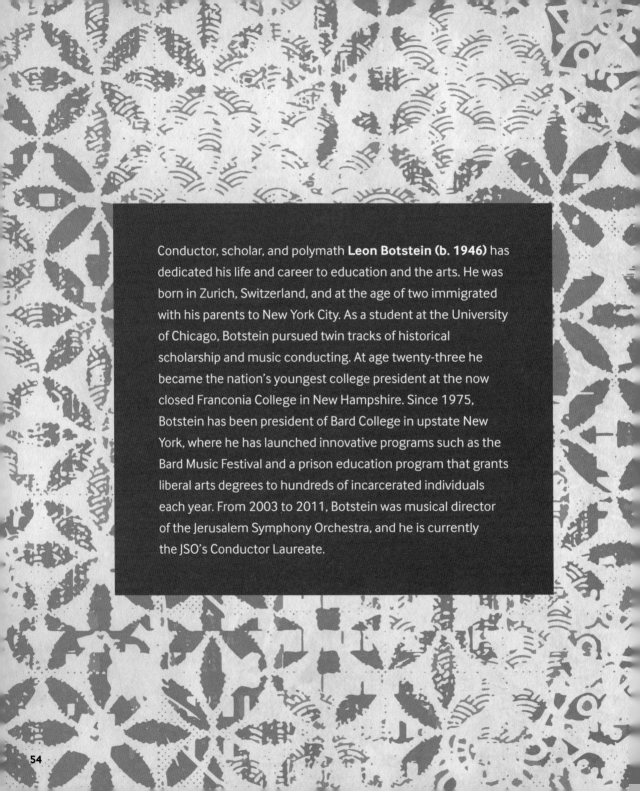

Conductor, scholar, and polymath **Leon Botstein (b. 1946)** has dedicated his life and career to education and the arts. He was born in Zurich, Switzerland, and at the age of two immigrated with his parents to New York City. As a student at the University of Chicago, Botstein pursued twin tracks of historical scholarship and music conducting. At age twenty-three he became the nation's youngest college president at the now closed Franconia College in New Hampshire. Since 1975, Botstein has been president of Bard College in upstate New York, where he has launched innovative programs such as the Bard Music Festival and a prison education program that grants liberal arts degrees to hundreds of incarcerated individuals each year. From 2003 to 2011, Botstein was musical director of the Jerusalem Symphony Orchestra, and he is currently the JSO's Conductor Laureate.

Our capacity to create something that is not useful, that's only understood by mortals, that's only within the human experience, and that is beyond the provable and everyday, that is unpredictable —that is the highest praise we can give for being human.

LEON BOTSTEIN, Swiss-American conductor, educator, and scholar

Those who burn books will in the end burn people.

HEINRICH HEINE, poet, writer, and literary critic

Heinrich Heine (1797–1856) set his 1821 play, "Almansor," against the backdrop of Spain's sixteenth-century conquest of the Moors. One line in that play, referring to the burning of the Qur'an, is considered one of history's most chilling prophecies. Heine was born into a Jewish family in Düsseldorf but as a young man converted to Lutheranism—which historians explain as his attempt to assimilate into European culture. Heine himself called it his "entry ticket," and he expressed ambivalence toward religion all his life. He went on to become one of Germany's most celebrated and esteemed authors. Long after his death, Heine's books, together with those of Albert Einstein, Thomas Mann, Ernest Hemingway, Karl Marx, and others deemed "un-German" by the Nazis— twenty thousand books in all—were tossed into a bonfire in Berlin. Heine's prophetic words are now engraved on a plaque at that same spot, on Bebelplatz, to memorialize Nazi atrocities.

LAUGHTER AND TEARS

From ancient times to the Borscht Belt, from Hollywood to Comedy Central, Jewish people have found wit and humor in the human condition, bringing smiles and laughter to Jews and non-Jews alike. Religion professor Howard R. Macy traces the roots of this sensibility to the Bible, where the word for laughter—"yitzhak"— makes an appearance when a ninety-year-old Sarah gives birth to Isaac. As Macy says: "Abraham laughs, Sarah laughs, everybody else laughs, and they name the baby 'laughter.'" But is there a particular Jewish flavor to the jokes? Like other forms of expression, Jewish humor emerges from the essential contours of the Jewish experience. Centuries of displacement, adversity, and hardships have left the Jews with a sober sense of reality. Comedian and actor Walter Matthau was once asked, "When are you going to do serious stuff?" His reply was, "Are you crazy? My serious stuff *is* my comedy."

Or, as the age-old joke goes: The Jewish pessimist says, "Oh my God, things could not be worse," while the Jewish optimist says, "Of course they could!" But the Jewish predicament has also imbued Jewish people with irrepressible optimism and faith in better times ahead. No matter how dark their suffering, they have always looked to a brighter future, from the Promised Land to the streets of America paved with gold to the coming of the "Mashiach," or Messiah. That signature optimism often finds expression in dark humor, irony, and satire. Some say that the Jewish brand of satire takes power back from oppressors; others say that it demonstrates resilience; and some call it an admirable form of self-preservation through self-depreciation. But one thing can be agreed upon: Jewish humor has contributed to the most significant achievements of comedy around the world and across time.

This section demonstrates the range of Jewish laughter and tears, two extremes of the emotional spectrum mixed into a bittersweet but truly hilarious brew.

artist | **Eleyor Snir,** *Open Hands*

What makes
Jewish humor unique
is that it has a deep
self-critical content. It is
an antidote to pomposity.
A good shtuch—a shtuch is
a jab—into an inflated ego
is what a good joke
can do.

MOSHE WALDOKS, teacher, storyteller, and comedian

Raised in a Yiddish-speaking home in Toledo, Ohio, **Moshe Waldoks (b. 1949)** is the son of Yidel Waldoks, whose wife and daughter were murdered by the Nazis in the wake of the *Einsatzgruppen*, the Nazi mobile killing units that entered Poland in 1941. His own mother, along with his aunt and grandmother, were survivors of a Nazi camp in Czechoslovakia. But this dark history did not rip humor from his household. Along with co-editor William Novak, he published *The Big Book of Jewish Humor* (HarperCollins) in 1981. He is credited for writing over two hundred cable television shows, *Aleph* being the first Jewish show to be televised in the Boston area. While his commendable reach can't be covered in only a few words, he is well known for his unparalleled stand-up comedy, storytelling, activism, and philosophy and has performed for hundreds of communities across the United States and Canada.

Crankiness is at the essence of all comedy.

JERRY SEINFELD, stand-up comedian, actor, writer, and producer

In 1988, **Jerry Seinfeld (b. 1954)** was invited by NBC to create a sitcom pilot. He turned to his friend Larry David for help with the premise. That show became *Seinfeld*, featuring a fictionalized version of Seinfeld and his close-knit circle of friends in New York City. The show had a distinctly Jewish sensibility, and many characters with Jewish backgrounds. But NBC president Brandon Tartikoff (himself Jewish) had doubts—it was "too New York, too Jewish"—before ordering the smallest possible number of episodes. *Seinfeld* ran for nine seasons, from 1989–1998, and is considered one of the most influential television shows of all time. As a stand-up comedian, Seinfeld incorporates the classic Jewish themes of pessimism, neurosis, self-deprecation, and kvetching (Yiddish for "complaining"). He has said he inherited his parents' sense of humor, especially his "wildly funny" father, who kept a file cabinet stuffed with jokes.

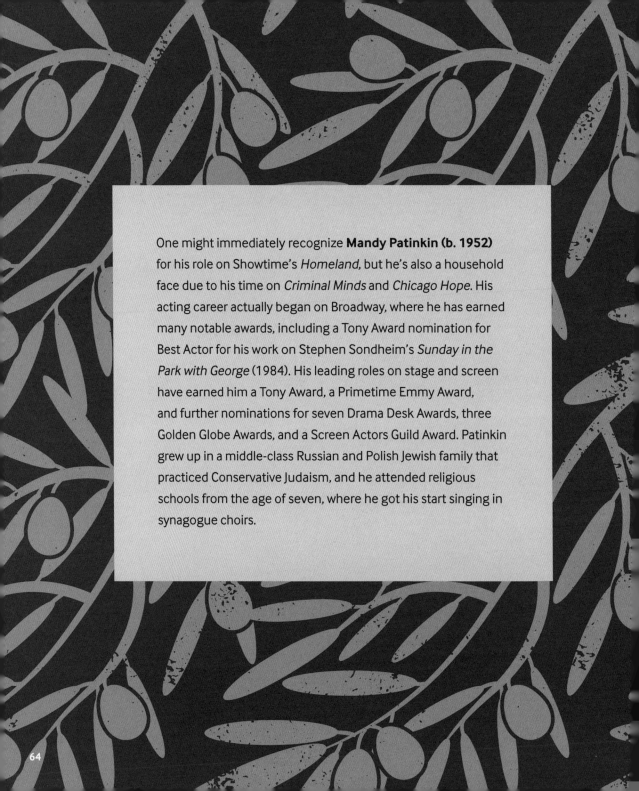

One might immediately recognize **Mandy Patinkin (b. 1952)** for his role on Showtime's *Homeland,* but he's also a household face due to his time on *Criminal Minds* and *Chicago Hope.* His acting career actually began on Broadway, where he has earned many notable awards, including a Tony Award nomination for Best Actor for his work on Stephen Sondheim's *Sunday in the Park with George* (1984). His leading roles on stage and screen have earned him a Tony Award, a Primetime Emmy Award, and further nominations for seven Drama Desk Awards, three Golden Globe Awards, and a Screen Actors Guild Award. Patinkin grew up in a middle-class Russian and Polish Jewish family that practiced Conservative Judaism, and he attended religious schools from the age of seven, where he got his start singing in synagogue choirs.

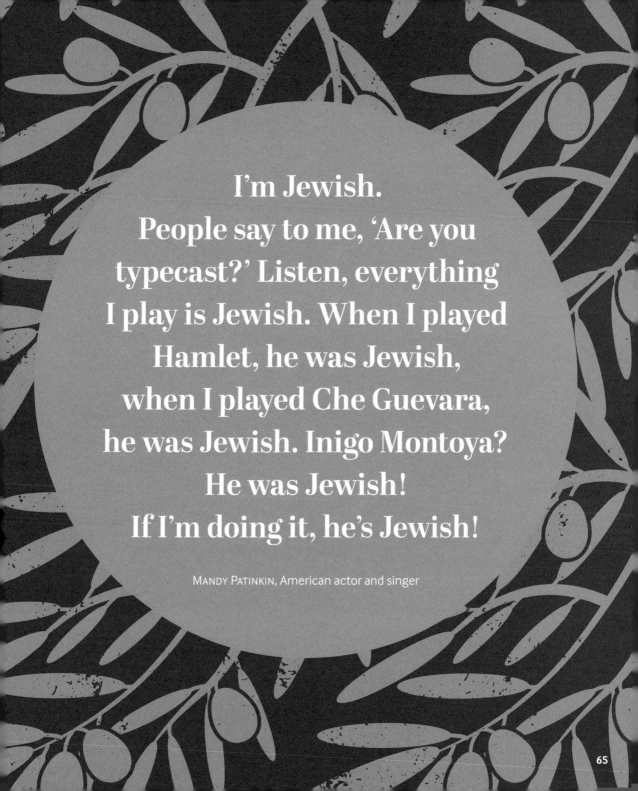

I'm Jewish.
People say to me, 'Are you typecast?' Listen, everything I play is Jewish. When I played Hamlet, he was Jewish, when I played Che Guevara, he was Jewish. Inigo Montoya? He was Jewish!
If I'm doing it, he's Jewish!

MANDY PATINKIN, American actor and singer

In our world right now, there is nothing more frightening than choosing life. It is an idea that will require the most brave, creative, and heroic efforts and strength imaginable for those who are willing—amidst ongoing trauma, angst, and suspicion—to build an idea of a future. In most conflicts, there are two sides, and neither side is going anywhere. So, all over our world, we have got to learn to live together. Or all over the world, we are going to die together.

RACHEL GOLDBERG-POLIN, American Israeli activist

Rachel Goldberg-Polin (b. 1970) is an American Israeli deeply committed to resolving the hostage crisis sparked by Hamas-led attacks on Israel in October 2023. Her son, Hersh Goldberg-Polin, was among the victims abducted during the Re'im Music Festival. Rachel quit her job to focus entirely on advocating for the release of her son and the other hostages. She has emerged as a prominent advocate for hostage families, engaging with world leaders like President Joe Biden and addressing the United Nations and Pope Francis. Her relentless dedication earned her recognition in *TIME*'s 100 Most Influential People of 2024 list. Originally from Chicago, Illinois, Rachel now resides in Jerusalem with her husband Jonathan and their children.

Laughter forces air into and out of our lungs—it keeps us alive and motivated even in the worst of circumstances.

Esther D. Kustanowitz, American writer, editor, and consultant

When teaching the skills of improv theater, **Esther D. Kustanowitz (b. 1971)** sees similarities with Jewish communal life: Everyone is equal, everyone is expected to participate, and everyone is responsible for the group's success. Based in Los Angeles, Kustanowitz explores Jewish identity and pop culture in *The Bagel Report,* a podcast she cohosts with journalist Erin Ben-Moche. A self-described "entertainment junkie," Kustanowitz also writes about television, film, and Jewish life in Southern California and beyond. She is the author of *The Hidden Children of the Holocaust: Teens Who Hid from the Nazis* (Rosen, 1999). Kustanowitz grew up in New Jersey and draws literary inspiration from her mother, Shulamit E. Kustanowitz, a writer of children's books, fiction, and journalism, who passed away in 2011.

Life continues, and while the pain never goes away, new blessings come into your life. And there is love and laughter, even with the pain.

CHANIE APFELBAUM, writer, cookbook author, lifestyle influencer, and blogger

Chanie Apfelbaum (b. 1981) is the author of the delightful cookbooks *Millennial Kosher* (Mesorah Publications, 2018) and *Totally Kosher* (Clarkson Potter, 2023), in which she blends traditional Jewish cooking with a contemporary millennial perspective. Devoted followers of her kosher lifestyle blog, *Busy in Brooklyn*, and her @busyinbrooklyn Instagram adore her reimagined traditional recipes and practical advice on keeping a kosher kitchen and lifestyle. Apfelbaum takes pride in her namesake, Rebbetzin Chana Schneerson, mother of the venerable Rabbi Menachem Mendel Schneerson, the Lubavitcher rebbe. In 1994, Apfelbaum's sixteen-year-old brother, Ari Halberstam, a close protégé of the rebbe, was killed when a gunman opened fire on a van of Jewish schoolboys on the Brooklyn Bridge. This tragedy irreparably transformed her family, but through their grief they find ways every day to celebrate life. Apfelbaum sees her exploration of contemporary Jewish tradition, ancient history, and deeply rooted culture as a way of paying tribute to her brother.

Ohad Naharin (b. 1952) is an Israeli dancer and choreographer whose innovative explorations of movement have become highly influential in the modern dance world. Raised in an artistic family on a kibbutz in northern Israel, he began his training in 1974 with the renowned Tel Aviv–based Batsheva Dance Company, founded in 1964 as an interpreter of the work of Martha Graham. Naharin then danced with the Martha Graham Company in New York City and attended The Julliard School and the School of American Ballet. Returning to Israel, he rejoined Batsheva as director and choreographer, transforming the company into a vehicle for an improvisational style of movement he called Gaga——a word that, to him, conveys a sense of openness and playfulness. Gaga training is intended both for expert dancers and the general public. After thirty years at the helm of Batsheva, Naharin stepped down in 2018 and now has the position of house choreographer.

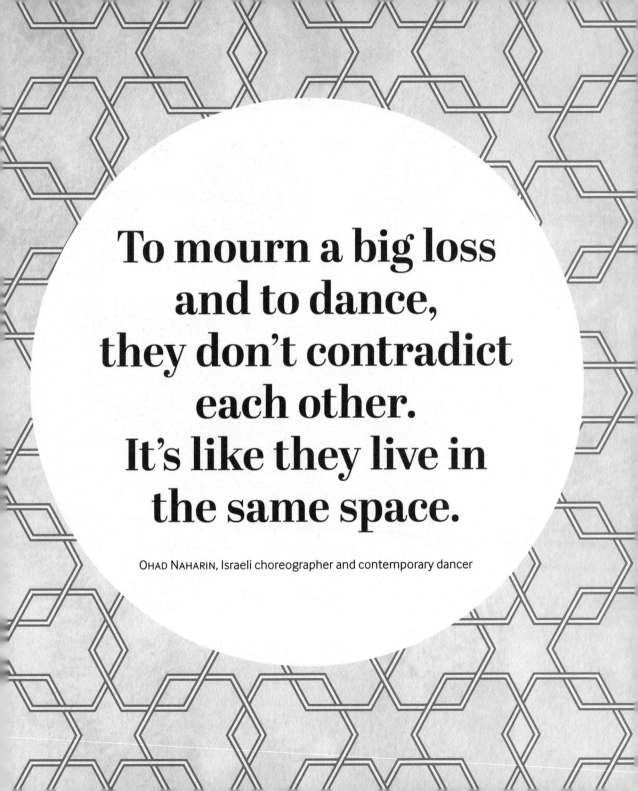

To mourn a big loss and to dance, they don't contradict each other. It's like they live in the same space.

OHAD NAHARIN, Israeli choreographer and contemporary dancer

I'm Black and Jewish, which means I'm proud, but I feel guilty about it.

RAIN PRYOR, actress and comedian

✡

Just as **Rain Pryor (b. 1969)** was starting to write her 2005 memoir, her father, Richard Pryor, passed away. Despite feeling "in a fog" during that time, eventually she published *Jokes My Father Never Taught Me*, in which she describes growing up in an unstable, mixed-race home with an absent father and a party-loving mother whose parents, Ashkenazi Jews, partly raising her. Their home was "a typical middle-class Jewish household" where she absorbed their culture and traditions. Pryor went into acting and had early success playing a rapping tomboy in the ABC television series *Head of the Class*. She also headlined alongside her father at The Comedy Store on Hollywood's Sunset Strip. In 2004, she hit the road with a one-woman show, *Fried Chicken & Latkes*, mining humor in her dual identity. Pryor is also outspoken about the need to develop new treatments for multiple sclerosis, the disease that incapacitated her father before he died.

ANTISEMITISM
AND THE HOLOCAUST

Historians say the first recorded antisemitic attack occurred in 38 BCE in Alexandria, then part of the Roman Empire. Writer and philosopher Philo Judaeus was an eyewitness; he saw synagogues attacked, Jews tortured and stoned, and entire families set on fire. That was the start of centuries of catastrophe for the Jewish people.

Antisemitic attacks increased with the rise of Christianity in Europe. Jews were accused of murdering children to use their blood in religious rituals, the notorious "blood libel." Tens of thousands of Jews were slaughtered in the Crusades, and in the following centuries, Jews in many parts of Europe were confined to ghettos, excluded from universities, and barred from countless trades and professions.

Then came the singular experience of the Holocaust, when the Nazis systematically and sadistically exterminated six million Jews in mass shootings, gas chambers, and through starvation, deprivation, and sheer brutality, a disaster known to Jews as the Shoah ("calamity" in Hebrew). Not until the creation of the State of Israel in 1948 could all Jewish people take refuge in their own land. Out of the ashes of the Holocaust came the resounding resolution: "Never Again."

Far from disappearing, antisemitism in the twenty-first century is on the rise. In 2018, eleven Jews were gunned down as they prayed at a synagogue in Pittsburgh, Pennsylvania. On October 7, 2023, Hamas terrorists from Gaza butchered more than 1,200 Israelis in cold blood, the largest number of Jewish deaths since the Holocaust. The cries of "slaughter the Jews" reverberate through century upon century of Jewish trauma.

This section brings together quotes that recall those searing memories, stare current antisemitism in its ugly face, and summon the Jewish resolve to create light in the face of evil.

artist | **Chavi Feldman,** *Dove Peace*

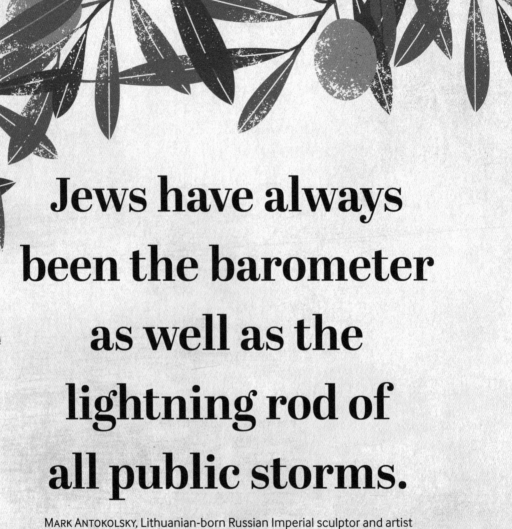

Jews have always been the barometer as well as the lightning rod of all public storms.

MARK ANTOKOLSKY, Lithuanian-born Russian Imperial sculptor and artist

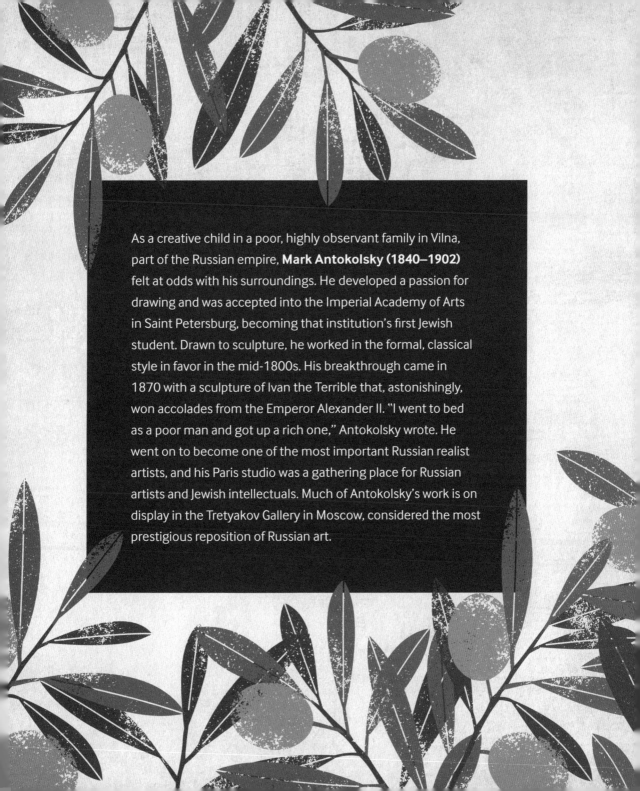

As a creative child in a poor, highly observant family in Vilna, part of the Russian empire, **Mark Antokolsky (1840–1902)** felt at odds with his surroundings. He developed a passion for drawing and was accepted into the Imperial Academy of Arts in Saint Petersburg, becoming that institution's first Jewish student. Drawn to sculpture, he worked in the formal, classical style in favor in the mid-1800s. His breakthrough came in 1870 with a sculpture of Ivan the Terrible that, astonishingly, won accolades from the Emperor Alexander II. "I went to bed as a poor man and got up a rich one," Antokolsky wrote. He went on to become one of the most important Russian realist artists, and his Paris studio was a gathering place for Russian artists and Jewish intellectuals. Much of Antokolsky's work is on display in the Tretyakov Gallery in Moscow, considered the most prestigious reposition of Russian art.

Hatred toward the Jew needs no system, discipline, or methodology. All you need do is allow yourself to be carried along, allow the hatred to drag you, overwhelm you, imprint itself upon you, arouse your imagination, your phobias, your areas of impotence and omnipotence, reticence and impunity.

JACOBO TIMERMAN, Soviet-born Argentine publisher, journalist, and author

Argentinian journalist and publisher **Jacobo Timerman (1923–1999)** gained international recognition for writing about the repression and antisemitism of his country's military dictatorship during the so-called Dirty War from 1974 to 1983. Arrested without charges in Buenos Aires, Timerman was imprisoned and tortured—from that experience came his 1981 bestselling memoir, *Prisoner Without a Name, Cell Without a Number*. Some said that Timerman exaggerated the extent of antisemitism and the vulnerability of the Jewish population in Argentina, the largest Jewish community in South America. But in 1994, a truck bomb at the Argentine-Israelite Mutual Association in Buenos Aires killed eighty-five people and injured more than 300. Security experts blamed the explosion on the Lebanese-based militant group Hezbollah, supported by Iran. Timerman remained an outspoken advocate for human rights until his death in 1999.

Daniel Pearl (1963–2002) grew up in Southern California and became a journalist, joining the *Wall Street Journal* in 1990. While reporting on terrorism after the attacks of September 11, he was abducted on his way to what he believed was an interview with a leading figure in the Islamic Movement. The kidnapping took place in downtown Karachi, Pakistan, and nine days later he was beheaded by his captor, Khalid Shaikh Mohammed. In the video produced just seconds before he was murdered, Pearl made this proud, unwavering declaration of his Jewish identity. He was thirty-eight years old and left behind his grieving parents, two sisters, and his wife, Mariane Pearl, who gave birth to their son just four months later. In his memory, his family established The Daniel Pearl Foundation to combat extremism and support voices of moderation through educational and cultural programs.

My name is Daniel Pearl.
I'm a Jewish-American from Encino, California, USA . . .
My father is Jewish, my mother is Jewish, I am Jewish.

DANIEL PEARL, American journalist

We all have a responsibility to stand up. Words matter. Hate speech begets hate crimes.

Josh Shapiro, 48th governor of Pennsylvania

Growing up in Philadelphia, **Josh Shapiro (b. 1973)** attended Jewish day schools and developed a strong kinship with fellow Jews around the world. Proactive from the age of six, he started a global letter-writing campaign on behalf of Soviet Jews, or "refuseniks," who were neither allowed to openly practice their Judaism nor leave the Soviet Union. He served in the Pennsylvania House of Representatives, on the Montgomery County Board of Commissioners, and in 2016, became the state attorney general. In that position, he became known for his dogged investigation into the Catholic clergy's sexual abuse cover-up. Shapiro has served as governor of Pennsylvania since January 2023 and is outspoken about his Jewish faith and support for Israel. In the wake of the horrific attacks in southern Israel on October 7, 2023, Shapiro used his visibility and platform to take a strong stand against destructive misinformation and hate speech.

Elie Wiesel (1928–2016) was born in the village of Sighet in the Carpathian Mountains of Romania. At age fifteen, the Jewish community was confined to a ghetto and then deported to Auschwitz, where Wiesel's entire family perished. He resettled in France and became a journalist. After ten years of silence, in 1955 he published a nine-hundred-page eyewitness account of his experiences, *Un di velt hot geshvign* (*And the World Remained Silent*), later abridged and published as *Nuit* (*Night*). For his dedication to speaking out against violence, repression, and racism, in 1986, he was awarded the Nobel Peace Prize.

We have been accused of everything in
the world for the last two thousand years at least.
Of poisoning the wells. Of creating diseases.
Of spreading diseases. Of being too rich or too poor.
Ignorant. Too learned. Too successful or not enough.
Too believing. Too religious, or too atheistic.
There isn't—literally—there isn't an accusation in
the world that has not been leveled against us.
All of these things, of course, were nonsense. Simply
hatred. They hated us because we were different.

ELIE WIESEL, Romanian-born American writer, professor,
political activist, Nobel laureate, and Holocaust survivor

I was bullied for being Jewish in the town I grew up in and was made to feel embarrassed for my Judaism. Now I am proud to be descended from survivors of Auschwitz.

AMY SCHUMER, comedian, screenwriter, producer, and director

Amy Schumer (b. 1981) has a gift for finding humor in the difficult challenges of life. Growing up on Long Island, she struggled to be socially accepted after her parents divorced. The kids called her Amy "Jewmer" and threw pennies at her. Humor became her defense. Her first big break came on the NBC talent show *Last Comic Standing*, which opened doors to higher-profile roles. In 2015, she wrote and played the lead role in the romantic comedy *Trainwreck*, which became a box-office hit. Since then, her career as a stand-up comedian, writer, and director has skyrocketed. She has been vocal about the dangers of antisemitism and her pride in her Jewish identity.

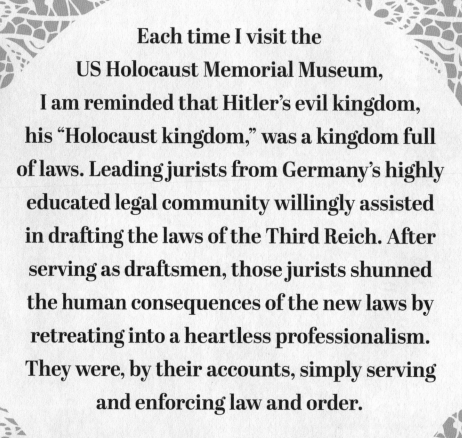

Each time I visit the
US Holocaust Memorial Museum,
I am reminded that Hitler's evil kingdom,
his "Holocaust kingdom," was a kingdom full
of laws. Leading jurists from Germany's highly
educated legal community willingly assisted
in drafting the laws of the Third Reich. After
serving as draftsmen, those jurists shunned
the human consequences of the new laws by
retreating into a heartless professionalism.
They were, by their accounts, simply serving
and enforcing law and order.

Ruth Bader Ginsburg,
Justice of the Supreme Court of the United States

Born and raised in an Orthodox Jewish home in the borough of Brooklyn in New York City, **Ruth Bader Ginsburg (1933–2020)** became a trailblazing American lawyer and judge who served as a justice of the US Supreme Court for twenty-seven years. Much of her long legal career was devoted to changing US laws to promote gender equality and women's rights. She spoke often about her pride in her Jewish faith and tradition and the Jewish values that formed the foundation of her jurisprudence. On the wall of her legal chamber was the commandment from Deuteronomy: *Zedek, zedek, tirdof*—"Justice, justice, shall you pursue." A champion of human rights, a role model to many, and a shining example of how to stick up for the underdog, Ginsburg is lovingly known as the Notorious RBG.

> # *To our non-Jewish friends, we don't need to know if you would hide us in your attics. We don't need people to hide us. We need you to come out of hiding and stand with us.*

Noa Tishby, Israeli actress, writer, producer, and activist

An accomplished actress, **Noa Tishby (b. 1975)** has appeared in a multitude of American television shows, including *The Affair, Nip/Tuck, The Island, Big Love,* and *NCIS.* This work has given her a gateway to help produce and adapt several Israeli shows into American entertainment through her production company, Noa's Arc. A Zionist activist, she founded the organization Act for Israel, which provides support and visibility for major Jewish issues, before publishing her first book, *Israel: A Simple Guide to the Most Misunderstood Country on Earth* (Free Press, 2021). She is a strong and outspoken advocate for Israel and many turn to her as a leader in the Zionist Movement.

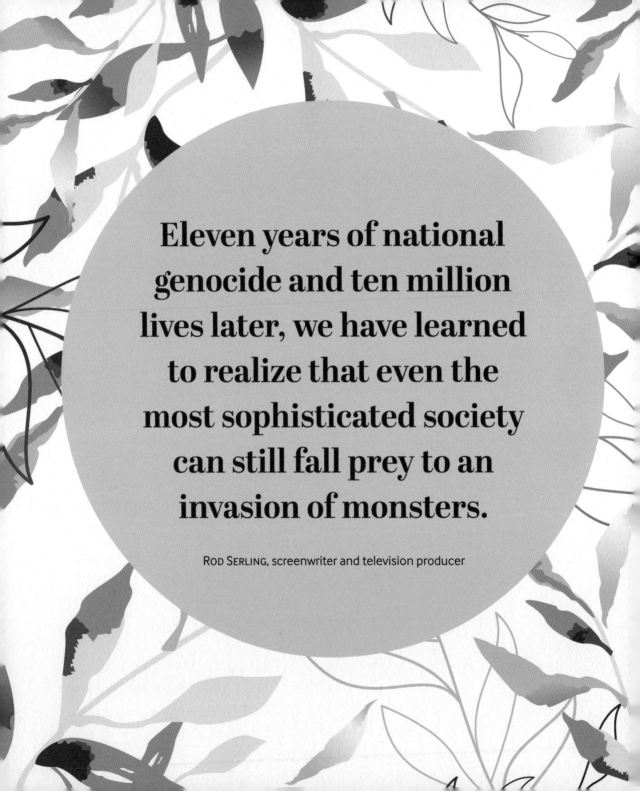

Eleven years of national genocide and ten million lives later, we have learned to realize that even the most sophisticated society can still fall prey to an invasion of monsters.

ROD SERLING, screenwriter and television producer

Raised in Upstate New York, **Rod Serling (1924–1975)** showed an early talent for public speaking and debate, putting him on a smooth path to journalism and writing. For his combat duty during World War II in the Philippines, he was awarded a Purple Heart and a Bronze Star. He sold his first radio script in 1949, paving the way for a career in radio and television. The work that eventually won him fame was the haunting, mind-bending show *The Twilight Zone*, a television series that ran for five years on CBS. Many of its themes—racism, intolerance, paranoia, and the unpredictability of death—reflected his wartime experiences and the specter of Cold War politics.

וַאֲנִי בְּקוֹל תּוֹדָה אֶזְבְּחָה לָּךְ אֲשֶׁר נָדַרְתִּי אֲשַׁלֵּמָה יְשׁוּעָתָה לַה׳

ספר יונה ב׳

MY SALVATION COMES FROM HASHEM   BOOK OF JONAH 2:10

EDUCATION AND LEARNING

Diplomat and financier Felix Rohatyn was a teenager when the Nazis were closing in on the Jews in Vichy France. He and his mother narrowly escaped with just a few hidden gold coins. "We had been well off, but that was all we got out," Rohatyn recalled. "Ever since, I had the feeling that the only permanent wealth is what you carry around in your head."

The notion that the most secure investment you can make is in your knowledge may not be exclusively Jewish, but it does have a powerful Jewish lineage. Education has always been an obligation and a priority for Jews. According to the Five Books of Moses, one of the principal duties of parents is the instruction of their children. This commitment to the transmission of knowledge has been a key factor in Jewish resilience and continuity from generation to generation: In many Orthodox communities, Jewish boys begin studying Hebrew as early as age three, and then at age five attend *cheder*, a Jewish Hebrew school. Every Jewish male after his bar mitzvah is required to engage in prayer, Torah study, and worship three times a day. In academies of Jewish learning called *yeshivas*, the emphasis is not on rote learning but on analysis and critical inquiry.

This tradition also applies to secular life. When Isidor Rabi, the Polish-born winner of the 1944 Nobel Prize in Physics, was asked why he became a scientist, he replied, "My mother made me a scientist without even knowing it. Every other child would come back from school and be asked, 'What did you learn today?' But my mother used to say, 'Did you ask a good question?'"

This section brings together quotations that express a variety of views about knowledge and learning, and the deep-seated Jewish commitment to lifelong education.

artist | **Chavi Feldman,** *Jonah and the Whale*

The advancement of learning is the highest commandment.

MAIMONIDES, Sephardic rabbi and philosopher

Moses ben Maimon (1138–1204), or Maimonides, was the leading Jewish scholar of medieval times. When he was a boy, his hometown of Córdoba, in the south of Spain, was conquered by the Almohad sect. The Jews were forced to either submit to Islam or flee. Maimonides and his family went into exile. For the rest of his life, he traveled, studied, published his work, and served as a rabbi, physician, and astronomer. His favorite subjects were Greek philosophy and rabbinical beliefs and practices. He compiled the Mishneh Torah, or code of Jewish law, when he was living in Egypt. It clarified and codified Jewish teaching, making it easier for the Jews of his time to follow. Maimonides was buried in Tiberias, in the north of Eretz Yisrael, where his tomb is a much-visited pilgrimage site.

To defend a country, you need an army. But to defend an identity, you need a school.

JONATHAN SACKS, English Orthodox rabbi, philosopher, theologian, and author

Jonathan Sacks (1948–2020) was a theologian, scholar, rabbi, and author who became a much-loved spokesman for a broad and inclusive vision of modern Judaism. When appointed to the position of Chief Rabbi of the United Kingdom in 1991, a time of widespread assimilation and secularization, he feared the Jews were losing their sense of identity and commitment to God's teachings, and he called for a "decade of renewal." Over time he became more universalist and shifted his focus to contemporary social issues and ethics. Sacks wrote more than twenty-five books, including *To Heal a Fractured World: The Ethics of Responsibility* (Schocken, 2005), and in his writing and lectures argued for a shared moral code that would overcome divisions and quell extremism. Sacks often had to walk a delicate line between opposing factions in the reform and Orthodox communities. He emerged as a respected, treasured voice of authority in Jewish circles and the secular world.

Revered as the founder of Hadassah, the Zionist women's social service organization, **Henrietta Szold (1860–1945)** was a woman of achievement in different spheres. Raised in Baltimore, she established a night school in her hometown where Russian Jewish immigrants could learn English and vocational skills. For twenty-seven years she served as editor of the Jewish Publication Society, which published scholarly and popular Jewish books in English. In 1912, she founded Hadassah, which introduced modern nursing in Palestine and funded hospitals, a medical school, dental clinics, and other facilities for Palestine's Jewish and Arab inhabitants alike. Szold was always a proponent of Arab-Jewish friendship and efforts to found a bi-national state. At age forty-nine, she took on the massive mission of directing the Youth Aliyah program, which rescued thousands of children from the Nazi regime and resettled them in Palestine. Szold passed away in 1945 in the very same Hadassah Hospital she had helped found in Jerusalem, and is buried in the Jewish Cemetery on the Mount of Olives.

The Jewish heart has always starved unless it was fed through the Jewish intellect.

HENRIETTA SZOLD, Jewish Zionist leader and founder of Hadassah

The most violent element in society is ignorance.

EMMA GOLDMAN, Anarchist revolutionary, political activist, and writer

To the press, **Emma Goldman (1869–1940)** was known as "Red Emma" for her fiery embrace of revolutionary politics. Over the course of a remarkable life of public engagement and advocacy, she threw herself full-bore into reform causes such as free speech, free love, birth control, atheism, feminism, the woman's vote, worker's rights, anti-militarism, free universal education, and prison reform. Born and educated in Czarist Russia and Prussia, she immigrated at sixteen to the US, where she was arrested many times for her radical politics. Her articles and essays filled the pages of her monthly magazine, *Mother Earth*, and she gave hundreds of impassioned speeches in Russian, German, English, and Yiddish. In 1919, the US government deported her to Russia due to her anarchist ideas. That didn't slow her down—nothing could—and Goldman resumed her political work abroad before being allowed back to visit the US. She died in Canada in 1940.

Each of us holds a torch of understanding, empathy, and solidarity. By educating ourselves and others, challenging biased views, and supporting those affected, we forge a stronghold of hope and unity.

SANDRA LAWSON, rabbi and director of Racial Diversity, Equity, and Inclusion

Sandra Lawson (b. 1970)—"Rabbi Sandra" to her devoted fans and followers—was not drawn to religion until well into her thirties. She was working as a personal trainer in Atlanta when a client changed her life. Joshua Lesser is a gay rabbi on a mission to unite Jewish spirituality with social justice, and through their deepening friendship he pushed Lawson to explore the richness of Judaism. In 2004, Lawson converted, and fourteen years later she was ordained as a rabbi. Her religious faith has given her a new way to combine her love of music with spiritual and communal values, and she can often be found with a microphone and guitar at hand. In 2020, she founded Kol HaPanim (in English, All Faces), an inclusive Jewish community that supports rabbis and rabbinical students of color. Lawson lives in North Carolina, where she and her partner keep a vegan kosher home.

Books were our portable homeland.
Books defined our national identity.
We call ourselves am ha sefer,
the people of the book. And yet
here were books being destroyed.

AARON LANSKY, founder of the Yiddish Book Center

As a graduate student in the 1970s, **Aaron Lansky (b. 1955)** discovered that the unique and vibrant literary culture of his forebears was on the verge of disappearing. In 1980, he founded the Yiddish Book Center in Western Massachusetts—now based in Amherst, Massachusetts—and began traveling the country, eventually the world, rescuing old volumes, sometimes literally from the dumpster. He also called on the public to donate their unwanted Yiddish books, and the volumes came flooding in. Lansky and his associates have since collected more than 1.5 million Yiddish books, and much of that content has been digitized and is now accessible the world over. In 2004, Lansky published *Outwitting History: The Amazing Adventures of a Man who Rescued a Million Yiddish Books*, describing how he came to dedicate his life to preserving the literary heritage of an endangered language, the priceless record of once-thriving, now-vanished Jewish communities.

Sharon Brous (b. 1973) is the senior rabbi and leader of the Los Angeles-based Jewish community IKAR, Hebrew for "essence." Founded in 2004, IKAR promotes a reinvigorated Jewish practice and a justice-driven mission. Under Brous' stewardship, IKAR has drawn in young Jews in Southern California and beyond, and Brous' sermons, speeches, and writings have been influential around the world. Her 2016 TED Talk, "It's Time to Reclaim Religion," has been viewed more than 1.5 million times. In 2021, Brous was invited to lead the White House Passover Seder, alongside Second Gentleman Doug Emhoff. Her book, *The Amen Effect: Ancient Wisdom to Mend Our Broken Hearts and World,* was published in 2024 (Avery).

A good sermon makes us cry and sometimes laugh, teaches us something we didn't know before, helps us see something we didn't know before in a new way, activates, engages, sometimes enrages, always inspires.

SHARON BROUS, senior rabbi of IKAR

אֵשֶׁת חַיִל

מִי יִמְצָא וְרָחֹק מִפְּנִינִים מִכְרָהּ:
בָּטַח בָּהּ לֵב בַּעְלָהּ וְשָׁלָל לֹא יֶחְסָר:
גְּמָלַתְהוּ טוֹב וְלֹא רָע כֹּל יְמֵי חַיֶּיהָ: דָּרְשָׁה
צֶמֶר וּפִשְׁתִּים וַתַּעַשׂ בְּחֵפֶץ כַּפֶּיהָ: הָיְתָה כָאֳנִיּוֹת
סוֹחֵר מִמֶּרְחָק תָּבִיא לַחְמָהּ: וַתָּקָם בְּעוֹד לַיְלָה וַתִּתֵּן
טֶרֶף לְבֵיתָהּ וְחֹק לְנַעֲרֹתֶיהָ: זָמְמָה שָׂדֶה וַתִּקָּחֵהוּ מִפְּרִי
כַפֶּיהָ נָטְעָה כָּרֶם: חָגְרָה בְעוֹז מָתְנֶיהָ וַתְּאַמֵּץ זְרוֹעֹתֶיהָ:
טָעֲמָה כִּי טוֹב סַחְרָהּ לֹא יִכְבֶּה בַלַּיְלָה נֵרָהּ: יָדֶיהָ שִׁלְּחָה
בַכִּישׁוֹר וְכַפֶּיהָ תָּמְכוּ פָלֶךְ: כַּפָּהּ פָּרְשָׂה לֶעָנִי וְיָדֶיהָ שִׁלְּחָה
לָאֶבְיוֹן: לֹא תִירָא לְבֵיתָהּ מִשָּׁלֶג כִּי כָל בֵּיתָהּ לָבֻשׁ שָׁנִים:
מַרְבַדִּים עָשְׂתָה לָּהּ שֵׁשׁ וְאַרְגָּמָן לְבוּשָׁהּ: נוֹדָע בַּשְּׁעָרִים
בַּעְלָהּ בְּשִׁבְתּוֹ עִם זִקְנֵי אָרֶץ: סָדִין עָשְׂתָה וַתִּמְכֹּר וַחֲגוֹר
נָתְנָה לַכְּנַעֲנִי: עֹז וְהָדָר לְבוּשָׁהּ וַתִּשְׂחַק לְיוֹם אַחֲרוֹן:
פִּיהָ פָּתְחָה בְחָכְמָה וְתוֹרַת חֶסֶד עַל לְשׁוֹנָהּ: צוֹפִיָּה
הֲלִיכוֹת בֵּיתָהּ וְלֶחֶם עַצְלוּת לֹא תֹאכֵל: קָמוּ בָנֶיהָ
וַיְאַשְּׁרוּהָ בַּעְלָהּ וַיְהַלְלָהּ: רַבּוֹת בָּנוֹת עָשׂוּ חָיִל
וְאַתְּ עָלִית עַל כֻּלָּנָה: שֶׁקֶר הַחֵן וְהֶבֶל הַיֹּפִי
אִשָּׁה יִרְאַת ה' הִיא תִתְהַלָּל: תְּנוּ לָהּ
מִפְּרִי יָדֶיהָ וִיהַלְלוּהָ בַשְּׁעָרִים
מ ע ש י ה

FAMILY AND HOME

When asked by the Dalai Lama in 1989 to explain how the Jewish people had endured through the ages, feminist writer Blu Greenberg had a ready answer. "In times of great danger," she told the Buddhist leader, "Jews responded by having children."

The baby boom she cited is real—in the period immediately after the Holocaust, there was a tremendous upsurge in Jewish births. But the secret to Jewish survival may well be found not only in birth rates and demographics but also in the Jewish emphasis on family and home.

What makes a Jewish home Jewish is more than the ceremonial objects and symbols such as the mezuzah on the doorframe, the Shabbat candlesticks, the kiddush cup, and the Chanukah menorah. Jewish family life is the core from which all else radiates: identity, belonging, and self-fulfillment.

The Jewish home is a place to raise children, cultivate a love of learning, celebrate the holidays, instill Jewish values, and enjoy what the Talmud calls *shalom bayit*—"peace in the house," or marital harmony.

However, shifting demographics, increased mobility, and social change are calling on many Jews to rethink the traditional family structure. Like people of many other faiths, Jews are grappling with tectonic shifts in matters of personal choice, lifestyle changes, and private habits. New networks and forms of Jewish connection are emerging. Marriages of mixed faiths, single-parent families, adoptive parents, and same-sex marriages are all becoming more common and accepted. Instead of seeing them as threats to Jewish identity and continuity, many religious leaders welcome them as a way to enlarge the community, to enrich and enliven Jewish life.

This section includes quotes about the Jewish family and home that highlight their central role in instilling a vital cultural and religious life and ensuring a continued existence.

artist | **Eleyor Snir,** *Woman of Valor*

The home should be perceived as a microcosm of the Universe: The harmony that permeates the home and the family extends beyond, fostering harmony between families, communities and ultimately, the nations of the world.

MENACHEM MENDEL SCHNEERSON,
Orthodox rebbe of the Lubavitch Hasidic dynasty

In 1951, **Menachem Mendel Schneerson (1902–1994)** became the seventh rebbe of the Chabad-Lubavitch dynasty, the largest Hasidic movement, with nearly one hundred thousand followers around the world. Under his four decades of leadership, the Chabad movement established a worldwide network of institutions committed to social services and outreach to Jews on college campuses, in far-flung communities, and under repressive regimes like China, Russia, and Saudi Arabia. At the Chabad headquarters in Crown Heights, Brooklyn, the beloved rebbe delivered marathon spiritual talks to followers who hung on his every word, and received visitors in private meetings that lasted all night until dawn. To this day, many of his followers believe he never died and is just waiting to return and be revealed as the Messiah. But Schneerson himself said the world would be prepared for the coming of the Messiah when every Jew is committed to performing acts of religious faith and kindness.

Though we come from different cultures and totally different worlds, we all want the same things— to provide a good environment for our kids to grow up in. To laugh and share experiences with family and friends. To see our children grow up and achieve their dreams.

Ben Stiller, actor, filmmaker, and comedian

Born to entertainment royalty, **Ben Stiller (b. 1965)** has made his own mark as an actor, filmmaker, and comedian. He grew up in New York City, the son of comedy legends Jerry Stiller and Anne Meara, who performed hilarious skits in the 1960s as "Stiller and Meara." In 1970, they ended their live act, telling their fans they broke it up before it broke up their marriage. Their son Ben Stiller is best known for his roles in comedies like *There's Something About Mary*, *Zoolander*, *Meet the Parents*, and *Meet the Fockers*. To complete the family circle, his older sister Amy Stiller is also an actor who has appeared in theater, film, and television roles. Ben and Amy have often expressed gratitude for their parents' devotion to family. "Show business was important, but family always came first," Ben has said. "That was the most important thing."

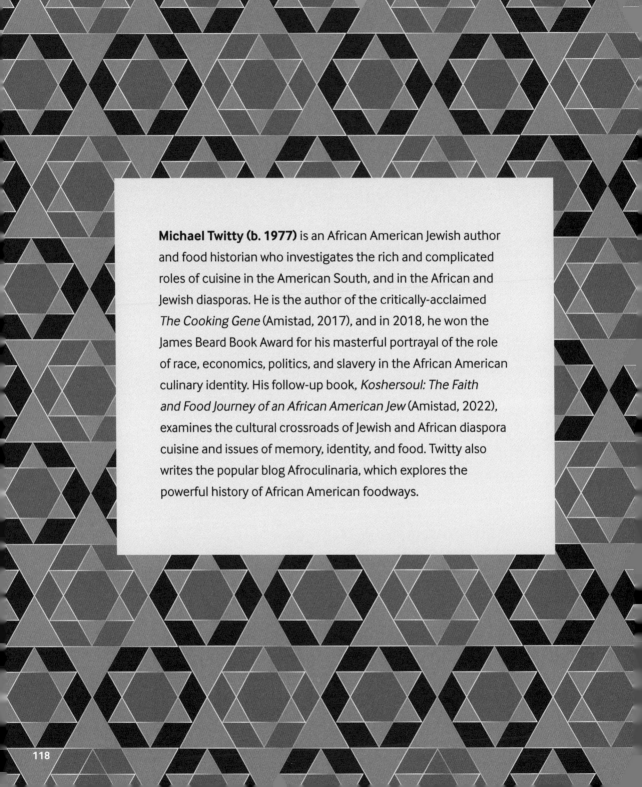

Michael Twitty (b. 1977) is an African American Jewish author and food historian who investigates the rich and complicated roles of cuisine in the American South, and in the African and Jewish diasporas. He is the author of the critically-acclaimed *The Cooking Gene* (Amistad, 2017), and in 2018, he won the James Beard Book Award for his masterful portrayal of the role of race, economics, politics, and slavery in the African American culinary identity. His follow-up book, *Koshersoul: The Faith and Food Journey of an African American Jew* (Amistad, 2022), examines the cultural crossroads of Jewish and African diaspora cuisine and issues of memory, identity, and food. Twitty also writes the popular blog Afroculinaria, which explores the powerful history of African American foodways.

You don't want any Jew to be alone. To not have a place at the seder table, a place to break the fast. In Judaism, being together is more than just community building, it is human sustaining. You are part of a family.

MICHAEL TWITTY, writer, culinary historian, and educator

All the chief virtues of the Jewish character have had the home, with its mighty incentives and its hallowed associations, for their nursing-place.

MORRIS JOSEPH, English Reform rabbi, preacher, and writer

A respected spiritual leader in Great Britain, **Morris Joseph (1848–1930)** served as a Reform rabbi for congregations in London and Liverpool. When the Boer War broke out in 1899, he struggled with reconciling patriotic militarism, the political justification for warfare, and Jewish teachings about the worth of human life. Those same issues surfaced again when World War I broke out and Joseph found himself delivering sermons on hope and resilience during wartime, giving eulogies for young men killed in action, and educating students who would shortly be enlisted in the British army. His ethical quandaries were complicated by the knowledge that hundreds of thousands of young Jewish men in Germany and the Austro-Hungarian Empire were fighting for their nations on the opposing side. Joseph also made his mark through his published works, including his popular *Judaism as Creed and Life* (Macmillan, 1903).

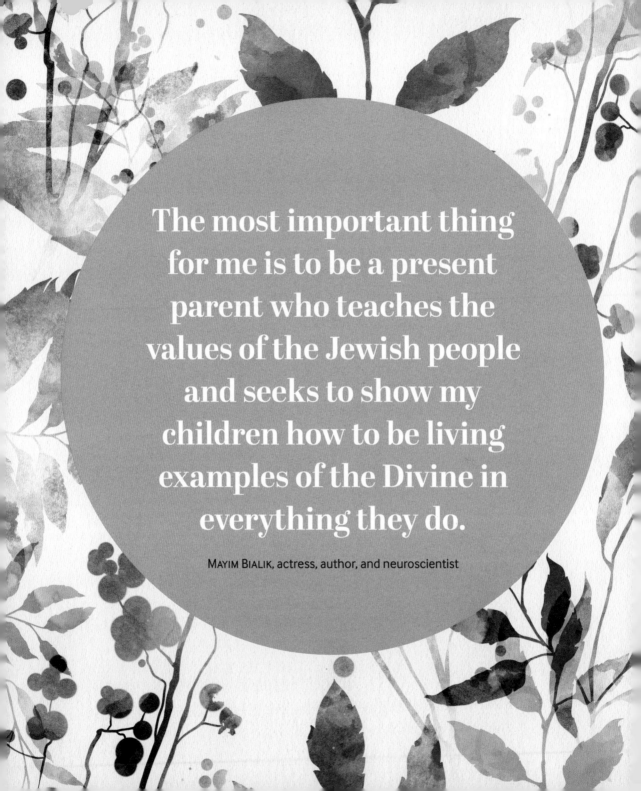

The most important thing for me is to be a present parent who teaches the values of the Jewish people and seeks to show my children how to be living examples of the Divine in everything they do.

Mayim Bialik, actress, author, and neuroscientist

Mayim Bialik (b. 1975) began her career as a child actress, appearing in a number of movies and television shows, including the 1988 classic *Beaches,* in which she played Bette Midler's character as a child. From 1991 to 1995, she starred as the title character on the television sitcom *Blossom,* and, from 2010 to 2019, she played socially awkward neuroscientist Amy Farrah Fowler on the sitcom *The Big Bang Theory.* Bialik, who holds a PhD in neuroscience from the University of California Los Angeles, hosts *Mayim Bialik's Breakdown,* a podcast about mental health. From 2021 to 2023, she co-hosted the primetime television game show *Jeopardy!* Bialik, a descendant of the pioneering Hebrew poet Chayim Nachman Bialik, identifies as Modern Orthodox — she calls herself "observantish." She's a fierce advocate for Israel and speaks and writes about Jewish rituals and culture.

Our job is to raise our children to leave us. The children's job is to find their own path in life.

WENDY MOGEL, psychologist and author

Wendy Mogel (b. 1951) was the mother of two young daughters and a practicing child psychologist in Los Angeles when she began to seek a new approach to the patients she counseled, and to her own parenting. Although she had been raised in a secular home with little knowledge of Judaism, she felt drawn to learn more, so she took a year off to study the Torah and Talmud full-time. As she explained in her bestseller, *The Blessings of the Skinned Knee* (Scribner, 2001), when she returned to her practice she incorporated the timeless wisdom and teachings of Judaism into her child-rearing advice. She found that the deep well of Judaic knowledge offers keys to helping parents raise sturdy, self-reliant children with a firm moral foundation, and with every opportunity for success and fulfillment. Mogel still practices psychology, is a popular public speaker, and is often interviewed as an expert on national media.

Judy Blume (b. 1938) is an award-winning author of more than thirty works of fiction for children, young adults, and adults. As a young New Jersey homemaker with children in preschool, she began writing and publishing stories. Her third book, *Are You There God? It's Me, Margaret* (Bradbury Press, 1970) was a breakthrough bestseller. Blume was among the first young adult authors to write novels that focused on helping young people understand the changes taking place in their lives and bodies as they matured, as well as psychologically challenging issues such as difficult social encounters, complicated friendships, abuse, interfaith relationships, death, and loss. She is known to talk frankly about the struggles that children can face and has the ability to address matters that kids might need guidance on but are too afraid or embarrassed to ask their parents. In her acclaimed 1977 novel, *Starring Sally J. Freedman as Herself* (Yearling), she wrote about her postwar Jewish childhood. A household name for kids and adults around the world, Blume's books have sold more than eighty-two million copies and have been translated into thirty-two languages.

Anybody who says, "My childhood was completely happy," is a person who isn't remembering the truth.

Judy Blume, young adult and children's author

Insanity is hereditary — you get it from your children.

SAM LEVENSON, humorist, teacher, television host, and journalist

Growing up during the Depression, **Sam Levenson (1911–1980)** was the youngest of eight children in an impoverished immigrant household in Brooklyn, New York. But as he explained in his bestselling memoir, *Everything But Money* (Simon & Schuster, 1949), their home was filled with warmth, love, and affectionate humor. Levenson developed his comedy routine as a hobby and appeared at church suppers, community luncheons, and classrooms before graduating to the Borscht Belt resorts of the Catskill Mountains. Eventually he quit his job as a high school Spanish teacher in East Flatbush, New York, to become a full-time comic. He had his own television show, *The Sam Levenson Show*, from 1951 to 1959, and appeared often on *The Ed Sullivan Show*, *The Price is Right*, *The Tonight Show Starring Johnny Carson*, and many more, winning over audiences with folksy nostalgic stories of his childhood in the tenements. "Poor, with books," is how he described those years.

בְּזֶה הַשַּׁעַר לֹא
יָבוֹא צַעַר. בְּזֹאת הַדִּירָה
לֹא תָבוֹא צָרָה. בְּזֹאת הַדֶּלֶת
לֹא תָבוֹא בֶּהָלָה. בְּזֹאת הַמַּחְלָקָה
לֹא תָבוֹא מַחֲלוֹקֶת. בְּזֶה הַמָּקוֹם תְּהִי
בְּרָכָה וְשָׁלוֹם.
Let no sadness come through this gate. Let no
trouble come to this dwelling. Let no fear come-
through this door. Let no conflict be in this
place. Let this home be filled with
Blessing and peace.

INSPIRATION AND HOPE

In 1878, a struggling Jewish poet in what was then the Austrian Empire wrote a poem about the Jewish longing for Eretz Yisrael. He called it "Tikvatenu"—in English, "Our Hope."

Naftali Herz Imber was a wanderer, a restless soul with a fanciful predisposition. But his words tapped into something stirring in the Jewish psyche, the dream of a homeland. With the founding of the Jewish state, the first two stanzas of his poem became the Israeli anthem, "Hatikvah": *Our hope is not yet lost/It is two thousand years old/To be a free people in our land/The land of Zion and Jerusalem.*

Set to music by Samuel Cohen in 1888, based on a Moldavan melody, "Hatikvah" was sung at a Zionist gathering as early as 1901, banned by the British Mandate, and chanted by Jews heading into gas chambers. In 1947, Holocaust survivors on the SS *Exodus* sang "Hatikvah" as the ship headed toward the port of Haifa, before they were forcibly sent back to refugee camps in Europe. Atypical for national anthems, the song is set in a minor scale that expresses the bittersweet quality of Jewish yearning.

The ability to reach for the light, even in life's bleakest moments, is shared by all faiths and traditions. Yet the form of optimism summoned by Imber seems to be particularly Jewish, an outlook that has been explored by many scholars and spiritual leaders. As psychologist David Arnow explained in *Choosing Hope: The Heritage of Judaism* (Jewish Publication Society, 2022), the Jewish faith provides a rich storehouse of responses to life's tribulations. But while God can provide spiritual uplift, it is human beings who must marshal their inner resources.

The following quotations are drawn from a deep reservoir of insight from individuals who have found inspiration and hope at every juncture of life.

artist | **Eleyor Snir,** *Home Blessing*

In 1942, when she was fourteen, **Vera Florence Cooper Rubin (1928–2016)** built a telescope out of cardboard and began to track meteors in the night sky. She followed her curiosity despite a high school teacher who advised her to stay away from the sciences. Rubin's early interest led to a PhD in astronomy at George Washington University with a dissertation that advanced a controversial theory on the distribution of galaxies in the Universe. She went on to study the rotations of galaxies and stars, supporting the notion that most of the Universe is invisible. What holds the galaxies together, she argued, was a mysterious invisible mass known as dark matter. Her research opened up a vast and entirely new realm of physics and astronomy that scientists are still probing today.

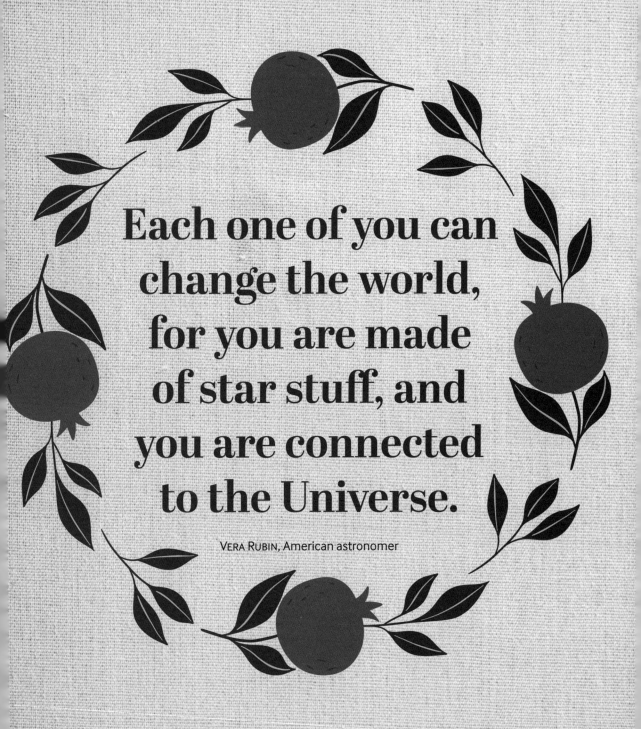

Each one of you can change the world, for you are made of star stuff, and you are connected to the Universe.

VERA RUBIN, American astronomer

I have never seen the world as "deaf" or "hearing" or "Jewish" or "gentile" or "black" or "white"... There is only one world, and many people live in it.

SHOSHANNAH STERN, actress, writer, and producer

Born in California to an observant Jewish and fourth-generation deaf family, **Shoshannah Stern (b. 1980)** is an accomplished actress, writer, and television producer. Although her first language is American Sign Language, she can read lips and speak English fluently. Shoshannah got her start in acting at her alma mater, Gallaudet University—a liberal arts college specifically tailored to the hearing impaired—where she made her film debut in the murder mystery comedy, *The Auteur Theory* (1999). From there, her career blossomed. Her breakout role was in ABC's *Threat Matrix*, as a member of an elite government anti-terrorist task force. She is also recognized for her work on Showtime's *Weeds*, the ever-popular *ER*, *Providence*, and *Cold Case*, to name a few. She notably had a reoccurring role on *Grey's Anatomy* as Dr. Lauren Riley (2020), the first deaf doctor role on a prime-time television network.

Hannah Szenes (1921–1944) was a playwright and poet who wrote in both Hungarian and Hebrew. As a young woman in Budapest, faced with rising antisemitism and the growing vulnerability of Hungary's Jewish population, she became a committed Zionist and moved to Palestine, then under British control. In 1944, as part of a joint mission of the Jewish community in Palestine and the British Army, Szenes was one of thirty-seven recruits who parachuted behind enemy lines into Yugoslavia, where she joined the partisans fighting to rescue Hungarian Jews. But while crossing the border into German-occupied Hungary, she was captured by police. Brutally tortured, she refused to reveal the details of her mission and was executed by firing squad. Szenes' poetry is treasured in Israel today. A beloved song based on "My God, my God" — in Hebrew, "Eli, Eli" — with haunting music by David Zehavi, has become an unofficial Israeli anthem.

My God, my God,

May these things never end:

The sand and the sea,

The rush of the waves,

The lightning of the sky,

The prayers of humankind.

HANNAH SZENES, poet, playwright, and partisan fighter

Many a man, when things go contrary, thinks he is suffering evil, yet the very thing we hold as evil may prove a blessing.

Gʟüᴄᴋᴇʟ ᴏꜰ Hᴀᴍᴇʟɴ, German-Jewish businesswoman and diarist

✡

Glückel of Hameln (1646–1724) was a businesswoman, wife, and mother, whose remarkable memoir provides an intimate glimpse of German-Jewish life between the late-seventeenth and early eighteenth centuries. She describes growing up in a prosperous Hamburg family, marrying and burying two husbands, and the joys and burdens of bearing fourteen children. She also writes about her Jewish faith, her large extended family, making and losing a fortune in business, her community's response to antisemitism, and her travels all over Europe. She wrote in her native tongue of Yiddish and made it clear she wanted her writing preserved for future generations. While the original manuscript of her memoir was lost, a copy survived and was published in 1896.

I dream about a time
when the idea of "woman" is no longer
troubling: because where there are questions,
something is still not right. If, however, I still have
had to answer the question of what pushed me, a
woman, to become a rabbi, here is what occurs to me
immediately: belief in my profession and my love for
people. God has imbued us with abilities and a sense
of mission, not asking about our sex. Thus everyone,
be it man or woman, has the duty to use the gift
given to us by God. Men and women alike
should serve the ideal and work on building
the world as human beings.

REGINA JONAS, Reform rabbi

Growing up in Berlin, **Regina Jonas (1902–1944)** longed to be a rabbi—an outlandish idea at the time, given that no woman in the world had ever been ordained by a theological seminary. After years of study and persistence, Jonas finally achieved her dream in 1935, when a broad-minded rabbi, Max Dienemann, agreed to the historic ordination. It was a time of profound upheaval for German Jews under the Nazi regime, and Jonas focused on her pastoral work, visiting the sick and caring for the needy. In 1942, she and her mother were deported to Theresienstadt, a concentration camp in Czechoslovakia. Even in such dire surroundings, Jonas continued to provide solace and counsel to her fellow inmates. Records at Theresienstadt show that she delivered forty-four talks on religious topics during her time there. On October 12, 1944, she and her mother were transferred to Auschwitz and likely murdered that same day.

If you don't respect yourself and if you don't demand what you believe in for yourself, you're not gonna get it.

JUDY HEUMANN, American disability rights activist

Judy Heumann (1947–2023) contracted polio when she was eighteen months old, one of the nearly forty-three thousand American children affected by the polio epidemic of 1949. When it became clear she would use a wheelchair for life, doctors advised her parents to put her in an institution. But as she explained in her memoir, *Being Heumann* (Beacon, 2020), her parents refused. They were German immigrants who had lost their own parents to the Nazis, who had exterminated the disabled. Heumann was raised to be independent and self-sufficient. She spent summers in the Catskills at a camp for children with disabilities, where the campers transformed themselves into activists—that experience was portrayed in a popular 2020 documentary, *Crip Camp*. Heumann became a teacher and a passionate advocate for the rights of the disabled, organizing rallies, successfully pursuing lawsuits to defend her rights, advocating for legislation, and serving as a powerful role model.

Jamie Geller (b. 1978) is a bestselling cookbook author, food and lifestyle blogger, and founder of a kosher food media company called Aish ("fire" in English). She was raised in a home with Jewish values in the Philadelphia suburbs, but in her twenties she decided to go deeper and embrace Orthodox Judaism. Geller worked as a writer and television producer for HBO, CNN, and the Food Network before publishing her first cookbook, *Quick and Kosher Recipes from the Bride Who Knew Nothing* (Feldheim, 2007). She has gone on to publish six more bestsellers that promote her commitment to no-fuss "quick and easy cooking." She and her family moved to Israel in 2012 and live in Beit Shemesh.

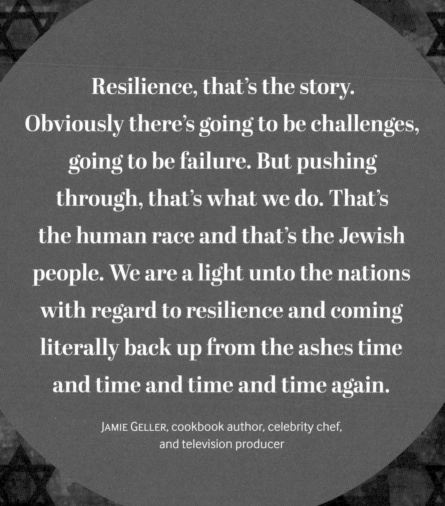

Resilience, that's the story.
Obviously there's going to be challenges,
going to be failure. But pushing
through, that's what we do. That's
the human race and that's the Jewish
people. We are a light unto the nations
with regard to resilience and coming
literally back up from the ashes time
and time and time and time again.

JAMIE GELLER, cookbook author, celebrity chef,
and television producer

What are the odds of Jewish and Native people actually existing after all of the genocide and erasure and attempts to detach us from our communities, and take away our languages, our cultures, and our practices? Here we are still hustling and working and thriving. To see the people in these communities who are thriving against all odds and are continuing to shift the narrative, it's a miracle.

SARAH PODEMSKI, First Nations actress and activist

Sarah Podemski (b. 1983) is an Anishinaabe/Ashkenazi actress and multidisciplinary artist most recently known for her role as Rita on the hit FX television series *Reservation Dogs*. On her mother's side, Podemski is a Salteaux, a tribe of First Nations people who are part of the Ojibwe Nations in Canada. Her paternal grandparents were Polish Jewish Holocaust survivors. After her parents' divorce, Podemski was raised by her father in a family immersed in Jewish culture. She went to a Jewish summer camp, joined a Jewish youth movement, and lived for a year in a kibbutz, a collective farming community in Israel. At the same time, she was also learning about the history and meaning of being Indigenous in Canada.

HOLIDAYS AND TRADITIONS

Judaism is a communal religion, a collective experience steeped in centuries of tradition. Jewish people do, of course, pray alone, out loud, and in silence. But the observance of most Jewish rituals and holidays calls for a group of people coming together with an awareness of shared purpose, belonging, and faith. In Jewish life, all public observances such as bar and bat mitzvahs, weddings and funerals, and the reading of the Torah require a minyan, a quorum of at least ten adults (traditionally men). Only once that group is in place can the rituals begin.

The Jewish holidays are celebrated communally, a cyclical procession of holy days and holidays that follow the lunar calendar, each one leading to the next with the unfolding seasons and the passage of time. Some commemorate key events in Jewish history, such as the long-ago triumphs and defeats of the Israelites, the Jewish exodus from Egypt, the giving of the Ten Commandments at Mount Sinai, and the destruction of the ancient temples. Others are tied to the agrarian cycle.

The one constant throughout the year is the weekly arrival of the Sabbath—*Shabbat* in Hebrew, *Shabbos* in Yiddish—honoring God's rest on the seventh day of Creation. It is a holy day set aside for renewal, an invitation to pause and contemplate the world and our role in it. With ceremony, symbolism, and song, Judaism provides a form of collective continuity and a rich blueprint for spiritual connection, inflected by rituals and customs emerging from the wide range of Jewish experiences around the world.

This section presents quotes that honor the rich depth and variety of Jewish holidays and traditions, and the ties that bind the Jewish people together across time and geography.

artist | **Eleyor Snir,** *Hanukkah*

Without traditions, our lives would be as shaky as a fiddler on the roof!

JOSEPH STEIN, American playwright

Joseph Stein (1912–2010) wrote more than a dozen Broadway shows, but none reached the heights of a musical based on a poor Jewish milkman struggling to preserve his religious and cultural traditions. *Fiddler on the Roof*, which opened in 1964, was a great commercial success, won nine Tony Awards, and shattered the record for the longest-running Broadway musical (3,242 performances). The story was drawn from Yiddish author Sholem Aleichem's tales of shtetl (village) life in early-twentieth-century Czarist Russia. In writing the book musical—Sheldon Harnick wrote the lyrics—Stein found his perfect subject. Tasked with transporting Tevye the Milkman's tales from the Old World onto the Broadway stage, he delved into his own background as the child of Yiddish-speaking immigrants who rarely ventured beyond their form of shtetl in the Bronx. Stein's "Fiddler" wove particularly Jewish themes into a universal story of family, tradition, religion, and the winds of change.

We started saying, where are our roots? We found out there were roots we hadn't learned about . . . the Jewish educators had skipped over them. It was important for us to find out who we were and where we came from.

HANKUS NETSKY, American multi-instrumentalist, composer, and ethnomusicologist

Musician, composer, and ethnomusicologist **Hankus Netsky (b. 1955)** grew up in Philadelphia at a time when Yiddish culture was close to extinction. Jewish educators were focused on Israeli music and on Hebrew language and literature, completely overlooking the rich, centuries-old storehouse of Yiddish literature, language, and music. Although he came from a family of musicians who played Jewish music at weddings and bar mitzvahs, Netsky was never encouraged to learn the music himself. But in 1979, inspired by the success of the folk revival movement, he began digging into his Jewish musical roots and founded the Klezmer Conservatory Band. Almost overnight the band found an enthusiastic audience and has played a key role in the resurgence of Jewish roots music. Netsky, who composes music for film, theater, and television, teaches at New England Conservatory in Boston.

Lawrence Kushner (b. 1943) is one of America's most beloved Reform rabbis and among the most widely read Jewish authors by people of all faiths. He has been particularly effective at opening up the deep Jewish mystical tradition, based on the writings of the Kabbalah, and making those teachings accessible and inspirational. Kushner was raised in Detroit and as a young man thought he was destined to be a fine arts painter, but he also felt an internal call to the rabbinate. After rabbinical ordination, he spent twenty-eight years at Congregation Beth-El in Sudbury, Massachusetts. During those years he wrote more than twenty books and developed a public voice as a commentator on Jewish faith and spirituality. Kushner is currently a scholar-in-residence at Congregation Emanu-El in San Francisco, but he now devotes much of his time to painting.

Shabbat is a daylong spiritual fiction by which we are permitted to stop planning, preparing, investing, conniving, evaluating, fixing, manipulating, arranging, staging, and all the other things we do, not for the sake of doing them, but with an ulterior motive for the sake of some future accomplishment . . . On Shabbat we do not have to go anywhere; we are already there. On Shabbat we do not have to do anything; it is already done.

LAWRENCE KUSHNER,
Reform rabbi and scholar-in-residence

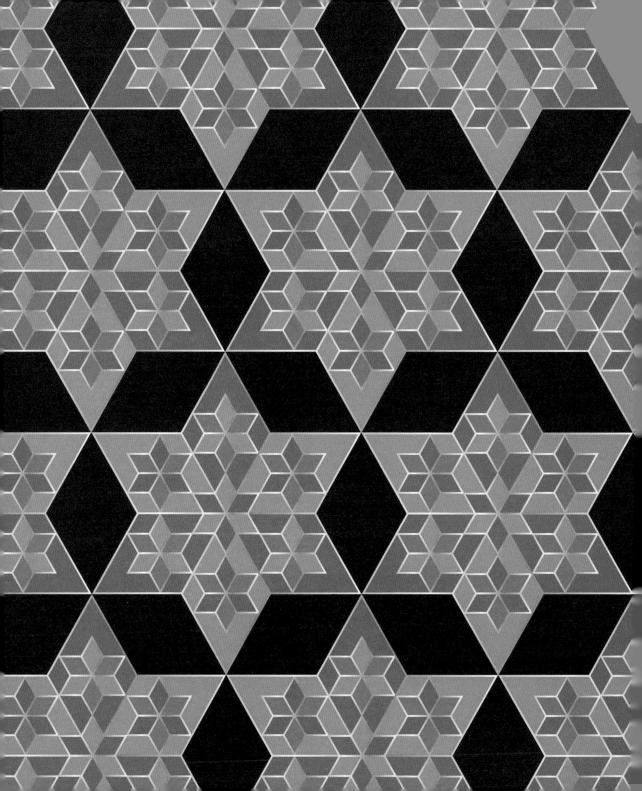

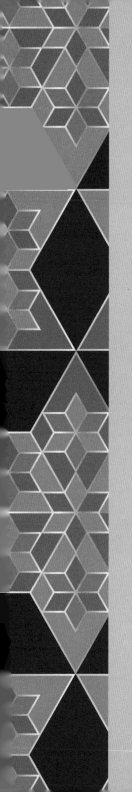

The Exodus from Egypt occurs in every human being, in every era, in every year, and in every day.

NACHMAN OF BRESLOV, founder of the Breslov Hasidic movement

By emphasizing a personal, intimate relationship with the Almighty, the early-nineteenth-century sage **Nachman of Breslov (1772–1810)** infused new energy into the Hasidic movement founded by his great-grandfather, the Baal Shem Tov. Through combining the Kabbalah with in-depth Torah scholarship, Rav Nachman encouraged exuberant worship and mystical communion with God as well as fasting and abstinence—practices continued even today by some of his contemporary followers. In his mid-thirties, Nachman contracted tuberculosis. He chose to die in the town of Uman, now in Ukraine, and promised redemption to his acolytes if they would come to pray at his grave. Each year on Rosh Hashanah, tens of thousands of pilgrims do exactly that, pouring into Uman to surround the rabbi's tomb and offer prayers, meditation, and joyful celebration.

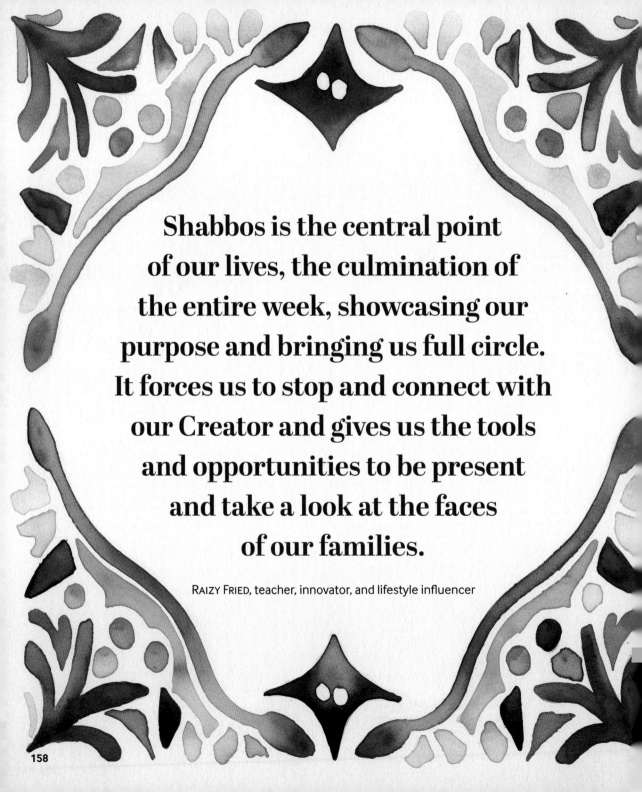

Shabbos is the central point of our lives, the culmination of the entire week, showcasing our purpose and bringing us full circle. It forces us to stop and connect with our Creator and gives us the tools and opportunities to be present and take a look at the faces of our families.

RAIZY FRIED, teacher, innovator, and lifestyle influencer

Known to her many social media followers as "the Jewish Martha Stewart," **Raizy Fried (b. 1981)** is a Hasidic Jew who combines traditional Jewish values with contemporary entrepreneurship. As a recipe developer, food stylist, food photographer, and lifestyle blogger, she sees the Jewish home as the source of creativity and innovation as well as the path to fulfilling the traditional role of wife and mother. Her platform, "Inspired Living," is devoted to helping women run their homes more efficiently by providing homemaking, organizing, and entertaining tips that comport with Halakha, or Jewish law. Fried is the author of *Lekoved Shabbos Kodosh: Infuse Your Shabbos with Love, Meaning & Joy* and *Lekoved Shabbos for Kids and Kids at Heart*, both focused on helping homemakers elevate and sanctify their families' sabbath meals and experiences.

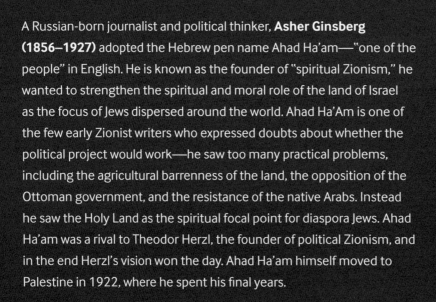

More than the Jews have kept Shabbat, Shabbat has kept the Jews.

AHAD HA'AM (ASHER GINSBERG), Hebrew journalist and essayist

A Russian-born journalist and political thinker, **Asher Ginsberg (1856–1927)** adopted the Hebrew pen name Ahad Ha'am—"one of the people" in English. He is known as the founder of "spiritual Zionism," he wanted to strengthen the spiritual and moral role of the land of Israel as the focus of Jews dispersed around the world. Ahad Ha'Am is one of the few early Zionist writers who expressed doubts about whether the political project would work—he saw too many practical problems, including the agricultural barrenness of the land, the opposition of the Ottoman government, and the resistance of the native Arabs. Instead he saw the Holy Land as the spiritual focal point for diaspora Jews. Ahad Ha'am was a rival to Theodor Herzl, the founder of political Zionism, and in the end Herzl's vision won the day. Ahad Ha'am himself moved to Palestine in 1922, where he spent his final years.

Alan King (1927–2004), who was born Irwin Alan Kniberg, was the son of Russian immigrants to Manhattan's Lower East Side, where his father worked as a cutter in a ladies' handbag factory. The neighborhood was tough, and Jewish kids had to deal with slurs and street gangs. A quick wit and chutzpah (roughly, Yiddish for "moxie") became King's defense and escape. At fourteen he sang "Brother, Can You Spare a Dime" on a radio talent show and got invited to perform on a nationwide tour. He dropped out of school and rose swiftly through the comedy ranks: the Catskills, nightclubs, opening acts for stars, and appearances on *The Ed Sullivan Show* and *The Perry Como Show*. Eventually he became an actor, and he was the longstanding host of New York City's famed Friar's Club. King is best remembered for his stand-up routines that exemplified the satirical, Yiddish-inflected, in-your-face comedy of the Borscht Belt.

A summary of every Jewish holiday: They tried to kill us, we won, let's eat!

ALAN KING, comedian, actor, and satirist

TIKUN OLAM

The concept of *tikun olam* dates to the Hebrew sages of the first century. But in modern times, this two-thousand-year-old idea has acquired new relevance, and many Jews today consider tikun olam to be the cornerstone of their religious identity.

Hebrew for "repairing the world," tikun olam makes use of the same verb—l'taken—that modern-day Hebrew speakers would use, for instance, when tinkering with a car engine or gluing together the pieces of a broken vase. Applied to the world at large, tikun olam places the well-being of humanity not just in the providence of God, but also in the hands of the Jewish people. But how can one people, a tiny sliver of the world's population, assume such an immense responsibility?

The key to understanding why tikun olam has become so central to contemporary Jewish life can be found in the depths of Jewish psychology and self-understanding. Jews identify with that broken vase. They know that like the broken shards, their people have repeatedly been smashed and scattered and that it can easily happen again. They know the world itself is broken and feel a responsibility to repair the cracks and fissures.

The following quotes show how fully many Jews consider tikun olam a cornerstone of the Jewish identity and purpose.

artist | **Chavi Feldman,** *Repair the World*

Whoever destroys a single life is as guilty as though he had destroyed the entire world; whoever rescues a single life earns as much merit as though he had rescued the entire world.

TALMUD

We live in a world in which, all too often, it seems that human life is cheap. Who cares that large numbers of people are suffering and dying? Judaism teaches that everyone must care. The key concept is not just that each life is precious, but that each life contains an entire world, just as the entire population of the earth descended from one human being, Adam. This quotation dates back to rabbinic commentaries on the Torah from the second to the fifth centuries. It arises during a debate about the judicial system and court procedures, specifically capital punishment. As the rabbis went back and forth, a clear message emerged: One human life can make all the difference.

> *If I was to be true to Judaism, I had to make it my business to care for the stranger—even if that stranger was my enemy.*

GEORGETTE BENNETT, sociologist, lecturer, and journalist

✡

Born in a bombed-out apartment building in Budapest just after the end of World War II, **Georgette Bennett (b. 1946)** immigrated to the US with her parents in 1952 and became a sociologist, lecturer, journalist, and philanthropist focused on interfaith relations and conflict resolution. In her career as a journalist she was a correspondent for NBC News and host of Walter Cronkite's PBS current affairs series, *Why in the World?* In the world of finance, she worked for the city of New York and The First Women's Bank. In 2013, Bennett founded the Multifaith Alliance for Syrian Refugees, raising more than $400 million in aid for Syrian war victims. She also cofounded the Global Covenant of Religions/Global Covenant Partners to delegitimize the use of religion to justify violence and extremism. She's authored five books, including *Thou Shalt Not Stand Idly By: How One Woman Confronted the Greatest Humanitarian Crisis of Our Time* (Wicked Son, 2021).

A senior rabbi at Manhattan's Central Synagogue, **Angela Buchdahl (b. 1972)** was the first Asian American to serve as either a cantor or a rabbi in North America—and she is both. Born in South Korea to a Jewish American father and a Buddhist mother, at age five she moved with her family to Tacoma, Washington. She was raised in a Jewish household and identified strongly with her faith, but has described the frustration she feels when people commonly assume she's not Jewish because of her looks. Buchdahl received her ordination in 2001 at Hebrew Union College-Jewish Institute of Religion. At Central Synagogue, her spiritual leadership has drawn scores of new followers into the community, and the livestreams and broadcasts of her services reach viewers in more than a hundred countries. Buchdahl and her husband mingle Korean and Jewish customs in their home and raise children who draw strength from their multi-cultural heritage.

Judaism teaches that each person is an entire world. Every one of you is here to do your part for something that is more lasting and significant than yourself. What you create will ripple out from you into the world in ways you cannot possibly imagine. While the vastness of awe can make you feel very small, it also calls you to transcend yourself—to moral beauty.

ANGELA BUCHDAHL, East Asian American rabbi

You are not obligated to complete the work, but neither are you free to abandon it.

RABBI TARFON, third generation of the Mishnah sages

A priest and Talmudic sage, **Rabbi Tarfon (70–135)** lived in the land of Judaea in the first century CE, around the time of the Second Destruction of the Temple in Jerusalem. He was a "kohen," a descendant of a priestly family, and as a young man served in the holy temple. Although raised in wealth, he developed a reputation for humility, good heartedness, and generosity. Tradition says that Rabbi Tarfon died in the Galilee, and followers today visit the spot believed to be his grave, under a stately old pistachio tree, not far from the mystical city of Safed. Rabbi Tarfon's scholarly and nuanced interpretations of Jewish law are respected and studied today by Orthodox Jews.

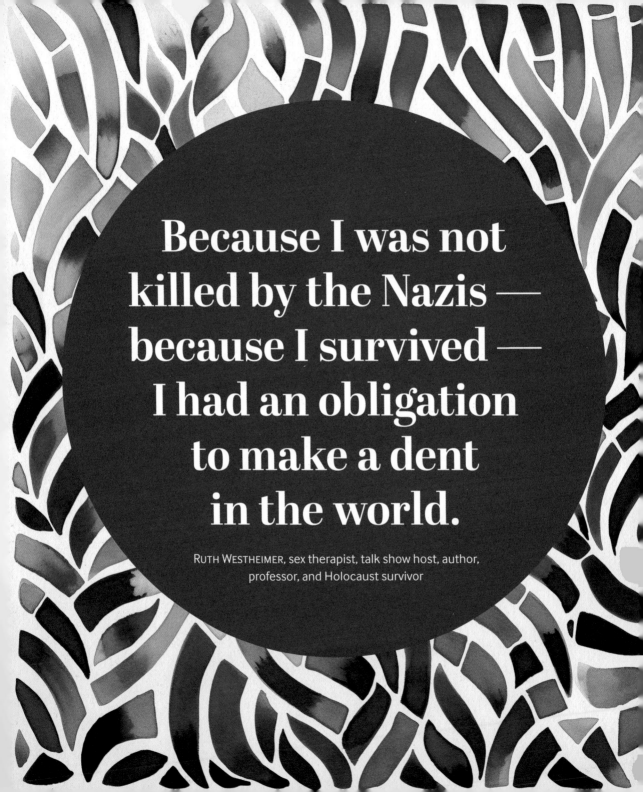

Because I was not killed by the Nazis — because I survived — I had an obligation to make a dent in the world.

RUTH WESTHEIMER, sex therapist, talk show host, author, professor, and Holocaust survivor

Long before anyone else was speaking openly about healthy sexual relationships, **Ruth Westheimer (b. 1928)** was born Karola Ruth Siegel in Germany, she was an only child in an Orthodox Jewish family. When Hitler came to power, the ten-year-old Karola was sent to Switzerland on a *kindertransport*, an organized rescue effort for Jewish children. Her parents, who stayed behind, were killed by the Nazis. She fought as a sniper for the new Jewish state of Israel, then she made her way to the US where she taught sex education and became a sex therapist. In 1980, Westheimer launched a radio call-in show, and her ebullience, charm, and straight talk about sex made "Dr. Ruth" a beloved public figure and led to a popular television show. Westheimer has written forty-five books on human sexuality, and in 2023, she became the first-ever Loneliness Ambassador for the state of New York.

As long as I am politically alive I shall continue to kick.

HELEN SUZMAN, activist and politician

The eyes of **Helen Suzman (1917–2009)** were opened to the reality of apartheid in South Africa when, in 1946, she was asked to collect evidence for a review of the national laws governing Black citizens. Until then she had been uninvolved in politics. She had grown up in a small mining town outside of Johannesburg, become a wife and mother, then returned to college for an economics degree. But when faced with evidence of the discrimination and hardship faced by Blacks, she ran for office and in 1953 was elected to the South African House of Assembly. Suzman spent the next thirty-six years as one of the most outspoken South African politicians opposed to apartheid—at times the only vocal opponent. She lived to see Nelson Mandela released from prison in 1990 and apartheid dismantled. When she died in 2009, aged ninety-one, flags all over South Africa flew at half-mast in her honor.

Abraham Joshua Heschel (1907–1972) coined the term "praying with one's feet" as a way of describing the notion of putting thoughts and intentions into action. A rabbi in Berlin, Heschel was arrested by the Gestapo in 1938 and sent back to his native Poland. Just ahead of the German invasion of Poland he escaped to London, then immigrated to the US. Most of the family he left behind were murdered by the Nazis. As a theologian and professor at New York City's Jewish Theological Seminary, he explored the relationship between God and humanity and wrote books of profound impact such as *God In Search of Man* (Jewish Publication Society, 1955). Heschel believed each person contained a spark of divinity, and that Jews were obligated to work toward alleviating the suffering of their fellow human beings. Literally "praying with his feet," he marched arm-in-arm with the Rev. Martin Luther King, Jr. in 1965, from Selma to Montgomery, Alabama, protesting racial segregation and discrimination. King called Heschel "a truly great prophet."

How many disasters
do we have to go through
in order to realize that
all of humanity has a
stake in the liberty of
one person; whenever
one person is offended,
we are all hurt.

ABRAHAM JOSHUA HESCHEL, Polish-American rabbi,
theologian, and philosopher

Say to yourself,
If there is a wrong
in our midst,
what can I do?
What is my responsibility?

LILLIAN WALD, American nurse, activist, and humanitarian

Born into a wealthy Jewish American family, **Lillian Wald (1867–1940)** spent her early life in Upstate New York attending Miss Cruttenden's English-French Boarding and Day School for Young Ladies. Finding there a love for science and medicine, she pursued a career in nursing, focusing on poor and underserved communities. Feeling compelled to serve, she began teaching home classes on health care to poor immigrant families on the Lower East Side of Manhattan, an area packed with immigrants from all walks of life. Focusing on poor Russian Jews, she founded the Henry Street Settlement, an organization that to this day continues to pursue its mission to provide every New York City resident with equal and fair health care, regardless of social status, race, gender, or age.

INDEX OF INDIVIDUALS

PERMISSIONS

LAND OF MILK AND HONEY

Melinda Strauss
Melinda Strauss @ therealmelindastrauss. "I stand with Israel because when I walk around Jerusalem, every step I take is a part of my history." Instagram, October 12, 2023. https://www.instagram.com/p/CyT1kFaR_8z/?utm_source=ig_web_copy_link&igsh=MzRlODBiNWFlZA==

Liz Rose
Liz Rose @jewishlyliz. "Israel has a duty to protect and defend its citizens, citizens who are Jewish, who are Arab, who are Christian, who are Jews, and every other minority who is living there." Instagram, October 7, 2023. https://www.instagram.com/jewishlyliz/?hl=en

Zelda Schneurson Mishkovsky
Zelda Schneurson Mishkovsky. *The Spectacular Difference: Selected Poems of Zelda*. trans. Marcia Falk. Cincinnati, Ohio: Hebrew Union College Press, 2004.

DIASPORA

André Aciman
André Aciman. *Letters of Transit: Reflections on Exile, Identity, Language, and Loss*. New York City, New York: New Press, 1999.

Hen Mazzig
Hen Mazzig @ HenMazzig. "Being Jewish means you are part of a family that spans across the globe, through different races, ages, sexualities, political beliefs, and histories. Being Jewish means that no matter where you are in life, you have a home." X, February 23, 2024. 6:26pm. https://twitter.com/HenMazzig/status/1761170605984874525

Kirk Douglas
Douglas, Kirk. Speech to Synagogue for the Performing Arts, Los Angeles, adapted in "More from Actor Kirk Douglas about Being Jewish." Maxine Springer. *Moment Magazine* Archives. October 30, 2008. https://momentmag.com/more-from-actor-kirk-douglas-about-being-jewish/

Waldemar Haffkine
The Chief Rabbi Joseph Herman Hertz. *A Book of Jewish Thoughts, Selected and Arranged*. Oxford, England: Oxford University Press, 1920.

ART AND CULTURE

Leo Baeck
Leo Baeck. *University Over the Abyss*, eds. Elena Makaarova, Sergei Makarov, and Victor Kuperman; transl. Victor Kuperman (Jerusalem: Verba Publisher, 2004). Quote by Leo Baeck courtesy of James N. Dreyfus and family, descendants of Rabbi Leo Baeck.

Leon Botstein
Leon Botstein. *Leon Botstein: Art Now* (Aesthetics Across Music, Painting, Architecture, Movies, and More.). Daily Motion. Originally released by The Floating University. September 2011. https://www.dailymotion.com/video/x6l6lcf

Leonard Nimoy
Leonard Nimoy. Leonard Nimoy's Oral History Interview. Christa Whitney. Yiddish Book Center's Wexler Oral History Project. Bel Air, Los Angeles California: October 15, 2013. https://www.yiddishbookcenter.org/collections/oral-histories/interviews/woh-fi-0000483/leonard-nimoy-2013.

Louise Nevelson
Louise Nevelson. *Dawns + Dusks: Taped Conversations With Diana MacKown*. New York City, New York: Scribner, 1976.

Stephen Sondheim
Stephen Sondheim. Stephen Sondheim: Award Winning Composer and Lyricist. The Academy of Achievement Interview, July 5, 2005. https://achievement.org/video/stephen-sondheim-full-interview/. Stephen Sondheim quoted with the permission of the Academy of Achievement; www.achievement.org.

William Shatner
William Shatner. "What I've Learned." Mike Sager. Esquire. Vol. 145. February, 2006. P. 116.

Zibby Owens
Zibby Owens. *Bookends: A Memoir of Love, Loss, and Literature*. Amazon Publishing, Little A, 2022.

LAUGHTER AND TEARS

Chanie Apfelbaum
Chanie Apfelbaum @busyinbrooklyn. "Life continues, and while the pain never goes away, new blessings come into your life. And there is love and laughter, even with the pain." Instagram, March 1, 2023. https://www.instagram.com/reel/CpQNkWjAaN3/?utm_source=ig_web_copy_link&igsh=MzRlODBiNWFlZA==

Esther D. Kustanowitz
Esther D. Kustanowitz. "Why Jews Laugh." Monica Osborne. *Jewish Journal*. October 20, 2021. https://jewishjournal.com/commentary/opinion/341541/why-jews-laugh/

Rachel Goldberg-Polin
Rachel Goldberg-Polin. Speech to the United Nations on Day 67 of the Hostage Crisis. Geneva. December 2023.

Jerry Seinfeld
Jerry Seinfeld. "Takes One to Know One." David Steinberg. *Los Angeles Times*, November 24, 2008. https://www.latimes.com/style/la-mag-nov302008-theear-story.html

Mandy Patinkin
Mandy Patinkin. *Mandy Patinkin: The Actor and Singer Who Could be Hollywood's Most Jewish Performer*. Francine White. *The Jewish Chronicle*, October 5, 2023. https://www.thejc.com/life-and-culture/mandy-patinkin-the-actor-and-singer-who-could-be-hollywoods-most-jewish-performer-paqwrj9b

Moshe Waldoks
Moshe Waldoks. Miriam Anzovin and Dan Seligson. *Getting the Joke: Exploring Jewish Comedy With Reb Moshe Waldoks*. Jewish Boston. Podcast audio. June 8, 2021. https://www.jewishboston.com/read/getting-the-joke-exploring-jewish-comedy-with-reb-moshe-waldoks/

Ohad Naharin
Ohad Naharin. Haymann, Tomer, director. *Mr. Gaga*. Heymann Brothers Film, 2015.

Rain Pryor
Rain Pryor. *Fried Chicken and Latkes*. Directed by Eve Brandstein. Jewish Women's Theater. August 17th, 2017. https://www.youtube.com/watch?v=w1ft-gnh8tY

ANTISEMITISM AND THE HOLOCAUST

Amy Schumer
Amy Schumer @amyschumer. "I was bullied for being Jewish in the town I grew up in and was made to feel embarrassed for my Judaism. Now I am proud to be descended from survivors of Auschwitz." Instagram, December 2, 2022. https://www.instagram.com/p/Clp9RXmOFUH/?utm_source=ig_web_copy_link&igsh=MzRlODBiNWFlZA==

Daniel Pearl
Daniel Pearl. "Family of US Journalist Daniel Pearl Marks 21 Years Since His Murder." *Themedialine*. February 2, 2023. https://themedialine.org/headlines/family-us-journalist-daniel-pearl-marks-21-years-since-his-murder/

Elie Wiesel
Elie Wiesel. "Antisemitism Redux." Richard Heffner. Richard Heffner's Open Mind: A Half-century of Public Affairs Interviews. June 6, 2002. https://www.thirteen.org/openmind-archive/history/anti-semitism-redux/

Jacobo Timerman
Jacobo Timerman. *Prisoner Without a Name, Cell Without a Number*. New York City, New York: Knopf, 1981).

Josh Shapiro
Josh Shapiro. *Locals Remember How the Pittsburgh Shooting Unfolded*. Jesse Bernstein. *Philadelphia Jewish Exponent*, October 25, 2019.

Noa Tishby
Noa Tishby @noatishby. "To our non-Jewish friends, we don't need to know if you would hide us in your attics. We don't need people to hide us. We need you to come out of hiding and stand with us." Instagram, December 2023. https://www.instagram.com/p/C0ZSKuYrkoj/?hl=en

Rod Serling
Rod Serling. "Rod Serling and Free Speech: Why 'Defeating by Ignoring' Doesn't Work." Originally published in *Playboy Magazine*. April 15, 1966. Shadow & Substance: Exploring the Works of Rod Serling. https://thenightgallery.wordpress.com/2017/08/03/rod-serling-and-free-speech-why-defeating-by-ignoring-doesnt-work/

Ruth Bader Ginsburg
Ruth Bader Ginsburg. "What Being Jewish Means to Me." American Jewish Committee. Reprinted from the *New York Times*, Sunday, January 14, 1996. https://www.ajc.org/sites/default/files/pdf/2020-09/Ruth%20Bader%20Ginsburg%20What%20Being%20Jewish%20Means%20to%20Me%20NYT%20Ad%201.14.96.pdf

Sarah Podemski
Sarah Podemski. For Jewish Indigenous Actress Sarah Podemski, It's a Miracle Just to Exist. Evelyn Frick. *Times of Israel*. October 22, 2021. https://www.timesofisrael.com/for-jewish-indigenous-actress-sarah-podemski-its-a-miracle-just-to-exist/

EDUCATION AND LEARNING

Aaron Lansky
Aaron Lansky. Ball, Sam, director. "A Bridge of Books: The Story of the Yiddish Book Center." Filmmakers Library. May 16, 2006. VHS, color, 13 min.

Jonathan Sacks
Jonathan Sacks. *A Letter in the Scroll: Understanding Our Jewish Identity and Exploring the Legacy of the World's Oldest Religion*. New York City, New York: The Free Press, 2004.

Sandra Lawson
Sandra Lawson (@Sandra Lawson. "Each of us holds a torch of understanding, empathy, and solidarity. By educating ourselves and others, challenging biased views, and supporting those affected, we forge a stronghold of hope and unity." Facebook. December 10, 2023. https://www.facebook.com/share/p/RSNKg5f796emGxuu/?mibextid=WC7FNe

Sharon Brous
Sharon Brous. "Sermons and 'Something Powerful': A Conversation with Sharon Brous." Isadora Kianovsky. Jewish Book Council. January 8, 2024. https://www.jewishbookcouncil.org/pb-daily/sermons-and-something-powerful-a-conversation-with-sharon-brous

FAMILY AND HOME

Judy Blume
Judy Blume. Judy Blume's Love, Writing About Kids Ages 9-12. Renée Montagne. *NPR*, December 25, 2008. https://www.npr.org/templates/story/story.php?storyId=98706074

Mayim Bialik
Mayim Bialik. Q&A with Mayim Bialik. Esther D. Kustanowitz. *Hadassah Magazine*, March 2017. https://www.hadassahmagazine.org/2017/03/09/qa-mayim-bialik/

Menachem Mendel Schneerson
Rabbi Menachem Mendel Schneereson, the Lubavitcher Rebbe. Reprinted from Chabad.org with permission. https://www.chabad.org/therebbe/article_cdo/aid/60862/jewish/Family.htm.

Michael Twitty
Michae Twitty. Culinary Historian Michael Twitty With Adeena Sussman. Adeena Sussman. *Hadassah Magazine*, September 2020. https://www.hadassahmagazine.org/video/watch-michael-twitty-in-conversation-with-adeena-sussman/

Sam Levenson
Sam Levenson. *You Can Say That Again, Sam!: The Choice Wit and Wisdom of Sam Levenson*. New York City: New York. 1979.

Wendy Mogel
Wendy Mogel. *The Blessing of a Skinned Knee: Using Timeless Teachings to Raise Self-Reliant Children*. New York City, New York: Scribner, 2001.

INSPIRATION AND HOPE

Glückel of Hameln
Glückel of Hameln. *The Memoirs of Glückel of Hameln*, trans. Marvin Lowenthal. New York City, New York: Schocken Books, 1987.

Jamie Geller
Jamie Geller. *#69: Behind the Bima - Jamie Geller*. Rabbi Efrem Goldberg. Behind the Bima. November 10, 2021. https://www.youtube.com/live/Y0qX8vH-JwU?si=6tA_xmVSQH9MqQM7

Judy Heumann
"Crip Camp." Crip Camp: A Disability Revolution, dir. Nicole Newnham and James Lebrecht, 2020. https://cripcamp.com/

Regina Jonas
C.V.-Zeitung, Berlin, June 23, 1938, and University Over the Abyss, eds. Elena Makaarova, Sergei Makarov, and Victor Kuperman; transl. Victor Kuperman (Jerusalem: Verba Publisher, 2004).

Shoshannah Stern
Shoshannah Stern. *Signing Up for Hollywood*. Gerri Miller. JVibe.com. https://web.archive.org/web/20070928125532/http://www.jvibe.com/popculture/signing_up_hollywood.shtml

Vera Rubin
Rubin, Vera. *Trailblazing Astronomer Vera Rubin on Science, Stereotypes, and Success*. Maria Popova. The Marginalien. Originally spoken at Berkeley University Commencement Address. May 17, 1996. https://www.themarginalian.org/2013/07/23/vera-rubin-berkeley-commencement-address/

Hannah Szenes
Hendel, Nechama. Eli, Eli, Halicha L'Kesariya. trans. Malka Tischler.Hebrewsongs.com: Your online Library of Hebrew Song Words. https://www.hebrewsongs.com/?song=elieli

HOLIDAYS AND TRADITIONS

Alan King
Alan King. *Matzo Balls for Breakfast and Other Memories of Growing Up Jewish*. Glencoe, Illinois: Free Press, 2004.

Hankus Netsky
40 Years in Yiddishland: The Yiddish Book Center Celebrates the Klezmer Conservatory Band. Amherst, Massachusetts: Yiddish Book Center February 3, 2021.

Joseph Stein
Jerry Bock. *Sheldon Harnick. Joseph Stein. Fiddler on the Roof*: Based on Sholom Aleichem's Stories. New York City, New York: Crown, 1965.

Lawrence Kushner
Lawrence Kushner. *I'm God, You're Not: Observations on Organized Religion & Other Disguises of the Ego*. Woodstock, Vermont: Jewish Lights, 2010.

Nachman of Breslov
Rebbe Nachman of Breslov. *Likutey Halakhot, On the Four Volumes of the Shulchan Arukh*. Rabbi Nachman of Breslov, Book One, Volumes 1 & 2. Keren Rabbi Yisrael Udesser Foundation Woodstock, Vermont: Jewish Lights,1994.

Raizy Fried
Raizy Fried. An Interview with Raizy Fried, Author of *Lekovid Shabbos Kodesh, a Shabbos Lifestyle* Book. Gila Stern. The Boro Park View. Issue 61. November 25, 2020. https://issuu.com/thebpview/docs/issue_61_low_res

TIKUN OLAM

Abraham Joshua Heschel
Abraham Joshua Heschel. "The Religious Basis of Equality of Opportunity, Race and Religion." January 14, 1963. Voices of Democracy: The U.S. Oratory Project. Abraham Joshua Heschel quoted with the permission of Professor Susannah Heschel. https://voicesofdemocracy.umd.edu/heschel-religion-and-race-speech-text/

Angela Buchdahl
Rabbi Angela Buchdahl. "The World is Built on Kindness (Yom Kippur 5783)". October 4, 2022. Central Synagogue. 25.18 minutes. https://www.centralsynagogue.org/worship/sermons/the-world-is-built-on-kindness-yom-kippur-5783

Georgette Bennett
Georgette F. Bennett. *Thou Shalt Not Stand Idly By: How One Woman Confronted the Greatest Humanitarian Crisis of Our Time*. Wading River, New York: Wicked Son, 2021.

Ruth Westheimer
Ruth K. Westheimer. Dr. Ruth Westheimer: My Family Values. Nick McGrath. The Guardian. November 9, 2012. https://www.theguardian.com/lifeandstyle/2012/nov/10/dr-ruth-westheimer-my-family-values

BIBLIOGRAPHY

LAND OF MILK AND HONEY
The Bible
Psalms, 137:5-6. *The Holy Scriptures According to the Masoretic Text, a New Translation*. Philadelphia, Pennsylvania: Jewish Publication Society, 1917.

Yisrael Meir ha-Kohen Kagan (Chofetz Chaim)
Yitzchak Berkowitz. Shimon Finkleman. Chofetz Chaim: A Lesson a Day: The Concepts and Laws of Proper Speech Arranged for Daily Study. Rahway, NJ: Mesorah Publications, Ltd., 1995.

Golda Meir
Golda Meir. Testimony before the Anglo-American Committee of Inquiry, Jerusalem, Mandatory Palestine, March 25, 1946.

Theodor Herzl
Theodor Herzl. Altneuland. Trans. Nahum Sokolow. Leipzig, Germany: Hermann Seemann Nachfolger. 1902.

Yitzhak Rabin
Statement in the Knesset by Prime Minister Rabin on the Israel-PLO Declaration of Principles. Yitzhak Rabin, Prime Minister. Knesset. September 21, 1993. Jewish Virtual Library. https://www.jewishvirtuallibrary.org/statement-in-the-knesset-by-prime-minister-rabin-on-the-israel-plo-declaration-of-principles

DIASPORA
Emma Lazarus
Emma Lazarus. *The New Colossus: The Poems of Emma Lazarus in Two Volumes*, Vol. I. Boston, Massachusetts: Houghton Mifflin and Company, 1889.

Simon Dubnow
S. M. Dubnow. *Pis'ma o Starom' i Novom' Evreistvi'e*, p. 225. Obshchestvennaia pol'za, S.-Peterburg,1907.

Anzia Yezierska
Anzia Yezierska. *Children of Loneliness*. United Kingdom: Cassell and Company, 1923.

ART AND CULTURE
Lillian Hellman
Lillian Hellman. Letter to Rep. John S. Wood. U.S. Congressional Committee Hearing on Un-American Activities. May 19, 1952. Pt. 8, p. 3546.

Heinrich Heine
Heinrich Heine. "Almansor," *Heines Werke in fünfzehn Teilen*. Berlin, Germany: Deutsches Verlagshaus Bong & Co. 1821.

EDUCATION AND LEARNING
Maimonides
Letter to Joseph ibn Gabir, Cairo 1191, II, 15a-16d. Kobez teshuvot ha-Rambam ve-igrotav *Collection of Maimonides' Responsa and Letters*. ed. Abraham ben Aryeh Lichtenberg. Leipzig, Germany: Ba-defus shel H.L. Shnoys, 1859.

Henrietta Szold
Henrietta Szold. "The Education of the Jewish Girl." *The Maccabaean*. Vol 5. No. 1. July 1903. 8–10.

Emma Goldman

Emma Goldman. Anarchism: What It Really Stands For. Anarchy Archives. Goldman Reference Archive. Marxists.org. 2001. Transcription and Markup Dana Ward and Brian Baggins. Originally published in *Anarchism and Other Essays*. New York City, New York: Mother Earth Publishing Association, 1910. https://www.marxists.org/reference/archive/goldman/works/1910s/anarchism.htm

FAMILY AND HOME

Ben Stiller

The Humanitarian Impact of Eight Years of War in Syria. Before the Foreign Relations Committee, U.S. Senate. Ben Stiller. May 1, 2019. https://www.foreign.senate.gov/hearings/the-humanitarian-impact-of-eight-years-of-war-in-syria

Morris Joseph

Morris Joseph. *Judaism as Creed and Life*. Milton Park, Abingdon, Oxfordshire: Routledge, 1929.

HOLIDAYS AND TRADITIONS

Asher Ginsberg (Ahad Ha'am)

Asher Ginberg. Ha-Shiloah. Berlin, Germany. 1898.

TIKUN OLAM

Talmud

The Talmud (AD 200-500) Collection of Jewish rabbinical writings. Mishnah Sanhedrin 4:9; Yerushalmi Talmud, Tractate Sanhedrin 37a.

Rabbi Tarfon

Pirkei Avot 2:16. Attributed to Rabbi Tarfon.

Helen Suzman

Dennis Lee Royle. "Called Joan of Arc...She Fights Racism." Associated Press. *Madisonville Messenger*, July 23, 1963.

Lillian Wald

Lillian Wald. Crowded Districts of Large Cities. First Convention, National Council of Jewish Women. November 17, 1896. Philadelphia, Pennsylvania: The Jewish Publication Society of America, 1897. 258-268. HathiTrust.org https://babel.hathitrust.org/cgi/pt?id=nyp.33433083637946&seq=9

ABOUT THE AUTHOR

Dana Rubin is a speaker, author, and consultant focused on expanding diverse voices and viewpoints in the public conversation. She works with organizations all over the world to develop their talent to be recognized experts, brand ambassadors, and role models for the next generation. In 2023, she published *Speaking While Female: 75 Extraordinary Speeches by American Women*, showing the extent to which women's voices have helped shape the ideas and institutions of the United States for nearly four centuries. As a companion resource, she created the Speaking While Female Speech Bank (SpeakingWhileFemale.co), a free online resource with thousands of speeches by women from across time and around the world. Instagram: @danagrubin

ABOUT THE ARTISTS

Chavi Feldman is a multi-disciplinary artist who left her birthplace in Canada to make her home in Israel thirty years ago. She lives in the center of her beloved adopted country with her husband, four children, and her dog. She is the granddaughter of Holocaust survivors and she was instilled with a love of Israel by her grandfather, who was never able to immigrate there during his lifetime.

Chavi is constantly inspired by the beauty of Israel's unique climate. She is a whimsical artist and loves hiding lovebirds on domed roofs, hanging laundry in the windows, and the odd cat on a roof.

Chavi has a simple goal—to create meaningful and spiritual artwork. Whether you are Jewish, Christian, or any other religious denomination, the quotes she uses are universal: They are about peace, joy, love, and unity.

Star of David (p. 6), *Dove Peace* (p. 76), *Jonah and the Whale* (p. 96), *Repair the World* (p. 164)

Leah Bar Shalom is an Israeli artist born and raised in California, but now living in the Israeli mountains with her family. Leah is passionate about creating vibrant art that captures the beauty of Israel and the spirit of the Jewish people. She also runs a spiritual cooking YouTube channel called Jew Got It. Leah's art shop at jewgotitart.etsy.com is the perfect place to find unique hand drawn items and gifts with a Jewish twist, including special apparel, art, home decor, meaningful personalized gifts, or beautiful reminders of one's heritage. Each item Leah creates is carefully crafted with love and 15% of all her shop sales are donated to support Israel.

Love (p. 2), *Figs* (p. 24)

Eleyor Snir was born and raised in Israel and grew up on a kibbutz with eight siblings, nurturing her creativity through drawing and dreaming. Inspired by her mother, Mirik Snir, a renowned children's poet, she honed her skills at Tel-Aviv's Vital Art Institute, majoring in illustration and design. By age twenty, Eleyor's acclaimed illustrations adorned children's books worldwide. In 2015, Eleyor embarked on a new chapter of her life, relocating to Canada with her partner and four children. Despite the geographical distance, she remains deeply connected to her roots. Her art blends traditional Judaic motifs with contemporary themes, integrating Hebrew text to convey profound messages, creating a harmonious balance of heritage and innovation.

Open Hands (p. 58), *Woman of Valor* (p. 112), *Home Blessing* (p. 130), *Hanukkah* (p. 148), *Love* (p. 191)

artist | **Eleyor Snir,** *Love*

First published in 2024 by Wellfleet Press,
an imprint of The Quarto Group,
142 West 36th Street, 4th Floor,
New York, NY 10018, USA
T (212) 779-4972
www.Quarto.com

Wellfleet titles are also available at discount for
retail, wholesale, promotional, and bulk purchase.
For details, contact the Special Sales Manager by
email at specialsales@quarto.com or by mail at
The Quarto Group, Attn: Special Sales Manager,
100 Cummings Center Suite 265D, Beverly, MA
01915 USA.

10 9 8 7 6 5 4 3 2 1

ISBN: 978-1-57715-459-4

Digital edition published in 2024
eISBN: 978-0-76039-192-1

Library of Congress Cataloging-in-Publication Data

Names: Rubin, Dana, author.
Title: Jewish voices : inspiring & empowering quotes
     from global thought leaders / Dana Rubin.
Description: [New York] : Wellfleet Press, [2024] |
     Includes bibliographical references and index. |
     Summary: "Jewish Voices offers over 70 powerful
     quotes on topics including family, activism, art
     and culture, entertainment, and more from
     the Talmud to well-loved contemporary Jewish
     voices"-- Provided by publisher.
Identifiers: LCCN 2024005125 (print) | LCCN
     2024005126 (ebook) | ISBN 9781577154594
     (hardcover) | ISBN 9780760391921 (ebook)
Subjects: LCSH: Jews--Quotations.
Classification: LCC PN6095.J4 R83 2024 (print) |
     LCC PN6095.J4 (ebook) | DDC 080.92/3924--
     dc23/eng/20240215
LC record available at https://lccn.loc.
     gov/2024005125
LC ebook record available at https://lccn.loc.
     gov/2024005126

Group Publisher: Rage Kindelsperger
Editorial Director: Erin Canning
Creative Director: Laura Drew
Senior Art Director: Marisa Kwek
Managing Editor: Cara Donaldson
Editor: Sara Bonacum
Cover and Interior Design: Tara Long

Printed in China

throughout Whitehead's way of seeing. Of course; but it is equally true of Jung, perhaps even more so of Hillman.

Against such a background it is very difficult to adjudicate the implied difference (if I read Cobb correctly) between Whitehead's eternal objects and Jung's archetypes. The "eternal objects" are "absolutely neutral": so also are Jung's "archetypes," which we never "know" as they are in themselves. They are *a priori forms of representation* (*CW* 18:1183), making them not too dissimilar from the "eternal objects" when given their "ingression" and their "gradations of relevance" within our experienced structures of order (*PR* 83–109). There is nothing "honorific" about the "eternal objects," as Cobb quite rightly indicates, whereas in Jung the archetypes are always "numinous." "God," perhaps, supplies this element for Whitehead. "God's purpose in the creative advance is the evocation of intensities." He is indifferent as to which of the "eternal objects" is actualized; but "his aim for it is depth of satisfaction" when and as it arises (*PR* 105).

I turn now to Cobb's correlation between images of depth and images of temporal past: to wit, the past is the depth of each occasion of experience; the depth of the Jungian psyche corresponds to the whole of Whitehead's "actual world." This is probably an improvement on my own proposal, and especially so if we concur with Whitehead (*AI* 51) that Plato stressed the psychic factors in the Universe as the source of all spontaneity, and ultimately as the ground of all life and motion, such spontaneity being of the essence of the soul. Also, "symbolic reference" (as the mediating power in interpretation between "presentational immediacy" and "causal efficacy") must be primarily understood as *psychical* efficacy. On the one hand, process must not be abstracted from existence; on the other, existence must not be abstracted from process.

Whitehead was persuaded that "the universe is laying the foundation of a new type [of order], where our present theories of order will appear as trivial" (*ESP* 118–19).

> The creativity of the world is the throbbing emotion of the past hurling itself into a new transcendent fact. It is the flying dart, of which Lucretius speaks, hurled beyond the bounds of the world."
> (*AI* 177)

But there is a sense, he also says, in which "the world is in the soul" (*MT* 163). Thus, coincident with the metaphor of the dart is the metaphor of depth, of the pebbles in the pool: we must wait long, as

Nietzsche put it, to know *what* is falling into our depths.[4] Philosophy, therefore, is "speculative," or "imaginal," as the Jungians say. It "hovers," both in Jaspers's sense and in Whitehead's, reading the cyphers, and projecting the "cosmological story" (Whitehead) beyond the utmost bounds of human thought. Crucial to this effort, however, is the notation of Hillman: "I do not want ever to separate ideas from psyche. *I would remove discussion of ideas from the realm of thought to the realm of psyche*" (*RVP* 120–21). It is just here that there is always a cave beneath the cavern beneath the grotto beneath the cave. . . .

I have tried to stress the problem of language. Whitehead recognizes it succinctly: "The account of the sixth day should be written. He gave them speech, and they became souls" (*MT* 41), which suggests a reordering of my epigraphs:

Something unknown is doing we don't know what.—Eddington

Something is taking its course.—Beckett

Something archetypal is going on.—Hillman

8

Psychocosmetics and the Underworld Connection

CATHERINE KELLER

I. Introduction

> Psyche travels back to the goddess of love bearing a box said to contain the secrets of beauty, and she has been told not to open this box. Yet she cannot resist, for she is curious; she wants to *know*. And when she opens this box she falls into a deep sleep, a sleep which must be full of human memory, but which is past consciousness, past culture.
>
> —Susan Griffin, *Pornography and Silence*[1]

> The innate urge to go below appearances to the "invisible connection and hidden constitution" leads to the world interior to whatever is given. This autochthonous urge of the psyche, its native desire to understand psychologically, would seem to be akin to what Freud calls the *death drive* and what Plato presented . . . as the desire for Hades.
>
> —James Hillman, *DU* 27

Psyche's curiosity opens the current task, the search for the elusive Eros between the cosmology of Alfred North Whitehead and the psychologies of Carl Gustav Jung and James Hillman: the quest of psyche in and for cosmos. In Apuleius's version of the tale of Psyche's quest for the flown Eros, Psyche has to descend into the Underworld as the last and most dangerous labor assigned her by her mother-in-law, Aphrodite. The goddess of love wants the beauty secret of Persephone herself, the Queen of the Underworld. Psyche succeeds in emerging alive from her quest, having, according to Apuleius, "received a mystical secret in the box."[2] The secret in the box—is it a distillate of "the world interior to whatever is given"?

133

In *The Dream and the Underworld* James Hillman enters Hades, the Greek realm of the dead, as a profound metaphor of depth itself, of soul and dream space. The underworld passage must also be undergone, I believe, for an effectual discussion of the "invisible connection" between archetypal or Jungian psychology and Whiteheadian philosophy. But whereas Hillman works his bridge to the Underworld through the dominant perspective of Pluto, the brother of Zeus and King of Hades according to classical mythology, Persephone will provide the present entrance. We approach this goddess then not as *anima*, as derivative femininity or vulnerable and violated Other within a masculine soul-world, but as primary perspective. And Psyche offers a human image for our empathy as endangered souls, sometimes sleeping, sometimes seeking, sometimes finding in the sleep itself.

In the beauty box, the ancient myth of Persephone, redolent with the mysteries of Eleusis, mingles with the later allegory of Psyche's quest. Aphrodite exhibits jealous sadism toward Psyche, behaving, in Susan Griffin's words, as "the most extreme of pornographers";[3] her request for the secret of Persephone stems from the secondary narcissism of the successful sex-object. But does her desire, and Psyche's test, move below the patriarchal surface of the text and "below appearances"? Or is the secret after all a glorified cosmetic kit, and Psyche's curiosity nothing but soporific vanity in competition with the goddess—a tertiary narcissism? Psyche reunites with Eros—now on her terms, requiring his *visibility*—upon awakening, and becomes a goddess: is this a cosmetic vision, rendered by allegory psychocosmetic? Or is it a new relation to the cosmic Eros gained from the sleep "past consciousness," a sense for "invisible connection" enabling radical— let us call it *psychocosmic*—vision?

This tale intersects the myth of Persephone and Demeter, the daughter and mother according to Homeric myth who were separated when Hades abducted and raped the maiden, wanting her as his underworld wife. Demeter, goddess of agriculture, searched for her daughter, withholding the earth's fertility in her raging grief until, in the famous compromise, Zeus agreed to return Persephone for part of every year: the season when all things flower and flourish.

The myths as we read them are products of the triumph of gods over goddesses. But inasmuch as these goddesses, primoridal yet in process, emerge against what Mary Daly calls a "deep Background," they do not remain in the pretty poses or nightmare shadows of the

"Eternal Feminine." One reaches this Background by reading backwards, as Robert Graves, J. J. Bachofen, Erich Neumann, and, more recently and systematically, Marija Gimbutas have done; but even more, by reading forwards, as feminism now does. If Lévi-Strauss could include Freud's use of Oedipus as a variant of the myth itself, then the reemergence of the Eleusinian motif, for instance, in contemporary feminism (as in Adrienne Rich and Mary Daly) counts as "dreaming the myth onward."

So we have an image of *Psyche*, soul, at odds with her shadow, that cosmetic idol of aphrodisiac culture, in search of her own eros, and gaining herself, her apotheosis, through the hardships of confrontation. Her search culminates—or, rather, bottoms out—when she must enter Hades and bring back a bit of this beauty as deep as death. And we have in the Divine Mother and Daughter a dual perspective upon World: Mother as upperworld, symbolizing with "a simple ear of grain"[4] the solidarity of culture and nature—that is, both aspects of what we usually name *world* or *cosmos*; and Daughter as underworld, place of what has perished, of the shades of the dead and, according to Hillman, of the dreams, depth, and death which locate "the endless activity of soul-making" (*DU* 27). Hades' abduction of Persephone need not explain her presence in the underworld any more than Zeus's headache need explain the birth of Athena: these tales of female contingency upon male agency may count as themselves requiring reversal if the violated female power is to show forth.[5]

We do not evoke these goddesses here as paradigms of the psychology of women; to whatever extent they do express specifically female psychology, that Psyche may carry a secret—the "invisible connection" indeed—for soul and world. Psyche and Aphrodite, Persephone and Demeter will now stand less for content in what follows, either for metaphysical allegory or for Jungian analysis, than, with this text, as con-text.

If this quaternary crossing of divine persons will evoke the ideas of Psyche and Cosmos, with the underworld as place where the two quests cross, we can pose our question: what "hidden connection" do we seek by setting Jung and Whitehead into this context? Whitehead wrote above all out of an eros for the world, in its self-knowledge, Jung out of desire for the soul's knowledge of itself.

When in the textual aftermath of the living author the Jungian and the Whiteheadian schemes of insight begin to close in upon themselves, becoming monolithic models of scholarly or therapeutic ilk, it is the worldliness of psychology and the soulfulness of cosmology that erode. When by contrast we seek to know them together, do we do this sensing that the outer edges of Jung's psyche and the inner limits of Whitehead's cosmos meet? Is a rendezvous between world and soul possible, precisely where there reigns a multiply institutionalized politic of disconnection? If so, we do not look for a connection between Jung and Whitehead for its own sake or theirs, but rather for the sake of the "invisible connection" of the world (which is in the soul) to the soul (which is in the world). To decompose the barrier, Hillman's underworld methodology of "dissolving, decomposing, detaching, and disintegrating" (*DU* 27) comes into play, as cure for alienation.

II. Psychocosmetic Surfaces

Psychocosmic radicalism suggests a fundamental continuity of psyche and cosmos. This continuity alters the traditional sense and locus of both. Psyche has been "in here," interior, private, subjective, self-enclosed, experienced in opposition to the attributes it assigns to cosmos, as "out there," exterior, public, objective, social. Body then bounds and binds soul, which tells tales of exile in its own home. Freedom becomes escape from body, from community, from world, because within the mundane conditions of alienation freedom means freedom from relatedness. Any intermingling of psyche and world is suspected of primary narcissism, or at best of monistic or mystical metaphor. Soulful self-knowledge gives way to knowledge of a metaphysical substance preoccupied with self-preservation: "the soul," substantial and self-enclosed. The very grammar of Indo-European languages falls captive to substantialism, presupposing enduring subjects presiding over outside objects lodged in passive predicates.

Dualistic metaphysics never completely captured the life-and-death energies of soul. For example, the black culture's soulfulness, replete with soul sisters, soul brothers, and soul food, evokes an emotion of suffering, music, and hope; it recalls a nonsubstantial grammar of psyche—adjectival, adverbial, qualitative, with the continuity of rhythm. But in the Western mainstream, world has been scraped out of soul as surely as soul has been ground out of world, leaving no influx of supplies for soulfulness.

When human creatures sustain such a bifurcation of their world and its soul, they lose the sense of intimacy, of interest, of eros, in daily encounters: the beauty has drained out of experience. They suffer what can be called a *psychocosmetic condition*. The world appears as a series of flat surfaces, characterized by opacity and objectification, upon which a certain decorative distraction replaces any depth of attraction. Gradually the plasticity of world-shapes is trapped in the ironically immortal substance of plastic, as ugliness overspreads the suppressed cosmos. Thus the ancient meaning of *kosmos*—which suggested decorative order, as a parthenon frieze or a woman's jewelry, a world-arranging beauty—is mocked.

The subject soul in such a state decorates the world with its own projections: because it does not already partake in cosmos, does not really have a world, it must make one up. The world—all that is object, as body, other, society, nature—must hold its faces still for a makeup job, letting itself be painted with *a priori* categories, with sense-data, with secondary qualities. The subject cannot then greet a color, a person, in the gratitude of eros; in its sophistication it suspects itself of projection, of endowing the other with whatever interest the self has felt. For the psychocosmetic self, world is a place of idols and aliens. Pathetically undernourished, with no world as soul food, yet intent on maintaining an illusion of substantial independence, it enters into parasitical relations with a few pieces of its outside world. It craves its own permanence to make up for the lack of a present. Death above all insults and embarrasses it; rather than enter its own underworld, it threatens to take the whole world under.

We hear the howl of Demeter, of the world turned barren; beauty is trapped in underworld, and surrounded by ugliness. Psyche must continue her presumptuous quest for eros, for the cosmic intimacy rendered ever more unlikely by an environment ugly and closing. In a man-made perspective the ever-ready surface has been provided by woman, who must with her sexual allure make up the psychocosmetic state, while with her emotional nurture she makes up for its alienation. Cosmetics hide decomposition—the aging, dying process by which beauty insists upon underworld, upon the secrets of Persephone.

It is no coincidence that woman functions as living fetish for the psychocosmetic subject. The soul-world barrier can itself be seen as *sine qua non* of patriarchy.[6] For the barrier, like a break made manifest, preserves the severance of ego-warrior from mother—not just from one other but from all that can be as undifferentiated as Great Mother, the stuff of origins and returns. Only by erecting a radical barrier against world, and so against itself *qua* soul, can the illusion of independence, permanence, and control remain standing.

III. Whitehead in the Underworld

The contrast between the comparative emptiness of Presentational Immediacy and the deep significance disclosed by Causal Efficacy is at the root of the pathos which haunts the world.

—Whitehead, *S* 47

In Whitehead's insistence upon the priority of causal efficacy as the "vague, haunting and unmanageable" (*S* 47) depth of experience, the inchoate source of every actuality, he registers a philosophical protest against the psychocosmetic self. *Causal efficacy* in his work refers to the immanence of objects in a subject. The presences of things to each other disclose, according to this idea, a throb of unconscious energies transmitting the interconnexity of *actual entities*. Causal efficacy describes the dark fringes of the present, melting from immediate past into immediate future, the threatening, promising atmosphere of transition.

Presentational immediacy, by contrast, "displays a world concealed under an adventitious show, a show of our own bodily production." Presentational immediacy, "for all its decorative sense-experience, is barren" (*S* 43–44). One can argue that the world of sense-presentation, when it lacks felt reference to causal efficacy, defines precisely its psychocosmetic condition. Traditional philosophical psychology has focused on the immediate presentation of the senses, especially visual, as the privileged model for all perceiving and knowing. The surface show of sense-presentation is not superficial intrinsically, in actual perception. But taken in abstraction from the causal connexity with the past and future worlds, sense-data become sheer projections upon the inner screens of a solitary monad.

Causal efficacy "is a heavy, primitive experience" (*S* 44). Hard as it is to imagine a Victorian gentleman like Whitehead ever having *had* such an experience, his doctrine here embodies an epistemological revolution. Whitehead mainly intends this new analysis of two modes of perception to counter the pet prejudice of philosophers since Hume: "Experience has been explained in a thoroughly topsy-turvy fashion, the wrong end first. In particular, emotional and purposeful experience have been made to follow upon Hume's impressions of sensation" (*PR* 162). His entire cosmological case rests upon the appeal to a phase of experience of which we are not or only barely conscious, but which is presupposed by all conscious phases of experience.

In this attempt to undermine the logical priority of conscious sense-presentation and so the entire epistemological imperialism (still) dominating philosophy, something more than academic esoterica makes itself felt. To draw this out, I want to situate Whitehead's notion of soul in the locale of causal efficacy. He himself does not explicitly make the connection, but I believe it valuable in the formulation of the continuity of soul with world, *via* the unconscious. For in Whitehead's development of causal efficacy, particularly in the descriptive language of his book *Symbolism,* an underworldly tone seeps through. Citing the inscription found on old sundials in religious houses, *Pereunt et imputantur* ("the hours perish and are laid to account"), he draws the contrast in a way that suggests a disconnection of upperworld and underworld:

> Here 'Pereunt' refers to the world disclosed in immediate presentation, gay with a thousand tints, passing, and intrinsically meaningless. 'Imputantur' refers to the world disclosed in its causal efficacy, where each event infects the ages to come, for good or for evil, with its own individuality. (*S* 47)

The contrast of presentational immediacy and causal efficacy suggests the divine dyad of Aphrodite in her frothy upperworld tints and Persephone dwelling in the secret world beneath, ravaged and repressed, yet efficacious and needed. Demeter is the older upperworld, not "gay or passing" but fertile and cycling, until her Persephone is lost among the ghosts. Then she voices what Whitehead calls (in the quotation at the head of this section) "the pathos which haunts the world." In the Homeric myth she causes the barrenness of the earth; perhaps we can interpret her as merely making manifest the barrenness that is already the case—a more apt reading of truly divine anger. When depth is severed from beauty, and soul from world, barrenness results.

Whitehead then uses an explicit reference to the Greek underworld mythos, citing the wartime prime minister, William Pitt, on his deathbed: "What shades we are, what shadows we pursue!" Whitehead diagnoses: "His mind had suddenly lost the sense of causal efficacy, and was illuminated by the remembrance of the intensity of emotion which had enveloped his life, in its comparison with the barren emptiness of the world passing in sense-presentation" (*S* 49).

Whitehead does not develop an account of some fundamental breach, some disconnective malady deeper than the prejudices of philosophers. Invariably, one must read into his analysis any sense of historic crisis, where he describes merely an intellectual misunderstanding. The urgency felt in both feminist and Jungian cultural critique—what has gone wrong with our world?—hardly intrudes into his analysis of what really is, even when one feels the deeply therapeutic intent of his metaphysic. Process theologians, notably John Cobb, nonetheless find in his harmonious score an adequate background against which to sound the alarm.[7]

In fact the notion of "perpetual perishing" developed in *Process and Reality* describes the causal transitions between moments: the momentary occasion comes to be in its "subjective immediacy," arising from a feeling of the efficacious but "dead datum" (*PR* 164) of the past, and then, having become, it perishes into an "objective immortality" by which it is datum for the future. In between these transitions is the "internal process" of becoming, the "concrescence," in which the data from the past are composed into a single subjective experience. But in transition there is a dying, a passing into underworld immortality, a perishing of the fleshy present tense of immediate subjectivity. This dying of the old into the new encompasses every moment's actuality in this scheme. The solitude of the concrescent individual thus avoids the "solipsism of the present moment" (*S* 33), because the present internalizes its world.

The notion of "perpetual perishing," paired with "objective immortality," replaces the traditional notion of a substance or soul in which the ego of one moment would be numerically identical with that of the next. Metaphorical affinities suggest themselves to Hillman's description of the deliteralizing process, whereby "the old heroic ego loses its stuffing and returns to a two-dimensional shade" (*DU* 102). Whitehead's objective immortality is not unlike Hillman's account of "the worldwide practice, especially Egyptian, of putting objects from life into the tombs of the dead. Their whole world was transferred with them. They had to have immense supplies, for psychic life is an unending process, needing ample materials" (*DU* 96).

Hillman is speaking of dream-work, which "takes matters out of life and makes them into soul, at the same time feeding soul each night with new material" (*DU* 96). Yet an analogous process can be spied at work in every ontological moment of Whitehead's notion of soul: the relevant past, with its literalism of achieved actuality, offers itself as the "dead data," not unlike the *simulacra* or *Tagereste*: both release their energies for incorporation in the present. Out of these supplies the actual subject works its beauty, its life—which then itself passes into underworld, into "objective immortality" (as opposed to "subjective immortality," which has little resonance with the Greek shades anyway and is a different sort of issue, concerned with literal death). Causal efficacy is the underworld of actuality: the past energetically decomposing as the very ground of the present's composition. Dreams would then constitute an instance of such a rhythm of decomposing and recomposing, an instance in which the mode of presentational immediacy is vastly subordinated in importance to that of causal efficacy.

Now, however, we can locate soul within this cosmology. The rhythm of perishing occasions creates a looping effect, something like a stylized border of waves on a Greek vase, joining the moments without merging or generalizing them into numerical self-identity: this is "soul." Soul is the "stream of experiences," the "succession of my occasions of experience, extending from birth to the present moment. Now, at this instant, I am the complete person embodying all these occasions" (*MT* 163). This is a soul socially grounded in body, sense, world, rather than a discrete substance finally reducible to rational intellect: "nature in general and the body in particular provide the stuff for the personal endurance of the soul" (*MT* 162). The creation of soul, out of the self-creation of the subject, represents an instance of the channeling of the world's subjectivities through causal efficacy. Causal efficacy as the internalization of the relevant world is precisely the place of soul—in the liminal zones of transition from subject to subject. Soul is the connexity of a subject to past and future; yet one's past personality is only one current in an ocean of influences entering the moment's experience. The momentary subject can be said in this system to perish into soul, or soul into the emergent subjectivity; but simultaneously, the world itself is perishing, melting, into each moment of soul, and soul perishing into world.

"Self" is here interchangeable with "actual occasion," as any given moment of soul. Self then includes both notions of process: the inward *concrescence* uses the collective and unconscious input of *transition* between occasions of concrescence as its soul-food. Self would then include the entire past with its harmonization in "the consequent nature of God," as well as the plenitude of possibilities "graded according to their relevance." This plenitude is personified by Whitehead as the *primordial divine Eros,* the moment's ideal, its daimon. Self is a unique spatiotemporal perspective upon the totality, selective in its self-creation. The "ego" according to Whitehead is just as clearly momentary; it is what can be said to perish, with the self, as the conscious crest of the wave of soul. Soul, as psychic process, does not perish, because it is not an entity with the claim to subjective immediacy as is self or its ego-tip, except as it is composed at any given moment. Thus for Whitehead the way the world is in the soul is precisely analogous to the way the past moment of soul is in the present self, as its desubstantialized, deliteralized offering of supplies for further soul-making. Hillman's advocacy of soul-making is certainly resonant with such a view as the following: "It is not a mere question of having a soul or of not having a soul. The question is, How much, if any?" (*AI* 208).

Soul-making in Whitehead is simultaneously an alchemy of world-making: the subjectivity that, through special connection, strings into a necklace of soul is the same subjectivity shared by all actualities. We see how soul gets into world. How is soul in the world, however? While it would be untrue to the Whiteheadian vocabulary to claim that souls are the fundamental constituents of the world, subjects in fact *are.* All actual entities—animal, vegetable, or mineral—are subjects, partaking of experience: feeling the past's feelings, awareness, purpose. Soul is only a special temporal arrangement of such subjects. Reality is pan-subjective, though not panpsychic. And so not only does soul, like any other subject, pour into the world as causal influence; the nonhuman world already exhibits soulful tendencies. If atoms should not be called "souls," each atom nevertheless is a series of subjective experiences, and hence a rudimentary analogue to a soul. And in a third sense, soul is in the world, as the "indwelling Eros," the "primordial nature of God," immanent in every occasion as its own "initial aim." Thus the daemonic stimulates all things to become themselves, being itself their soul, the world-soul.

But there are problems, perhaps more in Whitehead's manner than in the matter, for the attempt to put his thought to a radically psycho-cosmic use. His conviction that philosophy is more allied "with mathematic pattern" than with music (*MT* 174), his lack of mythos, his Victorian sanguinity, can leave psyche starved for images—one must go elsewhere. It is true that, as he reclaims the notion of the cosmic Eros, and the deep Beauty arising in the nature of things, he contributes perhaps as best a philosopher can to the reuniting of Demeter with her daughter. And this reunion does not force Persephone to abdicate her underworld powers, but rather allows her to reclaim them: reconciled, she embraces as from below, with an underworld coolness of perpetual perishing in her arms. But from Whitehead, in his ontological serenity, one learns little concerning the rape: the question of *why* the world is turning barren, why the mother cannot find the daughter, why—as Hillman puts it in another context—"the world is inundating me with its unalleviated suffering" (*S 1982*: 76). How did it happen? What is the mythic narrative, the historical precipitate, through which the World split into shallow surface and deadly darkness, and lost its delicate life in Soul? Why did psyche have cosmos scraped out of it?

Jung provides the diagnosis we do not find explicit in Whitehead. We will see, to be sure, that if Whitehead sublimates diagnosis too much into descriptions, Jung turns diagnosis too easily into prescriptions. But with insight hardly paralleled in depth and imagination, Jung sees the great dramas of unwholesomeness. Unfortunately, at vital points he proceeds to eternalize them and so prescribe them wholesale as the healing "eternal truth of myth."

IV. "Hence 'at bottom' the psyche is simply 'world'" (Jung, *CW* 9/I:123)

Is there a sense comparable to that in Whitehead in which Jung's psyche implies the world? A temptation for Jungian psychology, if not its intent, lies in a tendency to reinforce the dichotomy of world and self by pulling deep into the psyche, into its myths and processes, its religious function, in a way that avoids any atmosphere of reductionism or "mere psychology." The psyche has its own world, rich and dramatically satisfying, and can then leave the "external world" outside, simply uninteresting—except perhaps to extraverts, whom Jung finds uninteresting. In his passion for the reality of soul, against both the materialism of science and the dogmatism of theology, both of which shrivel psyche, Jung often disregards the "outer" world.

This tendency is perhaps most evident in his theory of projection (or introjection), which can support the very materialism he battles by rendering up the deadened world it seeks:

> If the historical process of world despiritualization continues as hith-
> erto, then everything of a divine or daemonic character outside us
> must return to the psyche, to the inside of the unknown man, whence
> it apparently originated. (*CW* 11:141)

The world then has no subjective life but that with which we endow it.
This notion that the soul not only lends the world its interest but takes
it back again, through projection and introjection, is at the heart of the
psychoanalytic version of the psychocosmetic condition. This puts the
paltry human self in a double bind: it must first make up, not simply
grow or cultivate, what it is to nourish itself on.

When it comes to anima projections, the teleology of which is to
reconnect a male to his unconscious soul, the psychocosmetic cycle of
projection and retrojection seems assured: the value of a real woman
for men is contained in her ability to excite projection—or to be so
anerotic, so plain, as to leave him to explore his psychic depth with
anima-hookers elsewhere.

One does not come to the Jungian tradition to seek direct affinities
to the Whiteheadian theory of relations—R. D. Laing or Thomas Szasz,
or contemporaries of Whitehead like William James or Harry Stack
Sullivan, display a more clearly process-relational view. But Jung's exploration of the depth of psyche leads, by way of breakdown or breakthrough, to a transpersonal or collective dimension of psyche, intrinsically
unconscious yet revealed by inference from its spontaneous symboli-
zations, in which the isolation of individuals ceases. Can we think of
this collective unconscious in terms of the interconnexity of causal
efficacy? Jung, like Whitehead, uses the language of microcosm for the
individual psyche. But is it in any sense true for Jung as for Whitehead
that the actual world is summarized in the individual as his or her very
stuff?

One may consider archetypes, the crystallized content of the collective unconscious, as partaking of its historical and cumulative character. That they are "present always and everywhere" (*CW* 9/I:89)
coordinates well with the Whiteheadian view of all actualities as potentials for the becoming of all other actualities: "each happening is a
factor in the nature of every other happening" (*MT* 164). The hypothesis
of the archetypes might also lend empirical and experiential content to
the more formal notion of the initial aim, especially as its "eternal
objects" come to function as "propositions," or "objective lures for
feeling." "Eternal objects" in Whitehead suggest pure, formal possi-

bilities of the sort characterized by any abstraction, and so in and of themselves cannot be equated with archetypes. The dynamic and telic functions of archetypes, as well as their numinosity, suggest a pure possibility entering into symbolization through the initial aim, itself a causally efficacious mode. In any case, Jung's idea of a collective reservoir of human and finally planetary experience sheds psychological light on Whitehead's view of the past as consequent and efficacious, transmitted *in toto* from one occasion to the next.

But as soon as archetypes situate themselves in process metaphysics, they are being stretched toward their least essentialist, most historical significance. They become capable of much more evolution than Jung implies when he emphasizes specific archetypes rather than the collective unconscious in its more powerfully evolutionary sense. For Whitehead it would be impossible to say: "This collective unconscious does not develop individually but is inherited" (*CW* 9/I:90). He would claim that the cumulative past is both individually developed *and* inherited, because the inheritance of the past by every occasion suggests that, while the past itself does not change, each individual both inherits the past and contributes something new to its total content. However minute the change—perhaps an almost negligible shift of perspective— something has been added to what the future will inherit. Inasmuch as the archetypal organization of the past expresses its own energies, its own personalities and causal influences, it has transcended the pristine eternity of pure possibility.

There is a world-inclusive and world-transformative power suggested by a more radically evolutionary interpretation of the collective unconscious. For example, we need not then acquiesce in repeatedly unchanging archetypes of the "Eternal Feminine" whose images function as complementary compensations for a collective consciousness based on androcentrism. We may then understand the growing mythic edge of contemporary feminism as a collective transformation of the archetype: the goddesses themselves change. Their new images break old feminine idols, evoking new possibilities in the "psychoid continuum" through the experience of women—through, in Adrienne Rich's parlance, the "gynergetic continuum."

There is ample evidence of Jung's interest in dissolving the soul-world boundary. He says, for example: "the human psyche is in no way outside nature. It is one of the natural phenomena." The world, both as nature and as culture, is evoked as psychic context. Jung carries this worldliness of soul through even to an explicit nondualism, thereby making causal interaction not unintelligible:

> Psyche cannot be totally different from matter, for how otherwise could it move matter? And matter cannot be alien to psyche, for how else could matter produce psyche? Psyche and matter exist in one and the same world, and each partakes of the other, otherwise any reciprocal action would be impossible. (*CW* 9/II:413)

That "one and the same world" would be the causal underworld where psyche and matter conspire in the dark—in the place before consciousness.

V. Shutting Him Out:
Alienation and Matricide

It is most telling for the present tale that Jung's psychocosmic radicalism never waxes stronger than when he approaches the archetype of mother, or of the mother-daughter dyad. But this is not surprising, because for him the entire unconscious symbolizes itself as *magna mater*. If *mater,* matter, and the collective unconscious root in the same stuff, the etymology holds good. Thus in his prophetic interpretation of the dogma of the Assumption (appreciated even by Mary Daly),[8] he derives hope for the reconciliation not only of "masculine" and "feminine" but also of matter and spirit. He complains that with "the decline of alchemy the symbolical unity of spirit and matter fell apart, with the result that modern man finds himself uprooted and alienated in a de-souled world" (*CW* 9/I:197).

A few pages prior he tells us that "for a man the mother typifies something alien, which he has yet to experience and which is filled with the imagery latent in the unconscious" (*CW* 9/I:192). In saying "yet to experience," he means with ego consciousness, because "mother" is always and already known with infant awareness. Whence this alienation in a relation of original intimacy? Jung's assessment holds good as phenomenological description, or as diagnosis, of male psychology within the reigning circumstance known as *patriarchy.* But is it possible that this "alien" mother and the "de-souled world" originate in the same moment? Perhaps indeed this is Jung's own implication.

Jung's work could be described as one long attempt to reconcile the hypertrophied ego of Western consciousness with its maternal source, the collective unconscious, without succumbing to the temptation to extinguish consciousness in her gaping womb. But might not the project remain an opus of impossibility within its present terms? As long as one presupposes the *necessity* of ego-development according to the model of the hero, I believe, one foredooms the case. By the time the hero enters the second half of life and might "individuate," the toll taken in alienation seems for most individuals and for the collective culture itself well-nigh incurable. As for women, they can find no viable role in this scheme, unless to embody compensatory oppositions and spurious symmetries—in short, to complement the hero.

In admirable distinction from Freud's myth of primary patricide (based on the greater importance of the father in Freud's thought), Jung recognizes that *culture rests on a recurrent matricide*. The fact that Jung overgeneralizes about hero myths, reading into them even more mother-slaughter than texts make evident, may be to his credit as a diagnostician of worldview. Furthermore he knows a debt to this mother is owed and must be paid, a major reconciliation effected.

Nonetheless, his habit of freezing historical, cultural conditions into archetypal inevitability here sets his work in solidarity with the status quo. He renders the primal act of matricide which founds patriarchy and its alienated consciousness an eternal necessity, a Luciferian (light-bearing) virtue:

> There is no consciousness without the distinguishing of opposites. That is the paternal principle, the Logos, which eternally struggles to extricate itself from the primal warmth and primal darkness of the maternal womb; in a word, from unconsciousness. . . . Unconsciousness is the prime sin, evil itself, for the Logos. Therefore its first creative act of liberation is matricide. (*CW* 9/I:178)

Consciousness and its requisite differentiation are consistently portrayed as a form of male ego-development based on hostility to maternity. As Marduk, he creates his world from her death. Genesis becomes gynocide.

> The world begins to exist when the individual discovers it. He discovers it when he sacrifices the 'mother,' when he has freed himself from the mists of his unconscious condition within the mother.

The violent symbolic equation of birth from mother with murder of mother displays the inflated solipsism of any world-discovery within a world-alienating condition. This ego reversed his dependence upon world: it now depends upon him. It is a world made up, secondary. Woman then reappears as drudge or decoration, dependent, contingent, worldly, and uncosmic.

The very opposite of Jung's above claim may be true. *What if this primordial matricide is precisely the process whereby the world is lost, not gained?* What if we observe at this point (which Jung has located better than anyone else) the severance of psyche from cosmos? Or, in Whitehead's terms, a process whereby the world of causal efficacy is definitively suppressed, replaced with that of the vivid, controllable, but barren world of presentational immediacy? Unless, after all, to gain the world is to conquer it, to subdue its chaos and possess its powers, what is the hero's achievement but the ontological severance of his soul from its matrix? The following passage suggests the impossible ambivalence of such a state of alienation:

> The myth of the hero seems to us to be the myth of our own suffering unconscious, which has that unsatisfied yearning—which can rarely be appeased—for all the deep sources of its own being, for the body of the mother, and in it for communion with infinite life in the countless forms of existence.

No wonder appeasement is rare: the hero himself has cut off the sources. Perhaps inevitably, Jung's developmental psychology takes the viewpoint of the heroic son seeking the re-sources of this world-mother in his state of alienation, finally seeking reconciliation: yet the theory itself does not question the necessity of severance. The presupposition of the heroic, belligerent male ego at once romanticizes and inhibits Jung's insights into the riches of a collectively shared psyche.

At certain moments another possibility emerges, however, here embodied in the relation of mothers and daughters:

> The psyche pre-existent to consciousness (e.g., in the child) participates in the maternal psyche on the one hand, while on the other it reaches across to the daughter psyche. We could therefore say that every mother contains her daughter in herself and every daughter her mother, and that every woman extends backward into her mother and forward into her daughter. . . . This leads to a restoration or apocatastasis of the lives of her ancestors, who now, through the bridge of the momentary individual, pass down into the generations of the future . . . so that all unnecessary obstacles are cleared out of the way of the life stream that is to flow through her. (*CW* 9/I:316)

One hopes that he is not referring to mere maternal biology when he speaks of a "life stream," but to his own more Bergsonian notion of libido, an *élan* energizing body and soul. The context of his awareness of the mother-daughter continuity is a discussion of the Demeter-Persephone mythos. He recognizes clearly that the myth "is far too feminine to have been merely the result of an anima-projection" (*CW* 9/I:383). To the "femme à homme" he juxtaposes these female figures as existing

on the plane of mother-daughter experience, which is alien to man and shuts him out. In fact, the psychology of the Demeter cult bears all the features of a matriarchal order of society, where the man is an indispensable but on the whole disturbing factor. (*CW* 9/I:383)

This is an odd statement. Woman again is "alien," other; and Jung never considers how myths of Father and Son, or indeed of Mother and Son, might shut women out. Moreover, there is no evidence at all that the ritual of Eleusis did exclude men.

Jung's colleague Carl Kerenyi sensed the importance for men of the Mysteries precisely because of the female imagery: "Men, too, entered into the figure of Demeter and became one with the *goddess*. To recognize this is the first step towards an understanding of what went on at Eleusis."[9] In the increasingly patriarchal Athens of the classical and Hellenistic periods, the mysteries at Eleusis celebrating the Two Goddesses provided in fact the major religious event of Athens for both male and female populations.

Thrice happy are those of mortals, who having seen these rites depart for Hades, for them alone it is granted to have found life there; to the rest, all there is evil.[10]

While it is certainly the case that the male, represented by Hades as rapist abductor, is portrayed as a "disturbing factor," his image suggests to Jung no violence, no alienation. The restitution of a mother-daughter bond of the goddess, beyond the rape, reestablishes the rhythmic rapport of life and death, of upperworld and underworld. At the heart of the mysteries seems to have worked a memory or prophecy of a nonpatriarchal (but not therefore matriarchal) harmony, symbolized by the modulations of mother and daughter but excluding no males except those who excluded themselves. The paranoid sentiment that this "communion with infinite life," some luscious bond of psyche and cosmos, is available exclusively to women itself expresses and institutionalizes the alienation.

VI. The-rapist

We see what is not there. We see visions. We know there is a world
without rape and this world is in our minds.

—Susan Griffin[11]

Mary Daly responds to Jung's jocular treatment of the mythos with what
might be the voice of the enraged Demeter:

> identifying with the gods, particularly with Pluto, who had abducted
> Demeter's daughter, Persephone, Jung says of the divine rapist hus-
> band that he had to surrender his wife every year to his mother-in-
> law for the summer season. With his semantic sleight of hand, the
> Divine Daughter is re-born as 'his wife' and the Divine Mother is
> baptised as 'his mother-in-law.' Thus the therapist proclaims his sol-
> idarity with the rapist, identifying himself, as many women have
> noted, as the/rapist.[12]

Identifying the psyche more as the violated daughter than as Hades,
Hillman evokes the "Persephone experience" as only one among many
modes of descent to the underworld. He apparently, nonetheless, en-
tertains a certain mythic solidarity with the rapist:

> To be a *psycho*therapist and work in depth, one must in some way or
> another cooperate with Hades.
>   The intervention of Hades turns the world upside down. The point
> of view of life ceases. . . . [W]e participate in Hades' rape, which is,
> let us remember, not just psychopathy, but a central initiatory mystery
> in the Eleusis myths. This rape threatens the intact psychological
> system that takes its strength from life, holding to human relationships
> and the natural ways of Demeter's daughter. Rape moves the Perseph-
> one soul from the being of Demeter's daughter to the being of Hades'
> wife, from the natural being of generation, what is given to a daughter
> by mothering life, to the psychic being of marriage with what is alien,
> different, and is not given. (*DU* 48)

Deep at work is the assumption that the realm of mother, of nature, and
of life is metaphorically less conducive to soul-making, to depth, than
that of wife: to transcend biology or first naïveté, indeed to descend,
demands the subordination of the female to the male sphere, the "marriage of death."

Some women write in full sympathy with Hades as well: "To be
Persephone, to be *this* goddess, Persephone *must* be raped. . . . I feel
I understand now how Persephone moves from defense against Hades

to love for him."[13] Within and without, women have indeed been required to make this move. But this sort of psychic acquiescence in the
patriarchal version of the myth endows the symbolism of rape with an
air of sacred necessity. It is a form of what Simone de Beauvoir calls
woman's "complicity" in her own oppression.

But what seems extraordinary at Eleusis, suggestive of its prepa-
triarchal origins,[14] is the capacity to recognize the tragedy and the
injustice of the violation *as* such in a cosmos already saturated with
divine rapacity. Countless rapes constitute the epiphanies of Zeus and
his brothers.

Rape complements matricide, reenacting the fundamental violence
in reverse: now the hostile ego moves into, rather than out of, the
female. In a victorious parody of eros, of connectivity, the male makes
up for the alienation of his made-up world. Rape completes the psychocosmetic cycle of alienated desire which keeps the androcentric psyche in its own context (this is why feminists must often take things
"out of context"). The slogan "take back the night" suggests the im-
perative of a new underworld journey: it becomes a metaphor for the
post-heroic culture, the "world without rape."

Of course, we violate the myth itself if we take *its* rape literally.
Yet one can well understand at such a point why Naomi Goldenberg,
as a feminist, criticizes the archetypalists for going too far in their
deliteralizing.[15] Yet we need not resort to weighing degrees of literalism
in order to hear the woman's experience encoded in the myth. The rape
of Persephone is certainly a metaphor for all the literal rapes of all
women, and at the same time for the violation of all the life in each of
us that is delicate, maiden-like, vulnerable. The rape expresses the
violence that rends the woman from her freedom, the body from its
place on earth, the underworld of eros and depth connection from the
upperworld of daylit interactions. These are interconnected violations,
suggesting the psychosocial matrix in which the systemic and growing
phenomenon of literal rape continues to present itself as a viable mode
of self-creation for males who are, perhaps, overwhelmed by power-
lessness and rage and their own fear of death.

Rape as metaphor and rape as act feed upon each other, but not as
isomorphic realities. The act, ritually played out in every city every
night, literalizes eros, denying bodies the translucency of their psychic
subjectivity. The act enacts the myth. It expresses the ultimate futility
of a psychocosmetic reduction. In the imagery and in the act of rape,

the alienated psyche renders itself soulless by canceling the world out as woman, and the woman out as world. As it belies the soul, or causal efficacy, of the victim, it pushes not only her but also the underworld itself into a realm of oblivion. Perhaps such deadly actions intend to deny death itself. Certainly woman has borne the brunt of mortality and its imagery of death, corruption, age, and finitude. When Persephone is raped and wived, the inflowing world, what Whitehead refers to so beautifully as "these sources of power, these things with an inner life" (*S* 57), are locked in unknowing, in the sleep of a dissociated underworld. It deadens the subtle hearing Hillman is calling up from below: "There is an opening downward within each moment, an unconscious reverberation, like the thin thread of the dream that we awaken with in our hands each morning leading back and down into the images of the dark" (*DU* 67).

The violation represents a systemic disorder in the cultural epistemology. Only through great labor do men or women begin to regain the connection to the life locked in the darkness—not so as to lose themselves in underworld exploration, but so as to let the deep underground support and energize worldly life, in all its death-bound finitude and frailty. Thus Adrienne Rich affirms the importance of a resurrection in which "it is a mother whose wrath catalyzes the miracle, a daughter who rises from the underworld." When Persephone appeared in a blaze of light with her infant son, demonstrating that "birth in death is possible," says Rich, she embodied a response to the systemic disconnection: "The real meaning of the Mysteries was this reintegration of death and birth, at a time when patriarchal splitting may have seemed about to sever them entirely."[16]

VII. Return

The splitting of death from life, of soul from world, has rendered the descent dangerous but necessary. The knowledge of their interplay, in what Whitehead calls *causal efficacy*, in what Jung calls the *collective unconscious*, eludes us, and Eleusis is no more. Thus Hillman's profound act of obeisance to the perspective of Hades, in spite of the failure to step outside of the patriarchal context which renders Hades so dreadful to begin with, must return to haunt this thought process. But does Hillman not in *The Dream and the Underworld* surrender the daylight world of Demeter and presentational immediacy to that death-defying-

and-denying ego he so brilliantly disarms in all his works? It is as though the hero and his Zeus-styled gods preside over life itself. Who is Hades but the shadow, the brother of Superego Zeus, the conspirator in the rape?

Hillman depicts the death-realm as an end in itself, the final cause of which is soul-making: "by the call to Hades I am referring to the sense of purpose that enters whenever we talk about soul" (*DU* 31). Yet can the underworld contain its own telos so well that it functions, as a concept, to counter the realm of unconscious interconnection of soul with world suggested by Whiteheadian primitivity? Hillman says:

> When we give an account of the dream's images and language by referring to other influences—other persons, sense impressions, past memories—we are in a materialism, although we may never have used reductive terms. (*DU* 70)

I have, by contrast, suggested that underworld is precisely the locus of influences, vast and particular; it is the place where the world flows in as "dead datum," as residues of subjectivities past, to be accepted as matter in the moment's fresh finality. That Hillman continues in the tradition of archetypal mother-repulsion precisely where criticizing the fixation upon which it is based should not come as a surprise. "Great Mother" has become so much a matter of projection of nostalgic therapists and male-identified camp followers that one must appreciate Hillman's assessment of "Monism as Momism" (*DU* 35):

> She is our materialism; the common derivation of both matter and *mater* . . . is neither an accident nor a joke. She is that modality of consciousness which connects all psychic events to material ones, placing the images of the soul in the service of physical tangibilities. (*DU* 69)

But his underworld emphasis leads him, in conjunction with the previous dismissal of "influences," to the unnecessary inference that any connection between the two worlds is tantamount to a subservience of under to upper. The Jungian Great Mother may merit Hillman's matriphobia, but his critique implicates the image of Mother *überhaupt* in a voracious materialism. Jung's association of the hero's matricide with both sides of the dualism—the triumphant rationalism, the resentful materialism—suggests (in spite of its problems) a crucial reading of cultural history. His genial analysis of the bodily Assumption of Mary as a prophecy of matter's need to re-soul, and spirit's need to find body, contributes to a psychocosmic perspective. Only through the violent split of the sense-world from its own underworld, its own mystery of influence, does matter become the subject of materialism.

In a pivotal essay proclaiming *"Anima Mundi*: The Return of the Soul to the World," Hillman lures psychotherapy back into the material world, calling it to turn its well-trained attentions upon a world saturated with soul. He inaugurates a dramatic widening of the range of psychotherapy: "a way might open again toward a metapsychology that is a cosmology, a poetic vision of the cosmos which fulfills the soul's need for placing itself in the vast scheme of things" (*S 1982*: 82). After indulging the soul's inner world of images over and against the outer cosmos, he now proclaims the *anima mundi,* the Platonic soul of the world, which, he tells us, Ficino translated as *Aphrodite.* "With the loss of Aphrodite cosmos has become cosmic—vast, empty, fantastic."

Yet we began with a mythic reading of Aphrodite as lost to herself, her more ancient radiance locked in the cosmetic farce of beauty which blocks precisely the *aesthesis* Hillman evokes. *World must be flowing through soul if soul is to shine forth in world*: this is the mutuality of a cosmic eros. Hillman suggests that, to grasp the Greek account of perception as a perception of the heart,

> one must already, as did Psyche in Apuleius' tale, stand in the temple of Aphrodite, recognizing that each thing smiles, has allure, calls forth *aesthesis.* "Calling forth," provoking, *kaleo*: this was Ficino's derivation of Aphrodite's main characteristic, *kallos,* beauty. (*S 1982*: 82)

This is precisely the *modus operandi* of the notion of the primordial lure, with at once Greek and Hebrew precedents, which for Whitehead describes the divine impact upon the inchoate occasion.

Feminism casts a dark glance—underworldly at that—upon mythic romanticism, and would here remind us that, though Psyche certainly grew and deepened immeasurably by contending with Aphrodite's sadism, the evil remained evil. So we might wonder whether the degradation of Aphrodite to patriarchal mother-in-law and pornographic idol does not prefigure "the brutal uniformity and degradation of quality" (*S 1982*: 72) that torment psyche and cosmos today. Is her loss of self, which is our loss of world, an image of the suppression of that *aesthesis,* the repression of that feel for primary quality and *Ding-an-sich*, upon which rests a culture of heroic egoism and external relations?

What then is the secret of the beauty from below? On the surface it is a caprice of vanity, suicidally reenacted by Psyche in her desire to attract her flown husband. She succumbs to narcissistic curiosity, and loses consciousness, then like Sleeping Beauty is rescued by her Eros. Awakened from her aesthetic slumbers, she marries him: a tale of hardcore psychocosmetics comes to its conclusion with the reconciliation of Psyche, Aphrodite, and Eros. But the tale has been calling all along for another reading. Is it possible that in the beauty from below, Persephone granted a mystery at once to Aphrodite and to Psyche—to the world as ensouled, to the human soul? Of course we can only *know* as Psyche, upon her awakening.

What is the beauty sleep that engulfed her? Its secret resists translation; we can perhaps trace its fragrance on the air, its echo in our effort. It seems to contain a knowledge that cannot become conscious as long as it remains below—no more, indeed, than can the "initial phase" of causal efficacy or the collective depth of the unconscious be rendered up to epistemological mastery. Yet something can be brought up, some sample of this beauty efficacious with perpetual perishing. Is there in its wake a new intuition, a clearer inference, into the internal relations in which Aphrodite becomes again world-soul? Through the underworld transitions, the moment-by-moment dying and rising, soul partakes in the "life and motion" that, according to Plato and then Whitehead, is its rhythm. Indeed, Plato suggests that the real name of Persephone is not Destroyer but *Perepaphe,* etymologically derived: "because she touches that which is in motion, herein showing her wisdom. And Hades, who is wise, consorts with her, because she is wise."[17]

The wisdom of Underworld reverses the perspectives of the ego-warrior's world. We sense in the curiosity that passes through the secret sleep a radical art of psychocosmetics, one that might again expose "the colors in the face of things, the radiance of the Gods shining in the material world" (*S 1982*: 82)—if the Goddesses will find themselves, find each other, find us. In direct allusion to the final task of Psyche, Susan Griffin suggests an awakening hope:

> For the part of the mind that is dark to us in this culture, that is sleeping in us, that we name 'unconscious,' is the knowledge that we are inseparable from all other beings in the universe. Intimations of this have reached us.[18]

9

Psychocosmetics

A Jungian Response

ROBERT L. MOORE

I want to begin my response to Catherine Keller's essay by placing my comments in a cultural perspective that can illuminate the wider context of our discussion. Much has been made of late of the challenge of creating a *postmodern* approach to culture and personality. The importance of this task can hardly be overestimated. The human achievement of modernity has indeed been a mixed blessing. Although it has reflected an important achievement of consciousness and its capacity for discrimination and autonomy, it has brought with it an alienation from the physical world, from the body, and from the unconscious. Much of Keller's essay can best be understood as a sophisticated critique of the culture of modernity. Her insightful analysis of the relationship between alienation in sexual relationships and alienation from the world is a telling indictment of the modern consciousness. From a Jungian point of view, this modern consciousness in part reflects the dominance of the archetype of the hero, resulting in what some have called the "heroic ego" of modernity. This ego is inflated, cut off from its roots, and seeks to deny its limitations and its embeddedness in the physical and social world.

A postmodern culture and consciousness will have to find ways to relativize the inflated modern ego and to reestablish appropriate relationships to the biosocial ground that is the ego's matrix. One sign of contemporary movement toward postmodern sensibilities is the current interest in ritual process and its role in human life. Inspired to a great extent by the seminal work of the cultural anthropologist Victor Turner, this renewal of awareness of the importance of ritual in human experience has been attracting the attention of scholars in disciplines ranging from neurophysiology to religious studies. Keller's reference to the "liminal zones" of the soul suggests that the place of soul is that sacred space which Turner called *liminality*,[1] a transformative space that is elicited whenever an old psychosocial adaptation has outlived its usefulness and must be transcended. This is an insight shared by many contemporary Jungian analysts. They recognize that liminal states are where the unconscious is most manifest, where the opposites are reconciled, where appears a center of orientation (called the Self) which is beyond the ego and which makes possible a relativization and reorganization of the ego complex that makes it more appropriate to the claims of the real world.

Process thinkers and Jungians alike would do well to explore the importance of ritual process in general and the work of Victor Turner in particular. Soul-work is certainly what one does with one's solitariness (to use Whitehead's phrase [*RM* 47]); but it is also done in a biosocial matrix with clearly discernible ritual dimensions. One agenda for us, therefore, should be to develop a Whiteheadian interpretation of the transformative dynamics in ritual process that could also be used to interpret the ritual dimensions of the interactions characteristic of analysis.

Another important emphasis in Keller's discussion is her criticism of some popular ways of reading the Jungian perspective on projection (see section IV). There is a tendency among some Jungians and other interpreters of Jung to reduce erotic relationships in general and those between men and women in particular to a by-product of "splitting" phenomena in the psyche. According to this point of view, the physical world becomes lifeless when projected inner contents of the psyche are withdrawn and recognized as having internal and not external significance. Also, as she has pointed out, a man's seemingly erotic connection with a woman is often interpreted as being in fact an autoerotic relationship with a projected image of the man's anima. This line of interpretation does indeed lead to a devaluation of both world and woman as realities beyond the inner life of the male. A more fruitful, and no doubt more accurate, interpretation would be that of considering projection as *interfering* with true erotic relatedness rather than enhancing it. Splitting phenomena do in fact lead to a kind of enchanted world, but an enchantment that blocks relatedness rather than calling it forth.

This gets us to an important aspect of Hillman's recent thought that needs a good deal of emphasis if we are to understand the controversy surrounding his work. Most interpreters of Jung have emphasized his relationship with Freud, and this has resulted in what we might call a predominantly Freudian reading of Jung. This approach, while certainly having much merit, neglects the importance of the influence of the great analyst Alfred Adler. Adler's approach to analysis and psychotherapy put far more emphasis on the social matrix of human behavior than did Freud's. For Adler, all *psycho*pathology was at the same time *social* pathology: a depreciation of the reality and claims of the social world. An unwillingness to cooperate with the realities of the social world, to find one's natural place in the cosmic order, always reflected a lack of what Adler called *social interest* and led to psychopathology. Such psychosocial pathology always manifested distancing behavior and depreciation of the other. Hillman's very reluctance to discuss the intricacies of structural elements in metapsychology, either Jungian or Freudian, together with his emphasis on the fictive character of imaginative processes and his turn outward to the world, make it clear that Hillman's reading of Jung has taken an important Adlerian turn. Keller's criticism of residual hierarchical modes of relatedness that may be discerned in some Jungian perspectives on the relations between men and women also echoes Adler's own vision of cooperation and mutuality between the sexes. Here both Hillman's and Keller's criticisms and revisions of Jungian theory support each other and merit further development and elaboration.

Perhaps the most interesting issue raised by Keller is whether a postpatriarchal understanding of masculinity is a contemporary possibility. Is there, in short, the possibility of a mature masculinity that is not grounded upon rape and alienation? Much progress is being made today in understanding the differences between the sexes in their psychological development. One of the most significant books on this topic is Carol Gilligan's *In a Different Voice*,[2] a treatment of the developmental psychology of women. Though a committed feminist, Gilligan teaches us not only about the developmental tasks of women but also about the way in which the development of masculine psychology differs from and complements that of feminine psychology. In a manner paralleling Keller's analysis she notes that the most difficult task for the woman is developing autonomy, whereas for the man it is achieving relatedness. Keller's criticism of the heroic masculine ego (see section V) reflects this difficulty that men have in grounding themselves in eros. Patriarchal masculinity is indeed lacking in eros, and sexuality in this mode is fundamentally an expression of power and domination—hence the appropriateness of the image of rape to characterize the sexual relatedness manifest in patriarchy.

A danger lies near, however: that of equating masculinity with patriarchy. It is a psychoanalytic commonplace that the mode of sexual relatedness feminists describe as patriarchal is in fact an expression of the phallic-narcissistic stage of psychosexual development, *not* an expression of mature masculinity. Mature genital sexuality in a man is characterized by the capacity for great tenderness for his sexual partner and deep respect for the integrity of her personhood. The mature male, contrary to what Keller seems to suggest, is deeply grounded in eros. We must be clear here that this masculine eros is not a derivative eros merely learned from females, but is a uniquely masculine eros which fully initiated males learn equally from older males who have achieved this level of psychosexual maturity. The fact that we see so little of this kind of mature masculinity attests not to its nonexistence, but to the difficulty males today have in achieving masculine initiation. Men have been so brutalized emotionally in childhood, raped if you will, by uninitiated fathers and other immature older men that they often despair of ever finding a healing eros-relationship with an older man. Without such an experience of erotic masculine gender solidarity, men tend to be either emasculated or phallic, or to oscillate between the two. This is the psychological situation that often leads to physical abuse of women by men. The prevalence of failed masculine initiation is a problem of such scope as to merit our recognition of it as one of our most critical cultural crises, one with far-reaching ramifications. Keller's clear awareness of the seriousness of this problem calls us to confront it forthrightly.

Finally, Keller's essay leads us to the question of whether there can be a truly post-heroic ego psychology, one that does not equate ego-development with alienation from the biosocial matrix. From a Jungian perspective the mature ego must, after differentiation, find its way back to a creative relationship with its transpersonal ground. I grant that the tendency to use the image of the hero as the archetype relevant for the development of the ego does not effectively reflect this key task of the maturation process. In my view, the archetype of the magician is a far better image for this process. The magus, unlike the hero, does not lurch from crisis to crisis, solving adaptive problems with the sword.

Solidly grounded in ritual process, the magus deliteralizes both sword and chalice and uses their symbolic power to assist in the task of finding the right relationship to, and balance of, personal and transpersonal powers. From this point of view, the ego characteristic of modern consciousness—the heroic ego, if you will—reflects the developmental level of the "sorcerer's apprentice." The current ecological crisis and the increasing threat of a nuclear holocaust are both expressions of a consciousness characterized by power drives unregulated by a mature systemic awareness—the problem of the apprentice. Both Whiteheadian metaphysics and Jungian analysis provide significant resources for correcting the alienated and alienating ego consciousness of modernity. If both traditions work toward a more sophisticated consideration of the role of ritual process in this revisioning of the nature and dynamics of ego-development and maturation, then we may be near a revolutionary step forward in our understanding of the actual relationships between psyche and cosmos. Keller's understanding of psychocosmetics has presented us with a challenge we can ill afford to ignore.

10

Reconnecting
A Reply to Robert Moore

CATHERINE KELLER

Robert Moore rightly places the critique of the heroic ego, with its achievements of an autonomy based on a pattern of obsessive dichotomy, within the context of the broader critique of modernity. Radical feminism—as distinguished from liberal feminism, which would satisfy itself with the attainment for women of the rights of the bourgeois individual—can itself be understood as a precursor and *sine qua non* of postmodernity.[1] The problem of patriarchal masculinity, however, hardly begins with modernity!

The ancient archetype of the warrior-hero seems rather to incite and preform all forms of androcentric culture, including those of modernity. His rapacious swordsmanship wields all future dualisms and dichotomies. And, as Moore would agree, the Jungian tendency to enshrine this (or any!) archetypal pattern in a sanctified eternity of the inevitable merely supports the warrior's dominion. The ego-style of this masculine warrior must be seen to undergird, in belligerent or sublimated form, the most cherished presuppositions of the Western world (and perhaps of the Eastern world as well). Intrapatriarchal alternatives to the dualistic oppositionalism of the warrior, who severs psyche from cosmos, finally fail, inasmuch as they fail to acknowledge the symbiosis of the heroic ego with the psychosocial conditions of sexism. And yet the Jung-based traditions do at significant moments (notably exemplified by Hillman's *Myth of Analysis,* not to mention Moore's own work) promise to break through, to see through, the traditional myopias of masculinity.

The heroic ego, indeed, takes its rise in archaic patriarchal ritual—for example, rituals of matricide, such as the ancient Babylonian New

Year Festival in which the warrior deity/king slays "the first mother" and founds the cosmos upon her carcass. Or consider tribal rites of male rebirth through the fathers, invariably involving repudiation of the mother, which initiate the pubescent male into the mysteries of *patriarchal* manhood. Nonetheless I find Moore's evocation of the role of ritual in human experience intriguing. While there is nothing intrinsically feminist about ritual *per se,* it does seem as if our culture's loss of meaningful rites of passage, of metaphoric intensifications of life-space and life-time, somehow accompanies the mounting emptiness and destructiveness of modernity's heroic ego. Eliade's notion of *homogenization* (however rightly his dichotomy of sacred and profane is criticized by feminists such as Mary Daly) aptly reflects the rape of cosmos and the loss of soul that characterize patriarchal consciousness. Furthermore, if there is any validity in my association of Whiteheadian causal efficacy with the Persephonean underworld, the nonsubstantial continuity of rhythmic reiteration modulates the depths of psyche and of world—the psyche and world from which the heroic ego has violently separated us. We might speculate that causal efficacy, like Jung's idea of the libido as a rhythmic phenomenon, would most immediately enter into communal awareness and creative use in the form of ritual. Would not ritual attunement to the soul in the world and the world in the soul then permit a non-raping entrance into the depths? Indeed many women are experimenting with ritual possibilities for the summoning and channeling of previously suppressed energies.[2] In this way the experience of social marginality transmutes itself into psychocosmic liminality.

Moore proposes that a mature, postpatriarchal maleness may become a contemporary possibility only if forms—rituals?—of initiation of younger men by older, "initiated" males emerge. As it is, younger men tend to be "brutalized emotionally in childhood, raped if you will, by older, uninitiated fathers." This is an important insight. The myths of patriarchal warrior deities brim over with the competitive violence between the generations of males (see Hesiod's *Theogony* as well as the *Enuma Elish*: the father's infanticidal fear of the rival son and the son's castrating or patricidal response interlink with the motifs of misogyny and matricide).

Yet I would guess that the misogynist Oedipal cycle will simply continue if males, in the quest for a holy grail of male liberation, stop with a strictly man-to-man process. Perhaps the grail at this point in history will be found only by some opus of reconnection with the pre-

Oedipal mother. In this sense Persephone's reunion with Demeter, like Psyche's quest, remains important for men (though, I agree, it is not enough). Nancy Chodorow shows that the violent break imposed *by* the father *upon* the son *from* the mother results in the post-Oedipal masculinity of the separate self.[3] This does not contradict Moore's point. On the contrary, the intimate involvement of men in early parenting that Chodorow proposes would offer a social basis for the sort of initiation Moore advocates.

Paradoxically, the inability of men (based on the early Oedipal competition) to forge intimate relations with each other goes hand in hand with the parasitical intimacy of traditional male-female interactions. Therefore feminists should not—and Moore's argument lends new reasons why they *cannot*—carry the burden of male initiation and liberation now. Would we not simply be refining our anima role of soul-guide? In the meantime, patriarchy is hardly lacking in an array of *rites de passage* for males, whether of initiation by women into "love" or by professions and warfare into "manhood." Moore proposes the archetypal image of the magician as an alternative to that of the hero, and so suggests forms of apprenticeship, boundary-testing, and transcendence that may indeed supersede the crude and subtle forms of phallic narcissism. This is a promising path. But forms of female initiation—besides those of menarche, marriage, and childbirth—are barely emerging for women. All the more reason that women must be focusing energies not on the transformation of males but on the metamorphosis of the structures—the rituals—of world and soul for women. Yet such transmutation of social, psychic, and cosmological forms does not take place in separation from the world which men and women and all other sentient beings jointly inhabit. Feminism is *not* a new dualism.

And, yes, "patriarchy" is not synonymous with "masculinity." If it were, patriarchs would have no choice; as it is, they have no excuse.

11

The Mystique of the
Nonrational and a
New Spirituality

JAMES W. HEISIG

I. The Nonrational and the Need for a New Spirituality

Among the most revered memories of Western civilization is the image
of Socrates standing condemned before the tribunal of Athens, delivering his apology. "The unexamined life is not worth living," he protests
with a master stroke of irony, at once asserting his preference for death
rather than conformity and turning the judgment of the trial against the
very ones who had just passed sentence on him. We treasure that scene
as a noble embodiment of the ideal of critical reflection that is our own
irrevocable inheritance: the highest value of human life is that it is life
empowered to question itself; its deepest fraud, that it let itself go
unquestioned. Now it was in the genius of Plato to have recognized the
mystical quality of that empowerment. The urge to know the things of
life, to doubt them and reason about them, became for Plato a daemonic
grace, a "force" of human nature that grabs hold of one, not a mere
"technique" that one is free to choose or not, not a mere slave to be
kicked about at whim. For Plato the rationality in whose name Socrates
accepted the sentence of death was not its own ground but the sublimest
form of participation in a divine "givenness." Even the "divine madness" that erupts in human reflection in the form of ecstatic prophecy,
ritual mania, poetic inspiration, and erotic release serves rationality in
a secondary, therapeutic role, as a catharsis for mind frustrated with its
own tardiness in attaining its full capacity, or as a check to the hubris

of mind grown smug with its own accomplishments. From there it was but a short step for Plato to identify the divine with the perfection of rationality, to see the *theos* as the consummate self-knowing to which the examined life of human beings compares at best as a shadowy reflection.[1]

The lure of the rational ideal is, to repeat, irrevocable, however one happens to respond to it. One may join issue with particular deliverances of critical reflection or ignore them outright; one may turn a skeptical eye to metaphysical arguments for a transcendent ground underlying the urge to reason; but none of this matters a whit to the mystique that bears the lure along from one generation to the next. Nothing short of a major catastrophe hurling us back into the Stone Age or leaving us genetically twisted to the point that language and social order can no longer be sustained would be required to dispose of the allurement. Socrates did not invent the mystique of reason. He worshiped it, and Plato gave it a theology.

The only real challenge to the mystique of the examined life in our present circumstances, then, is to advance the counterpoint of an opposing ideal, equally natural and forceful, to the effect that the unexamined life *is* worth living; or put conversely in the harsher words of Rousseau, that "a state of reflection is a state contrary to nature, and that a thinking man is a depraved animal."[2] At first sight the protest may seem little more than a mischievous bit of rhetoric aimed at those who would rather think about life than live it. After all, who among us has not felt the burden that education in rational reflection can impose on our simple longing to let go and savor the untutored passions of our nature? "You are a nanny goat, poor old soul," the poet (Kazantzakis) complains to himself. "You feel hungry, but instead of drinking wine and eating meat and bread, you take a sheet of white paper and inscribe the words *wine, meat, bread* on it, and then eat the paper."[3] The point here is not that the very act of writing those lines, or reading them and nodding one's head, confirms the mystique of the rational idea—which of course it does. It is rather to ask whether such thoughts are merely a flash of divine madness that is ultimately subservient to the divine force of reason, or whether it might not be the other way around: that letting go of reason represents another irrevocably given lure possessed of its own mystique and so essential as to be the proper lord of reason.

This is in fact the possibility that Rousseau pursues. *On the Origin of Inequality* opens with an allusion to the Delphic inscription that had been the inspiration of Socrates, and immediately he asks the reader to imagine the book as a discourse held in the Lyceum of Athens with Plato standing by as judge. Nevertheless, it is clear that, unlike Socrates and Plato, Rousseau did not consider self-reflection a necessity for all people but only a subordinate, epiphenomenal manifestation of the more fundamental desire for the immediate "feeling" of existence. The course of training he outlines in *Emile*, we recall, passes from instincts and sensation, through ideas, and all the way to the limits of rationality, where it passes over into sentiment. In much the same way that Plato enshrined the Socratic ideal of self-examination as a force innate in our nature, Rousseau shifted the weight of the mystique to a "divine instinct" for "self-interest" (*amour de soi*) wherein the person is attuned to the higher rhythms of an all-enveloping nature, and in terms of which rational reflection gains its importance. From there it was a short step for him to identify God with consummate self-loving, to which the life of human feeling weighed down by selfishness and social convention with all its rationalizing trappings can compare only as a journey to a lost continent.

I have drawn the distinction between Socrates and Rousseau rather more sharply than the complexity of their thought allows because it gives us the opportunity to look straightforwardly at the way we are accustomed to take sides on the role of the nonrational in human life. On the one side, the nonrational is taken as a sign of a radical human imperfection that is vindicated only insofar as it impels us toward using reason more fully; on the other side, it is portrayed as the closest approximation we have to the perfection that human nature is capable of reaching, if only it can be emancipated from its servitude to the imperium of mind.

It is precisely this opposition that I wish to undercut in suggesting that we locate the nonrational primarily in the realm of the daemonic, the divine givenness, the lure of a mystique that presses us now toward self-examination and now toward self-interest, now toward reason and now toward feeling, now toward thinking about the things of life and now toward savoring them, now toward starving ourselves on the asceticisms of mind and now toward glutting ourselves on the appetites of heart. Moreover, it is not to some ideal, healthy balance of these urges that I wish to direct my attention here, but to the unknown and uncontrollable impulse to forfeit that balance in order to move beyond our everyday humanity to that "vision of things unseen" of which religion speaks and which underlies the contrasting ideals of Socrates and Rousseau. In order to do that, it will be helpful to isolate the *nonrational* as a frame of reference that is to be clearly distinguished from both the *arational* and *irrational* dimensions, which belong to the *rational* frame of reference from which those ideals are typically viewed.

The examples of Socrates and Rousseau are further instructive in that they are personalities who appear to us, in hindsight, as "outsiders" who were yet more fully "inside" the spirit of their age than those blown about by the winds of opinion, even though they had no way of fully appreciating the fact. Socrates could not look to the future and see a Plato and an Aristotle immortalizing his experiments with truth into an ideal for all future philosophy; Rousseau had not the faintest idea that the likes of an Engels or a Lévi-Strauss would come along to lift him out of the attractive simplicities of eighteenth-century rationalism as an inspiration for their social theories.[4] Apparently lingering behind the progress of the world of their day, both now seem to us to have been ahead of it, whereas all they knew for sure was that they were opposed to it. And here it is not the mere *detachment* of speculative intellect that we admire, as for instance when we page through the notebooks of da Vinci and find sketches of mechanical inventions and anatomical observations decades if not centuries ahead of their time. It is rather an *attachment* to the moral dimensions of the questions of their age, a taking of problems to heart and making them the stuff of their own troubled existence that sets such figures as Socrates and Rousseau apart.

In a word, Socrates and Rousseau represent to us *the quest for a spirituality commensurate with the fullness of the human in the midst of an age grown blind to and uncritical of its own intellectual spirit.* The radically anthropocentric and psychological quality of the ideals they advanced must be judged not only on the basis of their theoretical schemes, therefore, but also and primarily in the light of the "healing unknowing" that each brought to a world tangled up in its own biases without knowing it. For all that, the ages in which they lived and the traditions of thought upon which they drew were not the same, nor are they of our own age and tradition. If the quest for a spirituality for our times can take courage in recalling the lives of those who divested themselves of the fashionable conventions of thought to arrive at a vision of abiding truth and then to return to do battle with the conventional, it cannot simply take over their responses or restrict itself to their intellectual environment.

It is against this background that I pulled the works of Whitehead, Jung, and Hillman off my office shelves for another perusal. The more I read them of late, the more I grow convinced that *each in his own way gives us the very footings we need for a new spirituality,* in a way that ancient Greece and the Europe of the Enlightenment cannot. They offer more than a convenient shelf of material for treating a topic that one might as well have treated through other books, even though I shall take advantage of that convenience in what follows. By the same token, criticism raised against one of them in the light of comparison with the others is really more than the mere academic exercise of bringing interesting thinkers into dialogue with one another in imagination and trying to surmise what they might have to say to one another. It is the attempt to discipline one's search for a place to stand and assert one's humanity in the present world. Accordingly, I shall be little concerned here with stating a question in the idiom of one thinker and replying to it in the idiom of another, or with recommending a synthesis of all three. For the most part the questions Whitehead is asking are significantly different from those that Jung and Hillman have asked, and many points of convergence and discrepancy that are critical to one side turn out to be incidental to the other. My aim here in focusing on the nonrational and its mystique in the context of their works has no ambitions in the line of correcting the conceptual schemes of any of the three, although that may turn out to be the logical consequence of some of my remarks. To borrow an image from the Japanese Buddhist philosopher Takeuchi Yoshinori, it is the standpoint of one standing outside on a dark street looking for something when suddenly light streams from out of a window overhead: "The window and the curtains cut me off from what is inside the room, and I probably have no way of ever really knowing what is in there. But if I am able with the aid of that light to see something that I might not otherwise have seen out here on this street, that is enough for me."[5]

What we are looking for, I have suggested, is a new spirituality. By *spirituality* I understand the essential temper of a person. A positive and explicit spirituality consists, on the one hand, of an increase of moral insight into the complexities of life combined with a vision of hope for the future, and, on the other, of an awareness of being possessed by a reality transcending the conditions of concrete individuality. It is a response to the nonrational by the rational, or perhaps better, an interaction between the two. It can therefore never be given adequate expression in purely conceptual terms, which always reduce the non-rational without remainder to the rational. A spirituality's appropriate idiom is the symbol, whose meaning is partly determined, or *collective*, and partly in need of discovery and interpretation by the individual, or *personal*. A spirituality can weaken and its symbols lose their grip on us if it does not keep pace with the advance of public knowledge, or if it represses the function of the individuals who entertain it, as the older spiritualities of the great classical religions and the new spiritualities of our scientific-technological age show, respectively. In such cases we cannot speak of a spirituality for our times because it can no longer be appropriated at both the corporate and personal levels.

Thomas Berry, who has devoted his writings to this problem as singleheartedly as anyone, gives us a hint as to how the classic Western spirituality, which carried both the religious and the scientific-technological thought of this century to their present forms of alienation, is really at odds with how we experience the world. He singles out four conceptions in that spirituality that have become negative forces: (1) the identification of the divine as transcendent to the natural world, so that the natural world became less capable of communicating divine presence; (2) the establishment of the human as transcendent to the natural world, so that the world was transformed into crass matter, raw material for human consumption; (3) the millennial vision of a blessed future accessible to history through technological progress; and (4) the stress on salvation dynamics to the neglect of creation dynamics, so that our eyes could be turned away from our abuse of the earth to focus on moral revivalism and dedication to pious causes.

What Berry suggests we now need is a new and "functional cosmology" that will be grounded on the symbols of *differentiation* (the recognition of the unique value of each articulated form of being), *subjectivity* ("the inner form, the radiated intelligibility, that shines forth from the deep mystery of each articulated mode of being"), and *communion* ("the relatedness of the universe in its every manifestation" so that it can be "a unity that enables us to say that the volume of each atom is the volume of the universe").[6] In an earlier essay, he adds to these three features of a functional cosmology a fourth: the *experience of a transcendent, numinous mode of being* as an indication of a new consciousness arising more from without than from within traditional religions. It is, he says, a "reassertion of the most primordial modes of religious consciousness," which function at a level beyond the specific religious focus of the immediate past. It is not that this consciousness is undifferentiated, but that the conditions in which such spiritual experience takes place, the basic methods of interiority, are similar enough for people of differing religious backgrounds to enter into profound spiritual communion with each other. This leads him to predict that "as this interior identity increases, the Oriental-Western differentiation of religious experience will be seen as more a differentiation in the human modes of consciousness than simply as a differentiation based on geographical or cultural factors."[7]

The scope of such ideas is gigantic, but it is not for that reason inappropriate to our situation, because if a spirituality commensurate with our age and its understanding of the world and the human is to function, it can do so only by facing *the twofold challenge of the scientific-technological achievement and the common search of the great world religions for common ground*. The antagonisms and competitiveness that have characterized our response so far are quite literally out of time.

The scientific and technological advances of this century have ushered in altogether unprecedented potentials for the human community. Scientific method has given the peoples of the world their first common language, and communications technology has made it possible for ever-increasing numbers of people to exchange vast amounts of information with one another across the globe in ever-shorter periods of time. Astronomy and space exploration have given us a glimpse of our planet from outer space and led us to appreciate its fragility as it pulsates through the immense energic movements of the universe. Ecological studies have taught us the dangers of abusing resources and the folly of tampering with atomic and subatomic explosives.

And yet the moral stature of our civilization is bent and dwarfed, laden with anachronistic myths of the place of the human in nature, sacralizing our apparatus to the point that our ultimate standard of value is to be "plugged in." Until such time as we can begin to see our knowledge and our tools as extensions of the human spirit and not simply as neutral kits of facts and equipment, we have no hope of walking erect in the world we now inhabit. In the same way that the farmer's plow, the fisherman's boat, and the shepherd's flock served as symbols in the classical religions for defining the values and hopes of what it was to be human for former civilizations, the television, the computer, and the robot need to be given a symbolic value in a new spirituality. And this can happen only if they are first experienced as expressions of the nonrational.

As for the encounter of the world religions, we can point with Wilfred Cantwell Smith to the growing aspiration among academics to see the religious history of humankind as a global continuum, which has its counterpart in "the fact that young people today not only are, but are beginning to see and to feel themselves as, heirs to the whole religious history of humankind."[8] Once the step has been taken toward the ideal that one religious outlook should understand another, he points out, nothing can ever be the same again. And once it is understood that religions are not merely something that humans create, have, and keep, but the expressions of a quality to human life itself, endlessly variegated across time and cultures, the absolutism of dogmatic apologetics no longer has a place to stand. The discovery on a logical plane is adequate to tear down; only the complementary discovery on the nonrational plane can sustain the building up of alternatives.

Although Whitehead, Jung, and Hillman have none of them put the issue in quite this form, there is an unmistakable sense in their works of the disservice done to our present civilization by structures of reflection inherited from the past, of being in a critical period of transition, and of the need to rescue the individual from the individualism in which we have trapped ourselves.

In his autobiography Jung sounded one of the keynotes of his life work when he wrote, "One half of humanity battens and grows strong on a doctrine fabricated by human ratiocination; the other half sickens from the lack of a myth commensurate with the situation" (*MDR* 331). Under such circumstances the only foreseeable future for an unrepentant world was that it would "destroy itself through the might of its own technology and science." The vision he offered in lieu of this impasse between inflated rationalism and crippling nihilism was based on the conviction that "we are living in a time which the Greeks called the *kairos*—the right moment—for a 'metamorphosis of the gods,' of the fundamental principles and symbols," and that it is only the individual who is the "makeweight that tips the scales," "that infinitesimal unit on whom a world depends" (*CW* 10:587–88). Hillman has taken this standpoint over into his own work, arguing that much of what goes by the name of revolutionary thought on contemporary intellectual battlefields lacks sufficient depth to extricate us from "that soulless predicament we call modern consciousness," based on a "positivistic nineteenth century system of mind" and reducing morality to the obedience of methods and conventions established according to requirements internal to science (*FG* 3; *RVP* 3, 132). We need rather to recognize that we are already being swept up in a "revolution going on in the individual soul . . . for a wholly new (yet most ancient and religious) experience of reality" (*I* 79).

When Whitehead speaks of grounding the hope for a rational order to things that metaphysics shares with science on "an ultimate moral intuition into the nature of intellectual action," he may seem close to confirming the very thing that Hillman and Jung have in mind to censure, and yet he goes on to acknowledge the "religious" quality of that intuition. By this he means that religion complements intellectual action by connecting "the rational generality of philosophy with the emotions and purposes springing out of existence in a particular society," and more particularly by dealing with "the formation of the experiencing subject." Like Hillman and Jung he was not interested in constructing an ethical system[9] and was aware of the damage wrought in the name of religion. The morality and religion he proposes are aimed at upholding the ideal of rational thought by "stretching individual interest beyond its self-defeating particularity" (*PR* 42, 15). The form that this self-defeating particularity takes for Whitehead is perhaps best seen in his account of the fatal impact that certain biases carried over from the nineteenth century have had on the morality of our own century. In this regard he speaks of the extension of the doctrine of the private, substantial mind into economic and political metaphors for industrial manufacturing, the wanton destruction of the environment, the unbalanced infatuation with professionalism and expertise, the repression of aesthetic values by scientific materialism, and the failure to appreciate that the ethical neutrality of technological power throws the ethical responsibility back on society.[10]

As to the challenge of religious pluralism, we find little in Whitehead other than a clearly nonparochial mood in approaching world religions and the history of religion, a hint that the day of the great religions may be coming to an end (*RM* 43), and a conviction that Christian theology is in need of reforming its attitude toward religious truth. When we turn to Jung and Hillman we find a quite different picture: not only considerable breadth of exposure to the doctrines, rites, and symbolism of primitive and institutionalized religion, but a commitment to viewing them all democratically from the selfsame perspective, that of the experiencing subject in its deepest reaches. As we have just indicated in the remarks cited above, this is also the standpoint from which science and technology are criticized as antireligious, which probably accounts for the general lack of social criticism of the sort that flavors so many of Whitehead's essays.

In any event, what makes these three thinkers important here is surely not only the analysis they offer of the challenges of science, technology, and religions, but the fact that their achievements already represent, each in its own way, a step in the direction of meeting those challenges. Rather than attempt to catalogue the details of their conceptual schemes relevant to these issues, I restrict myself here, as I have already stated, to trying to draw their thought closer to the task of uncovering a new spirituality for our times by showing how each has contributed to a recovery of the mystique of the nonrational, which is essential for any spirituality to take root, for in the last analysis the birth of a living spirituality equipped with appropriate symbols is not the invention of any one person or group, but the fruit of a process largely without our control, a process whose workings we perceive only dimly when we label it a *Zeitgeist* and try to follow its devious and unpredictable ways. At most we can hope to prepare ourselves critically for the uncovering. Like the sower in the parable, we prepare a field and till it in furrows, but we cannot stop the wind from scattering our seeds where it will.

II. The Rational,
the Arational, and the Irrational

Simply and initially put, the *nonrational* refers to a frame of reference within consciousness distinguished by events that intrude spontaneously and unannounced into the world of an experiencing subject in such a way and with such a force as to remove them from the reach of the rational operations by which the conscious subject knows and controls its environment. Although that frame of reference is never quite the same for each age, nor for each individual within a particular age, it should not be confused with an undeveloped mode of rationality corrigible by general advances in method or individual discipline; neither should it be limited to some transcendental and esoteric stage of enlightenment reserved for the few. It is a permanent, albeit imperfectly appropriated, feature of all human consciousness. In this section I prepare the way for a discussion of the nonrational by exploring the rational frame of reference, which includes the arational and the irrational.

There are almost as many definitions of reason as there are philosophers to cudgel their brains over trying to compose them. In a sense, we might say that the very notion of rationality itself does not point in the first place to some thing or faculty or set of operations, but to the perennial question of what it is that sets the human mode of being apart from the rest of the natural world. *That* the human being is so set apart, in some way or other, is an assumption we need not question here. Nor need we, for our present purposes, shy away from assuming that the distinguishing quality is in the nature of an essential and not merely historical condition. As Whitehead remarks, and archetypal psychology would agree, "however far we go back in recorded history . . . , it would be difficult to demonstrate that mankind has improved on its inborn mental capacity" (*AI* 48). As for what the capacity consists in, Whitehead would surely have been most comfortable with the traditional formula, *animal rationale*; Jung would likely have preferred Cassirer's alternative, *animal symbolicum*;[11] and Hillman seems to lean in the direction of yet a third possibility, *animal imaginale*. But what is common to all of them, and what is definitive of the rational frame, is the capacity for self-consciousness.

Now provided we grant that conscious experience entails both an attentiveness and an object or intention of that attentiveness, any further elaboration of the data of conscious experience that we speak of as rationality can be specified as a form of self-consciousness. As such, self-consciousness is the minimal essential requirement for all mental operations that entail abstracting from immediate or "pure" experience to a state of mediated reflection. In this sense we may speak of rationality as a frame of reference that enables not only *expression* in concepts, symbols, logic, art, and other forms of abstract language, but also a *critical review* of the way in which the variety of modes of intelligent activity can be disciplined, impeded, related to one another, and communicated, as well as of the limits—general and particular—under which intelligent activity functions.

This critical review is possible because the rational frame of self-consciousness itself depends on a distinction between the experiencing subject and its attended object, consciousness and its intention, the abstract idea and the concrete reality of experience. However much experience one may accumulate, attend to, organize, and express, and however rigorous the method by which this is accomplished, there can be no objective *data* in consciousness that are not to some extent affected by their genesis as subjective *capta*. Hence the commonplaces about ideas never describing experience fully, theory never embracing all there is to reality, and so forth—all of which come down to defining the rational relative to what is not of itself rational, namely the *arational*. When we speak of conscious experience as a stream (and, by association, of the ocean of events in the world of which consciousness is a tributary), we are speaking of such an arational. To say rational is to say arational; to say self-consciousness is to say self-consciousness *of* the non-self-conscious. This is the fundamental insight from which all critical review of self-conscious activity begins. Without that insight into the correlatedness of the rational and the arational, reason slips quietly and unobtruded into one of the many forms of unguarded rationalism of which self-consciousness is capable.

The critique of such unguarded rationalism occasioned by focusing on the arational takes three forms—or rather contains three elements, one of which is topically dominant—and each form in turn is characterized by its own ulterior, rational motive.

In the first and most obvious place, we find a trust in empiricism, which insists on the primacy of the actual world of experience and the inexorably hypothetical nature of all conceptualization and theory. The writings of Whitehead and Jung, and to a more modest degree those of Hillman, are replete with paraphrasings of this principle, occasionally technical but most often rhetorically flourished. Here too all three have expressed the same deep admiration for the example set by William James, whose whole intellectual life, in Whitehead's words, "was against the dismissal of experience in the interest of system" (*MT* 3; *CW* 8:262, 9/I:55; *RVP* 64). Despite Jung's repeated repudiation of all metaphysics as a nonempirical pretense to "knowing the unknowable," which Hillman has adapted to a censure of the "abstract literalness" of metaphysics, Whitehead's language and intentions could not be more congenial to archetypal psychology when he forthrightly rejects concern with any unknowable that might lie beyond the reach of human experience and admits to the "asymptotic" and even "metaphorical" nature of all attempts to formulate metaphysical first principles in precise terms (cf. *RVP* 136; *PR* 3–5).

Not only their statement of the empiricist principle but the motives behind it would also appear similar for all three. First, they clearly mean to acknowledge the need for that "imaginative flight" of reason that lifts one above the arational field of consciousness and opens up a perspective in which experience for the first time can become "fact" and "theory." Second, they mean to defend their respective conceptual schemes by appeal to an arational ground given apart from those schemes. And third, they wish to draw attention to the improvements they have wrought on existing theories by giving better accounts of the publicly accessible data.[12] In a word, although Whitehead was the only one of the three who seemed eager to say so,[13] for all of them empiricism meant nothing less than an open commitment to "that ultimate rationalism which urges forward science and philosophy alike" (FR 61).

In the second place, the critique against unguarded rationalism takes the aesthetic form of an imaginative wallowing in the sheer depth and immensity of the arational, which awaits rationality as its unfinished task. One thinks here of the passage in the Dialogues where Whitehead derides our human attempts at intelligence by looking at them as phenomena ocurring on "an insignificant planet swinging round a second-rate sun in no very important part of the universe" (D 192–93); or Jung's pausing in his seminars to liken our efforts to understand the psyche to a fly crawling about on the ceiling of the Sistine Chapel or a cockroach scurrying across the pages of Kant's Critique of Pure Reason.[14] Or again, we find Jung in the fever of a grave illness at age seventy-six expressing his sympathies for the author of the Apocalypse who was able, in the evening of a long and eventful life, to "see immense vistas of time stretching out before him," to rise up above the everyday world to "live in the sight of many aeons and in the movement of ideas as they pass from century to century" (CW 11:717). Although we shall return later to the place that feelings have to play in the rational frame, it is already possible to read these images as reconfirmation of the rational precisely insofar as they serve as rational reflections on the limits of reason. They are cut of the same cloth as the awesome idea of Whitehead that "each present occasion prehends the general metaphysical character of the universe" (AI 194) and Hillman's idea of the soul as the stage of an "eternal mythological experience" that transports centuries of past human history into the present (PP 4–5, 61).

In the third place, the most radical critique generated from within the rational frame is what we may call the problem of the "psychological circle." Simply put, it refers to the fact that consciousness itself cannot become an object to itself, that ultimately self-consciousness must be reduced to some form of reflection on a consciousness reflected through its intentions. Jung frequently complained of the impossibility of finding some Archimedean point above or beyond the psyche from which to view the psyche at work. "I am fully aware that I am entrapped in the psyche and that I cannot do anything except describe the experiences that there befall me" (*CW* 16:254).[15] Even in so-called unconscious experiences, which may be the closest that we can come to an objective experience of the psyche, Jung sees no escape from the circle that even the barest modicum of attention or mentation must circumscribe about those experiences (*CW* 11:774). The rational and arational thus define one another mutually not only when we have to do with the world outside of the psyche but also when the focus is turned on the psyche itself. Jung favored a Kantian vocabulary—without, we might add, the complexities of the Kantian argument—to pose this problem. For one thing it enabled him to include the psyche in the class of the *Ding-an-sich,* and thus resign himself to its ultimate unknowability; for another, it supported his model of the structure of unconscious functions (the theory of the archetypes) as an intuitive extrapolation parallel to the *a priori* structures of cognition that Kant had posited for consciousness.

Hillman has joined issue with the "container" imagery that splits the world and the psyche into "outside" and "inside" as unsuited to Jung's actual intentions, and goes further to dismiss Jung's appeal to the "noumenal archetype" as an "unnecessary theoretical encumbrance" (*FG* 33). While he honors the basic insight that "from the soul's point of view we can never get out of the vale of our psychic reality" (*PP* 57), Hillman is inclined to view this fact less as a vicious circle than as a virtuous one. When he writes that "whatever 'objective' idea we find in the pattern of data is also the 'subjective' idea by means of which we see the data" (*RVP* 126; cf. *LE* 6), he means that psyche or soul lends depth to our every experience by filtering consciousness, quite without the controls of self-consciousness, through its own innate and archetypal patterns, and that at the same time it restores the subjective dimension to the objective world by making every event an event of meaning available for conscious attention and reflection. "Truth is the mirror, not what's in it or behind it, but the very mirroring process itself: psychological reflection." This in turn leads him to an announcement: "I shall be adamant, even arrogant, in my claim for psychology. . . . The psychological perspective is supreme and prior because the psyche is prior and must appear within every human undertaking"

(*RVP* 109, 130). In so doing he brings to the fore the rational aim at work in Jung's allusions to the problem of the psychological circle, namely the appropriation of the unshakable assumption "that *everything belongs somewhere*" (*LE* 50), into the field of psychological inquiry, without falling back into the dichotomy of a subject assigning a place to the objects of its experience.

For Whitehead the assumption that everything has its place, apparent in his rational aim that "everything of which we are conscious . . . shall have the character of a particular instance of the general scheme" (*PR* 3), clearly lay behind his own efforts to dissolve the fiction of a world of subjects viewing a world of objects. He did not do so, however, by arguing for the priority of the intrapsychic generations of human meanings. Rather, he boldly and adamantly stated his hope in a universal order within which each event or actual occasion comes into being as a center that appropriates the world about it into a unique configuration or concrescence, which holds it in being as what it is. Whenever we may speak of consciousness in such an order of things, we may speak of the center as a subject and the surrounding world as its objects, but not in such a way as to constitute an exception to the wider principle of interconnectedness. The fact that there is self-consciousness to recognize this order does not therefore compel Whitehead to reduce the order itself to a mere metaphor of meaning for self-consciousness entrapped in its psychological circle. Rather, he drew the final entrapment as an *ontological* circle, which for him constitutes the supreme and prior perspective. The rational and the arational continue to define one another, as with Jung and Hillman. The difference is that the arational, that "everything of which we are conscious," embraces consciousness (and thus also the experiences psychology would call "unconscious") as one phase in a greater totality. In place of the psychological act of faith that the only possible meanings are meanings entertained by persons, Whitehead offers the wider act of rational faith that precedes metaphysics: that the only universe that can include intelligence is a universe that is itself intelligible (*SMW* 18; *PR* 42).

The correlation of the rational to an arational thus sets internal limits to the rational frame in terms of the distinction, though not necessarily the separation, of the world of subjective self-consciousness from the world of its objective intentions.

A second way of approaching the rational frame, already implicit in what has been said above, is to focus on the conditions under which that range of operations we call *reason* functions in virtue of the fact that it takes place within the concrete human personality, where directed self-consciousness is more the exception than the rule. The autonomic element permeates all the activities of self-consciousness with the force of both spontaneity and habit, forcing us to distinguish between mentation that lies within our power to control and that which does not. In other words, the non-self-consciousness that is entailed in all our talk of self-consciousness cannot be restricted merely to an arational world tolerant of our conceptions and misconceptions alike; it also must include mention of a range of functions taking place below the threshold of our attention and reflection in that shadowy world we call the *unconscious*. Whatever we may suppose about the structure of that subliminal underworld itself—the crucible in which all consciousness is concocted and to which it returns its yield—its eruptions into self-consciousness are too obvious and too important to omit from the essential ingredients of the rational frame. These eruptions are what we may call the *irrational*.

The coordination of the rational to the irrational is a common concern in Jung, Hillman, and Whitehead, and in all three it is connected to a notion of "feeling" that reflects the way subjects relate themselves to objects. As soon as we look at this more closely we get ourselves in a knotted tangle of noncoincident terms and distinctions,[16] which I have no intention of trying to unsnarl here. More important is to note that this is the case precisely because each of them has seen the need to take into account the complex patterns by which the rational operations of consciousness are affectively toned and guided by irrational processes whose functions are consciously perceived far less clearly than they are felt. For Jung and Hillman the complexity is due to their focusing on the problem within the psychological circle; for Whitehead the wider ontological circle demands that these higher levels of the problem first be rooted in a pattern of relationships already present in preconscious nature as a whole.[17] But let us then set these differences aside in order to look at two principal ways in which the irrational, in our particular use of the term, works correlatively with self-consciousness to constitute the rational frame.

In the first place, the irrational erupts in the form of intellectual intuition, that "instinctive apprehension," as Jung calls it, which carries with it its own "intrinsic certainty and conviction." In like vein, Whitehead speaks of proof and logical arguments as a "feeble, second-rate

procedure" providing "merely subsidiary helps" for the conscious realization of more basic intuitions.[18] Intuition breaks into experience
with the force of self-evidence no less strong than that of immediate
sense-perception, and for that reason is also liable to its own varieties
of illusion and error against which the only check is the integration of
intuitions into the totality of the rational frame. The clearest indication
of how this works is to be seen not in the theoretical explanations that
Whitehead, Jung, or Hillman offer of intuition, but in the quality of
their rational adventures as such. All three show a creative vitality of
thought that sees far more connections and speculates on far more possibilities than they are able to track down and reason out systematically.
And yet that creativity is shored up by the discipline of an equally vital
determination to make sense and to approximate fully logical explanations. Without such determination, the flashes of inspiration that appear so regularly in their writings would surely have been swallowed
up in the darkness of yesterday's news instead of continuing, as they
do, to attract the critical attention of us who reread them today. Jung
once diagnosed in himself a certain tendency toward "hypertrophy of
intellectual intuition";[19] Hillman has remarked in passing that he finds
intuitive thinking "automatic and unreflected" (*JT* 82); and Whitehead
freely acknowledged his own "muddleheadedness."[20] But in each case
it is confession of limits to the control of one's own rationality, not a
call to dismantle the rational frame altogether or disinherit methodical
thought from its right to a universal aim.

In the second place, the irrational shows up in the form of the
"double-meanings" that attach themselves to our rational products, a
sort of substratum of meanings, or an overlay, resulting from the interferences of mind working outside of our conscious dominion.[21] Here
the irrational denotes nothing other than the *depth* of depth psychology,
so that all attempts to dispose of it through the "single-meaning" genre
of literalism amount to a repudiation of that psychology itself. "Literalism is sickness," Hillman warns us. Even in the most materialistic
and objective of ideas, "nothing is literal; all is metaphor" for the
psychologist (*LE* 3; *RVP* 175). Whitehead, although less concerned
with any "meaning" involved in unconscious interferences in the rational process than with their surface meaning for reason, was certainly
aware of the phenomenon. For him all conceptualization, even the most
abstract, was emotional in its derivation, and this emotionality took on
personal qualities wholly lacking in preconscious "feelings." "The con-

cept is always clothed with emotion," he wrote, "that is to say with hope, or with fear, or with hatred, or with eager aspiration, or with the pleasure of analysis." He was also aware that such emotions are never simple but always complex, far too complex indeed for anything more than the vaguest of conscious analysis (*MT* 122; *PR* 237; *AI* 176, 215, 262). Aside from certain elaborations worked out in his notion of "importance" (which Hillman has linked to Jung's description of the "feeling function" [*JT* 107–8]), there is not much here in the way of actual psychological insight. It is more a matter of one of those inspirational intuitions we just referred to, whose underdevelopment is all the more in evidence when we move over into the field of archetypal psychology, where it has become a major preoccupation.

For Jung, the irrational belongs to the psyche because the basic unit of all psychological activity and the carrier of all meaning is the "complex," which is by nature ambivalent. The complex may be likened to a cluster of "feeling-toned representations" held together like electrons attached to a common nucleus, which gives it autonomy while preserving the plurality of forces that constellate it. One knows the complex only through the images or representations thrown up to ego-consciousness, which is itself a complex field of forces. When an image gains in clarity and power, we may presume that we are approaching nearer the nucleus, though never to the point of resolving all meaning into a single and univocal insight. As Jung's interest in the impersonal and collective aspects of psychic imagery grew, he gradually replaced "complex" with "archetype," a term he felt better represented the sense of archaic mimesis and teleology he saw at work in the basic ambivalence of the image. For all that, he never lost his critical sensitivity to the way that "illegitimate and thoughtless projections" can distort our view of reality, seducing us into every form of stupidity and superstition, blocking our way to fuller understanding. The irrational remained for him a mixed blessing that called for an increase in rational reflection, not its abandonment. Throughout his life he held to the principle that "man's worst sin is unconsciousness" (*CW* 9/I:455). Even if the power and function of the irrational cannot be made subservient to ego-unconsciousness, we must continue our attempts to analyze and evaluate the double-meanings that attach themselves of their own accord to our every effort at rationality (*CW* 8:5).

Hillman has emphasized even more strongly than Jung the self-regulatory nature of the archetypes in informing the way we "personify" experience to understand it and the way that our normal habits of understanding are "pathologized" to gain greater depth. Yet his treatment of "psychologizing" makes it amply clear that the "soul's reflection upon its nature, structure, and purpose," the psychological work that takes place at a rational remove from mere consciousness, is the point at which the archetypes first acquire meaning for us.[22] His writings on selected mythical motifs, straddling the borders of historical research and free reinterpretation, attest to the fact that he does not treat myth as a crude and chaotic heap of archaic fantasies there for the scrapping, but as rational products possessed of intrinsic conceptual forms that can aid us in the "transformation of consciousness," including the reformation of biases that creep into our most methodical and controlled modes of intelligence (*FG* 151). Even his anarchistic harassment of the ego as undeserving of the imperial status Jung gave it in practice, and his call for a democracy among the community of complexes to which the ego belongs (*RVP* 24–34), do nothing to shake his fundamental conviction of the solitary, rational subject who poses those questions and thinks through those possibilities. For all the "falling apart" we experience when we turn inward, self-consciousness stands firm as witness, arbiter, and final bearer of the responsibility that nature has laid upon humanity: know thyself.[23]

III. The Nonrational Frame of Reference

My purpose in the previous section in including the arational and irrational dimensions of experience within the rational frame—that is, of broadening our picture of the nature of self-consciousness beyond the narrow range of operations marked by deliberate and more or less methodical reflection—has been to prepare for an account of the nonrational dimension of experience as something distinct from the arational and the irrational, and therefore as something essentially disruptive of the rational frame as such. The problem is more than one of clearing up ambiguities by giving new definitions to words; it is a matter of *restoring to the nonrational its own unique and particular frame of reference*. On the side of Whitehead, this has been obstructed by overextending the rational frame to absorb the nonrational into the arational or the irrational, thus cutting short the full reach of his own insights into the nonrational. On the side of Jung, the obstruction has rather taken the form of overextending the nonrational frame to include what really should be classified as arational or irrational, thus cutting short the full reach of his obligations to rationality. To some extent Hillman has taken over Jung's bias here, as we shall see. But of all three, Hillman's understanding of the nonrational frame stands out as the clearest. His project of re-visioning psychology by recovering a vision of "soul" may serve as a catalyst to crystallize the nonrational frame in the thought of Whitehead and Jung, and to open their ideas further to the role they might play in the construction of a spirituality for our times.

The doctrine of "soul" that Hillman describes most fully in *Re-Visioning Psychology* cannot be said to challenge in any of its essentials the map of the psyche that Jung left behind in his *Collected Works*.[24] It is rather a change of accent, a turning away from a process centered on the work of individuation that goes on when ego interacts with unconscious with the aim of achieving a unity in the Self, and toward the pure dynamism of the psyche itself, multivalent and uncentered soul. Strictly speaking, *soul* and *psyche* are interchangeable for Hillman, but more often than not the latter carries a connotation of structure and interrelating elements, whereas the former connotes the totality of the dynamism as it is reflected in its every phase and product. The dynamism of soul makes itself manifest through everything that is *present* in consciousness, and infuses everything that is elaborated *representationally* through self-consciousness (which Hillman calls "spirit"). The fundamental activity of soul to which these manifestations point is "imagining," the transformation of concrete and particular experiences of life into meanings that draw the subject out of itself and into a wider reality. Thus he speaks of soul as the reenactment of collective myths and fantasies through the script and setting provided by everyday life, and conversely as the restoration of the collective to its seat in personal experience. On this understanding, the search for soul is not the search for some *thing*, the wizard behind the magical world of Oz, but the search to appropriate the *perspective* that psyche assumes toward itself and to locate oneself within that perspective. The subject of this search, the "imaginal ego," experiences life archetypally: everything becomes a part in an eternally recurrent play with a restricted cast of typical roles whose players are the Gods. Thus the imaginal discovery of archetypes among the things of life amounts for Hillman to a theophany. Once again "all things are full of Gods" because the Gods have become imaginal manifestations of the multifaceted perspective called soul.

Now if soul is the one perspective that encircles all others as an ultimate horizon, the one thing one cannot find is soul itself, because to do so would be to gain independence from soul, which is as impossible as living a physical existence outside of one's skin. The task of psychology is not to define soul in terms of anything else, but to "see through" all human experience to what is not human, to "make soul" by uncovering the imaginal structure of all the things of life that I otherwise presume to be thinking with *my* mind and feeling with *my* heart. It is to allow thought and feeling themselves to reappear as "the revelation of the uncontrollable, spontaneous spirit, an immortal, divine part of the soul, the *memoria Dei*" (*MA* 182). In terms of the examples of the opposing ideals with which this essay opened, soul is the mirror in which self-examination and self-interest are reflected as the mystique of the nonrational in one's life. Setting Hillman's re-visioning of psychology against the backdrop of the rational frame just outlined, I single out four characteristics of the nonrational frame that it is my concern to describe here.

First of all, the nonrational frame is the *locus of the encounter with the numinosum*. Unlike the experience of the "otherness" of the world as an arational, we have here to do with an otherness that can be named only the way that Otto has named it: *mysterium tremendum et fascinans*. It is an experience of an unknown and uncontrollable, yet awesome and enchanting, takeover of the everyday self by a force so sheerly other that we can speak of it only by denying it our words. Jung, as is well known, welcomed Otto's descriptions as pointing to the very events that had most impressed him about the psyche, and frequently spoke himself of the *numinosum*, not only in association with extraordinary religious and mystical experiences but also in referring to the commonplace experiences of dreams and fantasies and the allurement of symbols. To document the point is superfluous. There is no place anywhere in the Jungian corpus where one can drop one's nets without dragging up some allusion to the importance he accorded this sort of experience. To leave this out of account is to drain the very lifeblood from his work.

Hillman's description of soul as a middle ground between the perceiving subject and the world that is perceived helps to draw attention here to the "force" of the nonrational rather than merely to our own feelings of weakness before an apparently alien power. He speaks of "a sort of conscious unconsciousness" that is "non-directed, non-ordered, non-object, non-subject," in which elements separated in the rational frame seem to rise up in unison out of a common original and "transpersonal background" (*MA* 185; *I* 42, 66; *SS* 43–45).[25] Like Jung, he acknowledges a certain esoteric quality to such experiences—they remain of necessity ineffable and incommunicable because the experiencer does not "know" what has happened—and yet Hillman clearly intends for us to admit it as an abnormality that belongs to every normal life. It is the typical "pathos" accompanying the archetype along with the "logos" or meaning that the archetype represents. This is perhaps the main reason why he would have us imagine them as Gods, that is, as "forces I cannot control and yet which want something from me and intend something with me" (*RVP* 105, 129; *SS* 176; *PP* 57). The recovery of collective meanings in an individual life begins with the recovery of the nonrational, for "psychology may be based on archetypal themata, but psychology proper begins only when these dominants experienced as emotional realities through and within our complexes, are felt to pull and shape our lives" (*PP* 18).

Whitehead's interests in experiences of the *numinosum* are no more than tangents he drew occasionally but never ventured out on. We find him distinguishing between the "ordinary average experience of mankind" and "occasions and modes of experience which in some degree are exceptional." In reference to the latter he even alludes expressly to "the sublimation of the egoistic aim by its inclusion of the transcendent whole" (*AI* 294). But the context of his remarks makes it clear that his concern is with grounding the appeal of metaphysical notions. Even when he speaks specifically of religion, it is the theological content that is made to validate the experience. He notes the characteristic "intensity of the emotions" that religion generates as "evidence of some vivid experience" but immediately turns his attention to the interpretation of those experiences. On the one hand, it is the beauty of theological doctrine that attests to the "supernormal experience of mankind in its moments of finest insight" (*RM* 31). On the other, he rejects the notion of a special, subconscious religious faculty as symptomatic of the tendency to let religion slide into the "dark recesses of abnormal psychology," not because he intends to argue a place for religion in the psyche but because he wishes to preserve a "solid foundation for religious doctrine" (*RM* 120). I have no cause to dispute the point that the denial of rationality is as fatal for religion as it is for philosophy, but would only insist that the denial of the nonrational quality of religion is no less fatal. The "intensity of sensitive experience" that Whitehead upheld as a categoreal obligation is always and forever linked to a harmonious complement in the "breadth of thought," because "conscious, rational life refuses to conceive itself as a transient enjoyment, transiently useful" (*PR* 16, 340). If the concreteness of our conscious, nonrational life is to have any meaning other than that of symptom of our less than ideal existence, if the mystical element of life is to reach its "depth of feeling" and if its "direct insight into depths as yet unspoken" is to be attended to (*MT* 174), these things need first to be understood as disruptions of the rational frame.

The second characteristic of the nonrational frame rests upon the first. It is the self-conscious experience of the *providence of the craving for meaning*. Here it is no longer a question of the ideals that we deliberately entertain, nor even of desires deliberately rejected that return to haunt us. It is the experience of the directedness, the dynamism and vitality, of the entire rational project of a human life as a given. We have been provided with urges that govern our physical adaptation to a changing environment, and we have been provided with a lure toward the higher experiences of the conscious life. Even if we cannot say to what purpose we are so lured, and even if the flow of our lives never seems to respect the ideals we forge in response to that lure, the mere fact that we reach for the "more" of consciousness is a grace whose mystique we can acknowledge only by saying, "it is there." In this sense, the psychological circle of the rational frame can be said to disclose itself as a psychic circle. As Hillman notes, somewhat cryptically, it is not only that "psychology depends on the psyche of the psychologist" with regard to collective and individual limitation, but that "the psyche requires an adequate psychology to reflect itself" (*LE* 7).[26] Here soul is viewed less as a trap we are caught in than as the impulse of life to supply itself with meanings. The rational subject is the soul's way of looking at itself.[27] The otherness that impresses us in heightened moments of consciousness as an alien force is here felt as a permanent feature of our every attempt to be human.

Appropriately, Hillman speaks of a vision of "meaningness" in which all particular insights into meanings are gathered up. Here soul is viewed as an imaginal realm from which all images spring. Because we are "in" soul and not soul "in us," imagining is not something we freely choose to do or not to do (*RVP* 173; *I* 56, 119; *JT* 81). That the representations of self-consciousness may be linked to subliminal conditions is secondary to the primary miracle, that there are representations at all. Thus when Hillman states that the purpose of therapy is to increase awareness "that fantasy is a dominant force in life" (*LE* 2), he is saying in the first place that making soul means accepting one's responsibility as caretaker of the grace of rationality. We do not build a rational frame about us to shield ourselves from the unknown, so that the encounter with the nonrational would consist in leaving our artificial shelters. We build it because we must, and the encounter with the nonrational consists in confronting the providence of that "must." To see reason as fantasy is to restore to it its primary value as a force of nature; it is not to forsake its achievements under some pretense of mystical enlightenment.[28]

By his own admission, Hillman is following Jung here in grounding archetypal imagery in an instinct to reflect that belongs to human nature and determines the richness and essential character of the psyche. Like any drive of nature, of course, it is as liable to repression as to expression, and in fact becomes concrete precisely through the interaction of control and release. The main point here is not to get waylaid by the inadequacies of instinctual or energic models of description before one has caught the nonrational import of Jung's idea: that there is an "objective" psyche on which all "subjective" reflection rests, just as a bird takes to the skies or a fish to the sea (*RVP* 244–45).

It is, of course, true that Jung opposed this instinct for reflection to a "religious instinct" (or "religious function") impelling the conscious ego to confrontation with the collective unconscious through the use of symbols. But his concern was to disassociate the psychic value of religion from the dogmatic rigidity he found in rational, conceptualized religion, to which end he preferred to distinguish the former from reflection and align it closer to what we have called the arational and irrational components of the rational frame (*MA* 31–40; *CW* 6:passim). This is one of the clearest examples of the fact that Jung's failure to give the nonrational its proper place followed from his not seeing that the commitment to empiricism, the repudiation of dogmatism, the role of direct intuition, and the emotional background to ideas are the very things that place the capacity for reflection (or self-consciousness) within the *rational* frame of reference.

Whitehead's stress on the intelligibility of the world as the basic givenness from which metaphysics takes its start may be seen as the formal statement of the generally nondistinct and tacit reverence he paid the providence of the drive to intelligence in his writings. His impassioned strictures against anti-intellectualism and dogmatism as stifling potential and his recognition of the failure of reason due to the overwhelming complexity of the world or the internal complexities of emotional interference both attest to this reverence indirectly. Though he did not himself say as much, the craving for meaning may be seen as the way that the self-conscious subject experiences the "principle of empiricism" as dependent on the "ultimate irrationality" (read: nonrationality) of a "principle of concretion" (which was Whitehead's early term for God) (*SMW* 178). Although the existence of some world or other may be necessary, there is nothing necessary about just how our world is (*SMW* 178). When this idea is applied to the rational subject as one of the data given in the world, we are led to posit an act of faith in the craving for meaning and reason that, one way or another, has us in its grip. There is nothing any more necessary about that craving than about most other features of the world; it is a nonrational providence, belonging perhaps to the fact of "appetition" that underlies all concrete prehensions of eternal objects, in much the same way that "meaningness" and the "collective unconscious" underlie specific archetypes for Hillman and Jung. If there is a sense in which Hillman's infusion of "soul" into the psychological circle draws the whole question into the nonrational frame and out of its purely epistemological dimensions, an infusion of soul into Whitehead's ontological principle may help us to reread his commitment to rationalism as an unformulated acknowledgment of the nonrational frame. To fail to see the concrete mystique of the givenness of reason is to fall into a subtler form of the "fallacy of misplaced concreteness," of which Whitehead accused the abstraction-jugglers of the seventeenth century (*SMW* chap. 3).

These first two marks of the nonrational frame, as the locus of the encounter with the *numinosum* and as the providence of the craving for meaning, involve the conscious subject in a mainly passive capacity, and even the insight that is generated here tends to bear the form of a revelation more than that of a demonstrable conclusion. As we have shown, however, what defines the *rational* frame is not the self-conscious, rational subject but rather the naming of the objective and subjective conditions of reason as arational and irrational, that is, as accessible to the range of operations by which self-consciousness constitutes itself. What defines the *nonrational* frame, similarly, is not a repudiation of the self-conscious rational subject but rather a *new per-*

spective whose focus is on the radical inaccessibility of experience to our controls and conceptualizations.

The acceptance of such a perspective, or its rejection, remains the work of the rational subject. I shall refer to this acceptance as the *appropriation of the nonrational*, which takes two forms: spontaneous and deliberate. Viewed from within the rational frame, such appropriation would be called the interaction of the powers of reason with the arational and the irrational. But here rationality reaches satisfaction through the pure act of representational recognition of the mystique of its limitations. This "letting go" of reason does not contribute anything to the rational frame in the way of new conceptual controls; nor does it weaken the controls that are there in force. It is a reversal of the asceticism of the abstracting consciousness justified only by the intensification it brings to one's urge to savor the things of soul. Its *fiat* is at once passive and creative; it appropriates into consciousness a process that goes on working whether one reasons well or poorly about it. In fact, it is nothing more than the attempt to make the rational frame livable for the human beings that we are. It is here that we may speak of a spirituality for the life of self-consciousness.

The spontaneous form of appropriating the nonrational is the third characteristic of the nonrational frame. We may call it, with Hillman, *personifying*. Hillman argues that the major contribution of Jung's work lay in the "radical, personified formulation" he gave to the map of the psyche, in sharp contrast to the hydraulic and functional metapsychologies of Freud. Instead of thinking of mental events as hidden motives, instinctual drives, dim memories, traumatic events, and the like, Jung imagined them as persons. He imagined the complexes of the psyche as the players who people our dreams and fantasies; in myth, symbols, and rites handed down from tradition he saw not preconceptual *Ur-dummheit* but the projection of the depth of feeling that pervades all representation on whatever level of sophistication it occurs. And the whole process, for Jung, was not the outcome of deliberate attempts of gifted persons to allegorize ideas for the sake of rhetorical or emotional impact, but the work of a habitual, instinctual, ineluctable demand of the psyche to transform all of life into the image of persons so that it might have "real" meaning for us. When Jung says that "the psyche creates reality every day," Hillman understands this as the final justification for all soul-making, "to experience the fantasy in all realities," to see all ideas as metaphors of soul.

This personifying should not be confused, he cautions us, with "personalizing," a surrogate form of personifying, which is symptomatic of a coldhearted conceptualism that represses the imaginal in the name of clarity of thought and seeks compensation for its sins by coating its ideas with a layer of no-less-conceptualized moral values. Personalizing returns everything to the conscious ego, which passes judgments on its value; it reduces soul-making to a pampering of one's preferences for a world of neat and tidy meanings. Personifying by contrast protects the soul that mediates my way to the world by letting it do what it does, and what it has always done: imagine the world as the playground of daemonic forces which give vitality to the givenness of experience (*RVP* 1–51, 64). Through its personifying, personality ceases to be the private, skin-bound possession of individual subjects; it becomes an instance of a collective and transcendent realm, namely soul, which personifies everything it touches because it is the soul that possesses persons and not the other way around. In this way the arational and nonrational are no longer grist for the mill of reason but are drawn back, together with reason and the whole "spiritual" life itself, into the primordial mystique of the nonrational.

Hillman's arguments for personifying draw our attention to an aspect of Whitehead's metaphysics that tends to get obscured through purely philosophical appropriation. I do not refer to any slack-witted attempt, of which there are examples enough, to interpret the ideas as symptomatic of the private life of their author. I mean rather the curious predilection that Whitehead showed for expressing his most abstract notions, even in his strictly systematic language, in personal terms. He spoke of *feelings, consciousness, conceptual prehension, valuation, society, satisfaction, urge, subject, appetition, creativity, aim, harmony, symbolism,* and so forth, in reference not only to human persons but to the subhuman world as well. It is not enough to dismiss them as colorful "projections" cast on the world of nature. To do so would be to reconfirm Hillman's own complaint that "modern science and metaphysics have banned the subjectivity of souls from the outer world of material events" (*RVP* 2), which is surely *not* the case with Whitehead. His recognition that even technical terms "remain metaphors mutely appealing for an imaginative leap" (*PR* 6) points to something deeper than a mere statement about the arational. It is Whitehead's way of appropriating the nonrational spontaneously into metaphysics. I say "spontaneously" because it seems to me that his own justification for the procedure—that he was taking human experience as the prime analogue for lower forms of nature from which human life evolved (*PR* 112; *FR* 16)—is hardly sufficient to account for the lengths to which he followed this procedure. In personifying the categories of metaphysics, Whitehead was making his own rational adventures livable for human beings even as he stood firm against what Hillman calls personalizing (*AI* chap. 20). In this way Whitehead left an opening in his thought for the nonrational, whose charm we still feel as a distinct but hard-to-locate presence.

The fourth characteristic of the nonrational frame is a second and more deliberate mode of appropriating the mystique of the nonrational: *mythologizing*. Hillman follows Jung in using this word in a broad sense as a synecdoche extending the technical meaning of the Greek tales of the Gods to serve as a representative for all forms of symbolic narrative fictions that show universal, collective, and recurrent patterns of psychic response to the experiences of life. Although the myth itself speaks literally of a world of impossible events, "always a myth is the psyche telling of itself in disguise" (*PP* 155). What Hillman has in mind here is not only the fantastic tales of ancient times—whose genre as metaphor dressed in falsehoods we have been familiar with ever since the dawn of philosophy—but a quality of any human representation seen from the viewpoint of soul.

To recover this standpoint toward our science, philosophy, and everyday common sense, as well as toward our own fantasy life, Hillman insists we must first learn to see through their literalness and recover the God. This is a way of reversing the course of history in order to protect our own ties with history. "The myth that is alive is not noticed as mythical until seen through," and "seeing through" is the business of psychology. Hence only in the act of *remythologizing* does the mythological activity in which soul is constantly engaged come to light. Psychology translates back into the language of soul what has come to be spoken of in the language of the abstracting spirit. Hillman's aim is to dig under the tidy garden of our conventional idioms to unearth the tangle of "root metaphors" that join us to the soul of our humanity. There we find the basic types of life and thought, be they apparently of the most generalized or most privatized form on the surface, as part of a collective, unconscious, and polytheistic inheritance. In taking this step as resolutely as he does, Hillman backs away from Jung's lifelong insistence that psychology be accepted as a "science," locating it rather in the mode of a hermeneutics of soul whose primary method is not nonobjective empiricism but an unabashed absorption in imaginal activity (*FG* 33n5). "Remythologizing" means not anything so crude as the free invention of myths but a rereading of the stories we tell of our lives in the light of the archetypal stories which have come down to us in our corporate tradition, in order to discover the greater dynamic that is sweeping us along in our every rational adventure. It is "an exploration of soul by spirit for psychic fecundation" (*PP* 68). We do not set up a supreme court of reason in which the solitary ego can sit to pass judgment on the meanings behind the surface meanings of things, because even our psychologizing itself is in obedience to the archetype of soul-making. *All* things are full of Gods, even that statement itself. The archetyping imagination and the archetyped imaginal are one within the psychic circle.

In order to safeguard remythologizing from slipping into a subtle but uncritical form of reason, therefore, we must view soul as a perspective of *inexhaustible mythifiability*. This is the final rationale for Hillman's polytheism: to revere one God alone as natural to the soul is to constrict the nature of the soul into the expectations of the rational frame, and any spirituality so based rings shallow and unlivable in the concrete. No doubt Hillman is right to insist in this way on the uniqueness of the nonrational frame. We siphon off the mystique of soul when we dwarf it to the size of conceptual logic. Like the arrows the ancient Gauls shot at the heavens, the names we hurl at the divine never bring it tumbling down to earth. The experience of the givenness of life, whether felt through the presence of an otherness or through the craving for meaning, remains mystical. Remythifying accents the way the nonrational appears in life: in splinters, flashes, bits and pieces. What the speculative spirit weaves by day, the interior life unravels by night.

Nevertheless, the unity that Hillman denies our image of the divine, in refusing to speak of a single noumenal reality behind the plurality of phenomenal theophanies, returns in the form of the mythology of a common psyche participated in severally by all people everywhere, essentially unchanging, eternally repeating itself over and over again in the same patterns. The idea of soul as a universal temple of the Gods may not be the soul to which monotheistic theology turns as the locus of the experience of the divine. But for a psychology committed to viewing all realities as images, and to viewing the image-making soul itself as too transparent to "see through," one could hardly hope for any clearer "root metaphor" of the single Godhead behind all our ideas of God than the image of the one soul larger and more enduring than the individual humans who happen to inhabit it from one generation to the next. Any psychology that attempts to mythologize the interior life by remythologizing within the psychic circle is—for all its reticence to speak of the ontological status of the Gods apart from our images of them, and its lack of concern with the problems of theological relativism (*SS* 32)—more consistent with its principles if it terminates in a radical pantheism to complement its radical panpsychism.

In any case, the hermeneutic value of Hillman's polytheism is that it enables the process of mythologizing to survive all attempts to remythologize ourselves once and for all into a single myth to replace all others. If the point of mythologizing is to appropriate the nonrational factors or Gods which dominate the way we think and act, it is not in order to return them *tout court* back into the fold of the rational frame, where we can leave the mystique of the Gods behind and treat them as mere surrogate ideas (*SS* 32). In other words, although there is a solid base of systematic thought in both Jung and Hillman which is intended to be, and in fact amounts to, a fully rational *metapsychology* which needs to be judged on its own merits against the full measure of critical reason, the actual work of psychology as a *therapeutics of interpretation* deserves rather to be judged on its ability to locate the mystique of the nonrational in "a vivid, intense realization, transcending ego and revealing truth."[29]

The danger is at once obvious: confronted with metapsychological inconsistencies in its handling of the conceptualizations of the arational and irrational aspects of the psyche, such a psychology can beat a quick retreat to the mystical nature of its subject matter and indeed all our conceptualizations of it. Jung at least tried to keep these separate by focusing on the demand to be scientific. Hillman has taken over the conclusions Jung arrived at in these attempts but tends to slip away from the demands of the rational frame in which they were posed. The most telling example is the way that Jung's arguments regarding the psychological circle have been taken over by Hillman into the nonrational context of the psychic circle, thus begging the epistemological questions that Jung's metapsychology sought to answer and that philosophical inquiry comes to his thought prepared to ask.[30] A more common and more frustrating example is the way that allusions to myths are used as arguments to bolster up logical connections between abstract ideas or even take their place altogether, a practice adopted unscrupulously by many who have gotten their feet only a little wet in archetypal psychology's methods of interpretation. The process is simple: one cites a general idea, supplies it with an image from the world of myth to demonstrate its archetypal nature, identifies the idea with the image and leaves the idea behind to follow the image through its mythical context, and finally wends one's way back to the original idea, which one clarifies in terms of the conclusions reached through the mythical excursion. Sometimes this takes place in the course of pages of writing, sometimes in a single sentence, but always there is the same confusion of frames of reference.[31] Hillman's elucidation of the imaginal work of soul as a remythologizing is, to my knowledge, the best case anyone has presented for the uniqueness of the relationship between therapy and mythology, but we are left wondering too often what to do with the conceptual generalizations offered to appeal to our abstract sensibilities without any clear, logical archaeology behind them.

Probably the closest Whitehead has come to an appropriation of the nonrational by mythologizing is in his *Adventures of Ideas,* particularly in the final five chapters on Truth, Beauty, Truth and Beauty, Adventure, and Peace. Although he does not there, nor anywhere in his work, revision ideas as mythologems, he does perform the mythological function of affirming the enchanting power of ideas in history, and centers attention on how this enchantment both controls "the formation of mentalities of different epochs" (*PR* 338) and draws the individual out of the isolations of personality into the collective drives of the race. Here we see Whitehead at his most inspiring "muddleheadedness" in the medium of an extremely dense and technical idiom, trying to locate that "impulse towards higher things" which is the heart of all civilization because it is a permanent feature of all human nature. What we are given is more than a scattering of intuitions densely concentrated and in need of being pulled apart again by the reader, though that is surely our first impression. It is also an infusion of soul into ideas, in virtue of which ideas are set free to walk about as freely and uninhibitedly as the Gods that people Hillman's essays or the chemical substances that are personified in Jung's alchemical studies. The major difference is that Whitehead does not himself appear to see what he is doing as an essential departure from the rational frame. If there is anything like a nonrational mystique to the power that ideas exercise over us, the only way he could conceive of appropriating this mystique was to "rationalize mysticism," which means conceptualizing it (*MT* 174). In fact, one cannot escape the feeling that Whitehead ends up at times "mystifying the rational."

One might take his treatment of art as a description of this process. He begins by ascribing to art the task of bringing to consciousness the shadows cast by our conventional habits of thought, thus protecting us from becoming inflated with the workings of our reason. But then he goes on to note, entirely reminiscent of Hillman's characterization of therapy as a reenactment of the lives of the Gods in one's own interiority: "The origin of art lies in the craving for re-enaction. In some mode of repetition we need by our personal actions, or perceptions, to dramatize the past and the future so as to re-live the emotional life of ourselves, and of our ancestors" (*AI* 270–71). This is as succinct a statement as one could hope for of the way that Whitehead wrestles with the mystique of ideas in the midst of his frustrations at dragging them into the rational frame. In suggesting that art is "a psychopathic reaction of the race to the stress of its existence," he points to his own adventures with ideas as a pathologizing response to the stresses of rationality. This deliberate appropriation of the nonrational is Whitehead's way of mythologizing.

In contrast to the remythologizing of Hillman and Jung, however, Whitehead's mythologizing is more in the nature of a *demythologizing* of ideas, which sees "clear" as always only "clear enough" (*ESP* 123). If this amounts to the antithesis of religion as soul-making on Hillman's terms (*I* 67), it is of the essence of religion for Whitehead: "The progress of religion is defined by the denunciation of gods. The keynote of idolatry is contentment with the prevalent gods" (*AI* 11). But all demythologizing that is fair to its subject matter, as Whitehead's tries to be, rests on a recognition of the function of myth, which is the same as it is for the remythologizing attempt: to make rationality livable, to make it accord with the nonrational urges of our nature that reason expresses. I take this to be what Whitehead has in mind when he ascribes the abiding appeal of types of Platonic philosophy, with all their "arbitrary fancifulness and atavistic mysticism," to their instinctive grasp of the way that the abstractions of philosophy are limited by the inexplicable creativity with which the facts of experience encounter the inquiring mind (*PR* 20). Accordingly, I would venture to characterize Whitehead's attitude to the dominant power of ideas as *inexhaustibly demythologizable*. This lands him to err more on the side of ignoring the right of the nonrational to its own frame of reference, just as the attitude to soul as inexhaustibly remythologizable inclines Hillman and Jung to an isolation from the right of the rational to its own frame of reference. In the end, however, depth psychology is not served by dictating to science and metaphysics what they can and cannot pursue with their methods to the benefit of the general advance of our knowledge of the human; and conversely, science and metaphysics are not served by dictating to depth psychology what procedures it must follow to speak meaningfully. Some understanding of what the rational frame *can* do is as important, for the full exercise of self-consciousness, as some understanding of what it *cannot* do.

IV. The Popular Imagination and Inspirations for a New Spirituality

To paraphrase Whitehead's prediction about religion (*AI* 33): that spirituality will take hold which can render clear to popular imagination some eternal greatness incarnate in the passage of temporal fact. If, as I suggested at the outset, we are in a time of transition between the passing of classical spiritualities developed in isolation from one another and the coming to birth of new spiritualities global in scope and dialogical in their development, it is not surprising that increasing numbers of those for whom conventional habits of thought were once adequate are suddenly finding themselves adrift in a torrent of fundamental questions and struggling to keep afloat.

What makes thinkers like Hillman, Jung, and Whitehead so suitable for attention in such a mood is not only that they recognize the transition; nor only that their works rise up like islands in the sea, giving us a place to stand and weather the changes; but most of all because their hunches about our predicament are so downright full of inspiration to the adventure and creativity we need to carry on our journey into the future.

Three qualities account for this inspiration. First, we enter into their books not to find fixed ideas trapped inside a kaleidoscope and bouncing off of one another like pretty little bits of glass, but to see ideas brought to life like angels and demons of nature to be wrestled with before they yield of their promise. Second, at the same time as we find there an intellectually respectable portrait of the human painted in all its bright uniqueness as steward of the world of reflection, we are shown its essential continuity with the wider world of nature, which the individual experiences at the highest level when it aims at self-transcendence. And third, each of them confesses a faith in the temporal process tossing us about with the surface winds and waves even as in its depths it is pulling us with currents stronger and steadier.

These three qualities are what I have tried to point to as the non-rational appeal of their works, grounded in the mystique that the non-rational has for each of them. When we stand with Jung and Hillman and watch the things of life transformed into archetypes and Gods, when we stand where Whitehead stands and see the incessant urge toward novelty pulsing through the interrelatedness of all things, more is going on than a disciplined exercise in conceptualization. We are joining in the work of conversion to a new spirituality. Whatever else needs to be said about the utility of process metaphysics and archetypal psychology—and *far* more needs to be said than has been said so far—there is no denying the impact the major thinkers of these traditions have had on those who teach and write about them, evaluate their ideas, apply their schemes and follow through on their intuitions, and in general experiment with the truth of their achievements amidst the host of questions that life throws up at us all. A few hours spent reminiscing over the past decade of *Process Studies* and *Spring* give one a sense of the conversion this entails.

But now, to return to my paraphrase of Whitehead's comment about religion: the task awaiting completion is that of *weaving into the fabric of popular imagination* insights about eternal value flowing through the temporal. The fact is, few people are likely to be persuaded to give their leisure hours to books on metaphysics or psychological analysis to resolve actual moral decisions and settle on hopes for the future. Life in spiritual anomie will always be more popularly appealing than the rarefied air that professional intellectuals breathe. Popular imagination leans on ideas appealing for their concrete, symbolic value, and it is this world of popular imagination that occupies the greatest part of the attention and interest of the intellectual as well. It may be little consolation to say so, but the failures of our inherited spiritual traditions to guide us here stand out more clearly than proposals for alleviating the situation. And yet nothing of lasting value has been done until the popular imagination has been reformed and put to work on reforming civilization self-consciously.

One should not get the idea, of course, that the requisite metanoia of imagination has already taken place in the universities, institutes, and academies that house the intellectual establishment around the globe, and now needs only to filter down into the general population to take root properly. Quite the contrary—such change begins with the vaguest of sentiments widely diffused throughout a society and long seething there before it reaches the halls of learning. Take only the two instances cited earlier.

The demand for true religious catholicity, deeper and more serious than an academic spirit of fairmindedness that pounds the religious diversity of humankind into a single mass of dough, flattens it out, and then impresses it with a shiny kit of cookie-cutters, is a demand most obvious in experiments in religious pluralism being carried out uncritically by a whole generation of young people following their hearts from church to temple to cult. Likewise, the demand for humanizing technology is more appealing and creative when spoken in the idiom of the artists and fantasizers of science fiction, who animate our technology by giving robots a life of feeling and turning computer circuits into communities of little people, reminding us indirectly that in the course of investing our science in our machines we have also invested in them the scientist's heart, no less good or evil than the rest of ours. Most of the moralizing carried on at academic conferences about the "perils of technology" lags far behind the shadowy sentiments already astir in the popular imagination. One turns with such enthusiasm to the sort of rationally disciplined and revolutionary thinkers discussed in these pages, who give voice to needs neglected and aspirations trivialized by the force of conventions embedded into institutions, precisely because they are so few. Or, which is to say the same thing, because they seem to be recounting to us the spiritual story behind the story of our times from within the very nonrational mystique that we experience as we are living that story out.

12

Imaginal Soul and
Ideational Spirit
A Response to James Heisig

CHARLES E. WINQUIST

James Heisig has provided us with a useful and learned comparative analysis of philosophical issues surrounding the mystique of the nonrational in the thought of Whitehead, Jung, and Hillman. In this service he has addressed the theme of this volume, but it is clear that the deeper agenda of his paper is the search for a new spirituality. He wants to root the "awareness of being possessed by a reality transcending the conditions of concrete individuality" and to increase "moral insight into the complexities of life" (171) by the articulation of a frame of reference that credibly addresses the realities of the rational and the nonrational. It is also clear that, of the cast of characters that are here critically examined, it is Hillman who is given center stage. And yet Hillman's thinking is the least amenable of the three for the development of a spirituality, as it subverts spiritual aspirations in a dewy, downward movement of soul-making.

Hillman's published work contains clear evidence that he considers the search for a spirituality a barrier to his own agenda of soul-making, and he explicitly identifies the translation of the psychic into the pneumatic (spiritual) with "Christianism" (*DU* 85–87). There is no evidence of a hidden Christian apologetic in Heisig's paper, but the new spirituality is associated with a "demand for true religious catholicity" (201), which, in a mind less complex than Heisig's, might signal a hidden monotheism at opposition to Hillman's imaginal polytheism.

In spite of these *prima facie* difficulties, Heisig is working with a frame of reference, the nonrational, that nudges rational operations off center in a way that lends at least provisional credibility to a project of enlisting the aid of Hillman as well as Whitehead and Jung in the search "for a new spirituality." The real question will be whether thinking out of this frame of reference, in which the "mystique of the nonrational" is acknowledged, will give Heisig a way to overcome or at least temper the obvious oppositions between the thought of Whitehead and that of Jung and especially Hillman.

The quality of his comparative analysis of the three thinkers demonstrates that Heisig is not unaware of the oppositional problems in the trajectories of archetypal psychology and process metaphysics. In the expression of intention, the differences between these movements are not subtle. Although both movements are critical of traditional structures of reflection, Whitehead's grounding of the hope for a rational order on "an ultimate moral intuition into the nature of intellectual action" (175) is a good distance from a psychology that effects a poetic revolution and affirms pathologizing as "a hermeneutic which leads events into meaning" (*RVP* 111). These movements differ not in their elaborations so much as in their basic sense of what is real and important. As Heisig points out (177), Whitehead sees the human animal as fundamentally rational and Hillman sees this same animal as fundamentally imaginal.

Whitehead stresses the intrinsic intelligibility of the world and he is careful not to depart from the rational frame. There is the unknown but not the unknowable in his metaphysics. Whiteheadian philosophy is dominated by a vision of the whole and is generally wholesome. With subtlety, Whitehead brings the vagaries of experience into an increasingly illuminated organic context. Even the connection of the dim and the vague with importance is not understood as an epistemological *aporia*. The reformed subjectivist principle together with the ontological principle fashions an understanding of the subject-superject that would be darkened by a tragic flaw only if the reader reconstructed Whitehead's cosmology without the consequent and primordial natures of God. His likening of the speculative use of reason to the flight of the airplane that lands to renew and intensify observation (*PR* 5) reveals a confidence in rational thinking that has no parallel in Hillman's post-critical psychological hermeneutic.

Process philosophy does seem to have a tone that would resonate with Heisig's project of developing a new spirituality—*if* it were a credible vision of reality for a postmodern culture. The gap in credibility for the detractors of process philosophy is that it does not have a philosophical anthropology or psychology that can put to rest the suspicions, introduced into Western thinking by Freud, Marx, and Nietzsche, that life cannot be explained in terms of how it appears. The shattering of language as an adequate mirror of reality subverts confidence in rationality and its expression. It has at the same time valenced an unrealizable order of the unconscious as a concept that metaphorizes all descriptions of the human condition. This is the beginning of postmodernism in philosophy and psychology. Heisig needs an anthropology or psychology for the conceptual elaboration of a new spirituality. The problem is not just to develop a process psychology, but to develop a psychology that is honest about the wounds inflicted upon the intelligibility of its project.

The turn through Jung to Hillman is not going to help in the development of a process psychology or anthropology, and, to the extent that Heisig needs process metaphysics to guide the search for a new spirituality, this turn obscures his project.

Although process thinkers see the need for a philosophical anthropology to match Whitehead's cosmology and metaphysics, Hillman is not developing a philosophical anthropology. He is re-visioning psychology. His commitment to the experience of experience is at the same time a commitment to saving the appearances—saving the image, saving the imagination. Psychologizing or soul-making is not philosophical description or explanation.

Until his very recent metaphysical turn in his essay in this volume, Hillman was not looking for a cosmology or metaphysics at all, and even now he is envisioning a *psychological* metaphysics. Through the telling of events, random images and happenings are made into lived experiences. Only if philosophy disengages from its naturalistic literalism and becomes a rhetorical theater does it serve psychologizing. His struggle is with the presence of the image, and he will not repress the imagination even when it is not wholesome.

Hillman does not hesitate before the recognition that psychological reality is experienced at first as pathological. Things fall apart as the one becomes many. The fabric of psychological experience is not whole cloth; to present a unity one would have to stitch together seams, and the consequent philosophy would have to be seamy. Hillman will not allow us to stand above the pathology. He does not think that the psyche exists without pathologizing. In pathologizing, we experience the imaginal. The wound becomes an eye and not an *aporia*. Fragmentation with decenteredness is for Hillman an opportunity. The healer is the illness and the illness is the healer. The opportunity is not to restore the self or generate a new spirit, but to experience the soul.

Hillman envisions the work of thinking in a way that acknowledges the importance of giving priority to the imagination in the scheme of human experience. "Interpretation, like dreaming, becomes a dying to the dayworld by ruminating it from literal realities into metaphorical realities" (*DU* 96). This is a work. It does not presuppose a critical or precritical understanding of understanding. It does not satisfy the demands of a metaphysical logocentricism, and it does not claim to satisfy these demands.

If the conversation of these essays is to go forward, I think that we must acknowledge that Whitehead and Hillman are doing something very different. Whiteheadians are not ruminating the dayworld from literal realities into metaphorical realities. This is clearly not the thrust of the ontological principle.

Whitehead's trust in critical and speculative thinking has not been undermined by psychoanalytic, Marxist, or Nietzschean lesions, and Hillman has too much of Freud in his thinking for an easy rapprochement with process thought. The wound is implied by the primacy of the image over the idea. It would be easier for process thought to find resonances in the analytical psychology of Jung than in archetypal psychology. However, this is not the solution that Heisig seeks. He, along with Hillman, has dreamt the Jungian dream forward so that a retrograde rapprochement would be a dismissal of the postmodern experience, which is the matter to be transformed into a *new* spirituality.

I do not think that Heisig stays with the project of process philosophy in his paper. He pays it respect and acknowledges a debt to its vision, then moves on to Hillman. But I am not sure how far he can go with Hillman in his search for a new spirituality. The "requisite metanoia of imagination" (200) called for by Heisig draws him so close to Hillman's intentions that the reader of Heisig's paper may suspect that the opposition of soul to spirit is really a distinction without a difference. That is, we might conceive of the new spirituality as an expression of soul-making. Heisig could then bring his search for a new spirituality into the already-rich discursive domain of archetypal psychology.

The problem with this resolution is that there is still some interest due on the Whiteheadian debt, and, although the project is no longer a project of process philosophy, the actual practice of thinking demonstrated in Heisig's paper is ideational rather than imaginal. This statement does not question the imaginative quality of Heisig's ideational frame, but it does suggest that issues go into solution for Heisig not in the alchemy of the imagination but in a "clear, logical archaeology" (197) that in turn gives a place to the mystique of the nonrational. If Hillman were to develop an archaeology rather than an imaginative genealogy, he would ask to what mythological region, to what Gods, the archaeological task belongs. For Hillman, *archai* are not ideas but root metaphors.

Heisig is uncomfortable with a practice that "identifies the idea with the image and leaves the idea behind to follow the image through its mythical context" to an imaginal epiphany (197). This is not simply a matter of difference of temperament between Heisig and Hillman. Heisig wants to get behind the imaginal and Hillman wants to get behind the ideational. The distinction between soul and spirit is elaborated and thematized in the *work* of these two different projects. Heisig rightly notes that it is the practice of Hillman's elucidation of the imaginal that leaves him wondering.

It is here in the midst of Heisig's wonder that I have my most serious reservation about the Heisig project of a search for a new spirituality. We no longer have the rational assurance of Whiteheadian metaphysics to justify the expectation that we can articulate a clear, logical archaeology behind imaginal epiphanies, and yet the elucidation of the imaginal is not enough for Heisig to ground this new spirituality. Heisig's answer is to ground the expectation that we can articulate a clear, logical archaeology in the conceptualization of a nonrational frame that recognizes the imaginal but is not reduced to it.

The problem with this conceptualization is that it is empty until the rational subject does the work that Heisig refers to as the *appropriation of the nonrational*. This is a work of representational recognition of the mystique of the nonrational. Heisig does not do this work in his essay. He identifies these modes of appropriation with Hillman's work of soul-making and uses the specific modes articulated by Hillman in *Re-Visioning Psychology*. In effect, the attempt to appropriate the mystique of the nonrational draws us into a tangle of root metaphors that adjoins this work to the imaginal soul and not to the ideational spirit. Unless he holds Hillman's work in check, the use of these modes of appropriation will convolute and then contravene the search for a new spirituality.

The text of Hillman's practice has imaginal and mythological texture. It resonates psychologically. Its appropriation of the mystique of the nonrational makes soul. The text of Heisig's search for a new spirituality is an as-yet-unfulfilled invitation. The modes of appropriation need to be pneumatic inventions that issue from the powers of reason. I question the felicity of the Heisig project because I do not think that the notion of appropriating the nonrational can be seriously countenanced at the same time that we recognize the subversion of subject by the power of the nonrational. The danger of subordinating the nonrational mystique to rational appropriation is that the glitter of pneumatic lights can again blind us to the power of the nonrational, and, although we will talk about the nonrational, the power of the nonrational will remain unthought.

13

A Riposte

JAMES W. HEISIG

Any attempt to slice the human psyche up into distinct categories according to the various things it is supposed to do, the organs or faculties with which it is supposed to do them, or the changes that result in the world outside the psyche inevitably comes up against the great anomaly that besets all psycho-logy: the psyche works as a unit, not as a set of logically discrete operations. In the *logical* sense, it is altogether right to argue that "appropriating the nonrational" runs the risk of converting the nonrational into the rational, or vice versa. It is only through this sort of sense that the *psyche is able to construct a psychology,* both to describe to ourselves what is going on, and to evaluate it in order to maximize its healthy operation and to protect ourselves against what can go wrong. In the *psychic* sense, however, we know in fact that the psyche, in one or the other of its various moods, can "appropriate" just about anything in just about any number of ways, without much regard for the logics we devise to talk about it. And this is the sense in which we must admit that *no psychology,* for all its sophistication, *can ever construct a psyche.* Not "none of our existing psychologies" or "not yet," but simply "no psychology can ever."

The criticism I find in Charles Winquist's thoughtful response, that Hillman's project has undercut the rationality of psychology by insisting on the imaginal nature of its deliverances, is a serious one and not without its evidences in Hillman's own writings. Often enough in these writings we come upon a certain looseness of logic where we might wish for reflective rigor, and also a certain refusal to face the public realm of moral and commonsense judgment, which seems to cut it off from the everyday world to which our psyches invariably return from all reflective or internal operations. For this latter reason, if I understand him correctly, Winquist finds Hillman's work a threat to any authentic spirituality in the sense in which I have used the term. In large measure, I concur.

Jung's lifelong passionate insistence that he was doing "science" is all but absent from Hillman's writings. *What kind* of science Jung was doing is another question, but his commitment to the demands of rationality is clear. With Winquist, I agree on the need for any process psychology "to be honest about the wounds inflicted upon the intelligibility of its project." It is indeed true that a large segment of the academic community, having accepted various deconstructive ideas as starting-points, would find my project unintelligible. My project, however, is based on a rejection of just those ideas. For one thing, I hold that one can fully recognize the irrational, arational, and nonrational dimensions of experience without giving up the claims of the rational dimension. Hillman's tendency to ignore the demands of rationality, which sets him apart from Jung as well as Whitehead, is, in my view, the main weakness in his position.

A second wounding involves the issue of ethics. The strong antiethical stance that Jung first thought necessary in order to maintain his search for a scientific psychology softened as his work developed. After the war, his tone changed markedly. Indeed, I would say that his equally passionate insistence on the reality of evil and his refusal to dispense with it as a mere *privatio boni* indicates, obliquely, that Jung's concerns had left the confines of intrapsychic maladjustment to confront the abuse wrought on the human community by the individuals that make it up. With Hillman, we would seem to retreat again to the amorality of the imaginal to seek refuge from this world. Here, too, Hillman seems to part company with Jung.

At the time I composed my comments, the openings in Hillman's writings to wider concerns of a social and ecological nature were scanty, I admit. It was because I see the need for a "mythical" dimension to sustain and transmit these concerns that I tried to pry them open. To my surprise and delight, a copy of his paper, *"Anima Mundi*: The Return of the Soul to the World," fell into my hands at the time of our conference and showed that this was the very area into which Hillman himself had decided to move. I cite briefly from this essay because I think it merits mention in this collection:

. . . psychology reflects the world it works in; this implies that the return of soul to psychology, the renaissance of its depth, calls for a return of psychic depth to the world.

I find today that patients are more sensitive than the worlds they live in. . . . I mean that the distortions of communication, the sense of harassment and alienation, the deprivation of intimacy with the immediate environment, the feelings of false values and inner worthlessness experienced relentlessly in the world of our common habitation are genuine realistic appraisals and not merely apperceptions of our intra-subjective selves. My practice tells me I can no longer distinguish clearly between neurosis of self and neurosis of world. . . . This further implies that my theories of neurosis and categories of psychopathology must be radically extended if they are not to foster the very pathologies which my job is to ameliorate. (S 1982: 72–73)

The shift is a gigantic one, and it surely leads back to a more severe rational critique of the role of rational moral judgments in psychic health than Hillman has been willing to engage in so far. But more important for his life work, it suggests that the realm of what I called the "inexhaustibly mythifiable" has left the private soul and moved out into the soul of the human community, of social institutions, of nature, and of things. In this sense, it is altogether appropriate to the project of constructing a spirituality commensurate with our contemporary experience.

14

Back to Beyond
On Cosmology

JAMES HILLMAN

The difficulty of philosophy is the expression of what is self-evident.
—A. N. Whitehead (*MT* 68)

I. Something Further Is Needed

Some years ago for a conference in Geneva I wrote a paper called "On Mythical Certitude." I revised it for publication in French.[1] Later, Ed Casey sat with me giving it a very careful going over and I began a new revision for our present symposium. But a month ago, I fell ill while in the midst of the revision. Two weeks ago, still ill, I recognized that the paper, despite Casey's help, was not worth what I was trying to do to it. It did not have enough importance in Whitehead's sense— "Have a care, here is something that matters!" (*MT* 116). Nor did it seize the opportunity of speaking with colleagues whose concern is metaphysics. I put that paper aside in favor of bringing to voice matters I felt more urgent and more directly related to the occasion at hand.

This act of not following through with a declared intention—breaking the contract implied by the announced title of my public lecture— is unusual enough in my habits and serious enough in its possible disappointment of the audience to need some defense. But how? On what principles did I decide this change of course: moral? aesthetic? Do they differ? What determines the proper subject of a public talk—mere feelings and moods? mere deadlines for submitting a title long before the immediate presentation at an actual occasion? What is the relation of

213

the paper to the audience? private to public? soul to world? The questions raised by the failure to follow through with the plan have become central to the theme of this essay. How do we determine importance in a psychological cosmos? We are led back to First Principles, Metaphysics, Cosmology.

In my work so far I have shunned metaphysics. I have kept mainly within the critical tradition. The action of psychology I have called "seeing through," "psychologizing." And I have often enough spoken against norms for psychological actions because they become normative and normalizing, against ideals because they become idols to be smashed, against positive goals for psychology and therapy because they become positions and positivisms, against affirmative actions and supportive grounds because they become delusional densities that prevent the primary critical activity of seeing through. I have contended that all prescriptive moves reinforce the heroic ego (the bane of our culture), promulgate guilt, and continue to entrap us in the subjective *inspectio* of the Western Cogito: self-searching, correcting, directing, and thereby, in the concern to get *oneself* right, losing the faces and voices of others.

If anything, the depth psychology of soul-making as I have been formulating it is a *via negativa*. No ontology. No metaphysics. No cosmology. A knight errant, always off at a tilt, iconoclastic. Archetypal Psychology's main claim to positivity has been its paradoxical insistence on allowing the shadows to be lit by their own light—hence the long encounters with pathologizing: the underworld, depression, suicide, senex, and the pathologies of the puer.

The insistence has been on the *vale* of soul-making, staying in the valley of the shadow, turning even at times against the initiator of my own tradition, Jung, for his ascensionist prospects, his pronouncements from the mountain tops about the meaning of life, the worldviews, the generalized theories of typology, the Self and mandalas. I have tried to follow Jung the psychologist of the soul but not Jung the metaphysician of the spirit. And, for all its puer impetus and anima aroma, my work has been stringently dedicated to lowland tactics, to the discipline of image, of phenomena, of pathologizings, in the mode of critical skepticism.

Something further is needed, and I have known this for some time.

II. Metaphysical Praxis

In October 1979, the French national radio invited a group of thinking men and women to Córdoba in Andalucía, that extraordinary Spanish seat of culture where varieties of monotheists—Christian, Jew, and Mohammedan—collaborated and conflicted for centuries. We were some thirty people from physics (including Nobel laureates), neurophysiology and experimental psychology of mental imagery, Jungian thought, and, let us call them, metaphysicians of the Eranos circle, such as Gilbert Durand, Toshihiko Izutsu, Kathleen Raine, and David Miller.[2] We sat for five days at a raised green horseshoe table in a great hall in the palace where Queen Isabella gave Columbus the charge to go out to discover America. During those days, the spirit of Henry Corbin was very much present. Why, I wondered? Jung's eminence was less significant; he seemed to have been absorbed by the prevalent worldview, through his concern with science: the paradoxes of rational thought (union of opposites), matter and spirit conundrums, synchronicity, the psychoid. Corbin, however, stood apart from the age, or reflected it from another place, as a metaphysician who wanted to "briser l'histoire"—break through history into theophany: the revelation of the gods and thereby a restoration of the world to the temple of the imaginal.[3]

Corbin does not move eastward from the material world in which we are immersed to the orient for reorientation, or upward to a spirit that is, nonetheless, based in brain or biology or the physicist's matter—like Karl Pribram and Fritjof Capra. Corbin starts where Neoplatonism must start: in the blue,[4] in the imaginal or *mundus imaginalis,* viewing the dismay of the world from there. Not physics first, but metaphysics.

When in Córdoba the physicist and metaphysician David Bohm admitted frankly and sadly that physics had released the world into its perishing, and that physicists had neither learning nor ability to think the world out of its peril—and that this job was not the job of the physicist anyway—we saw that our plight was way beyond the discipline of the men who had advanced this plight. I saw the terrible need for metaphysics. The physical threat of the end of the world results from a metaphysical catastrophe.[5] I understood then why Corbin, during the final days of the meetings in Spain, had become so prominent, and I understood what was expected from Jung: it is to him as *metaphysician* that so many turn, and I am indeed a deviant from this main line of interest in Jung because I have been avoiding, even working to annul, his metaphysics so as not to lose his psychology. But in Córdoba I realized that psychologizing was not enough. The critical tradition of seeing through, of perspectivalism, of metaphorical ambiguity, of relativism and desubstantiation—my *via negativa* in the vale of soul-making—is necessary but not sufficient. It is sufficient neither internally nor externally.

The internal needs of the soul require that its psychology meet the soul's concerns about the nature of the cosmos in which it finds itself. The smallest Freudian child asks Aristotelian questions about coming-to-be and passing-away. Soul seeks to understand itself beyond itself; it attempts, in a strangely persistent and universal way, always to fantasy beyond; otherwise, would we have the many sciences and philosophies, the theories of origins and ends? This paranoid restlessness of the soul to be metaphysically satisfied by ultimates of meaning must be acknowledged as one of its internal needs.

Externally, the soul is situated differently from any time since the Flood. There have often been apocalyptic expectations. But now extinction is a predictable possibility. We are at the edge of the Final Solution. Sure, the Turks were once at the Gates, and there was the Black Plague—but there could always be imagined a remnant, or another place to go. And at least the buildings and the trees would go on. Now, however, the bell tolls for the whole earth, and its catalogue of all and everything. If the *anima mundi,* the soul of the world, is in this unprecedented situation, then psychology must also speak to and from the soul in this situation.

It struck me in Córdoba that what I had been doing was merely another strand of Western skepticism and nihilism. Worse: by declining to engage in metaphysics I was abetting the decline of the civilization into the catastrophe of concretized nihilism. My *via negativa,* though different in content because of its call of soul-making, the vivification of imagination, and the restoration of the Gods, still retained as method the critical, skeptical analysis such as we find in bare existentialism, linguistic philosophy, operationalism, and deconstruction theory. Was I really so different from those I opposed? One thing we held in common: the failure to grapple constructively, positively, with metaphysics.

I could no longer blame our plight on natural science, on Descartes and Hume, even on Christianity's apocalyptic and world-disdaining theology: Mary over Martha, the unconcerned lilies of the field, the earth's garden as a place of Agony. The blame was mine too, even if I seemed to have escaped into soul-country, issuing ennobling calls for enlistment in the ranks of soul-makers. Patriotism, even of soul-country, is still the last refuge of a scoundrel.

But how to face metaphysics with a friendly countenance? And how to change a whole style toward construction, development, positings? And how to do all this without taking back what is clearly the case: metaphysics has in the main failed the psyche. Collingwood, in his *Metaphysics,* entitles a chapter "Psychology as Anti-Metaphysics," but this has to be because metaphysics usually allows soul a place no bigger than a pineal gland, reducing soul to subjectivism and feelings, to an epiphenomenon of material nature, an invisible form of a living body, keeping it only human, or according it permanent value only by positing a home for it in an afterworld. What soul does—make fantasy images— has, moreover, been condemned by metaphysics as untrue, unreal, and amoral. Could one stay in soul and yet take seriously the soul's need to go beyond itself? I had been literalizing the need to stick *with* the soul by staying stuck *in* soul. In other words, how to fulfill Jung's suggestive phrase *esse in anima* (*CW* 6:78–80) with a psychological metaphysics?

In the years since 1979 I have been setting down jottings in a folder labeled "Cosmology." That word will occupy us in a moment. Because these jottings are scattered and schematic, is it legitimate to say I am engaged in metaphysics?

When we think of metaphysics what comes to mind are the great systematizers like Aristotle discounting his predecessors but integrating them nonetheless; Saint Thomas Aquinas's huge edifice; Leibniz; Hegel; Ouspensky; Teilhard de Chardin reaching from paleontology to the spheres and aeons. Metaphysics—the all-encompassing vision in synthetic construction.

But these can be distinguished—the metaphysical vision and the metaphysical synthesis. Coleridge, for instance, succeeded at the vision, but failed to hold it in coherence. Locke was fairly coherent, and the anti-metaphysical metaphysics that he published certainly gave the mind foundations for politics, psychology, epistemology, scientific method— but was it a metaphysical vision?

Nor is coherence itself the key criterion. A metaphysics does not have to unfold deductively *à la* Spinoza, but can be eclectic—that is, selective, pragmatic, heuristic—perhaps even the work of a *bricoleur*. Whitehead was accused by Stephen Pepper of just this eclecticism.[6] The skew of metaphysics toward logic is a bias we need not share. The metaphysical basis of our Western mind, after all, is as much in the tales of Genesis and the sayings of Jesus, in the fragments of Heraclitus and the aphorisms of Nietzsche, as in the antinomies of Kant and the logic of Mill.

This distinction between vision and synthesis encouraged me, for my access to mind is sporadic, fragmentary, polemic, and certainly not all-encompassing. Mars guides me more than Saturn, Hermes more than Athene. I feel claustrophobic when submitting to generalizations and laws, and call out "paranoid" when required to enter any unifying system.

This distinction encouraged me, furthermore, to note more carefully the style that mind takes in psychological hands. Here I found a third way of doing metaphysics, besides vision and synthesis, which is metaphysical *praxis*. I think *this* is the psychological mode. Theories of depth psychology, its metapsychology, have been born side by side with its practice. A psychological metaphysics will continue to be tied to its twin, practical *therapeia*. We are less metaphysicians in a visionary sense or a synthetic sense than we are practicing metaphysicians in therapy. We dare not think a thought without noticing its effects on the twin of practice: when I go toward transcendence in thought, does this brother blanch and push away his food, does he sail off sunward, or does he squat in the dust and snarl? Thought may not be rationally consistent with behavior. But the fantasies in the thought and the images shown by behaviors reveal common themes. For instance, Western metaphysics with its inherently world-denying, abstractive tendencies has been thought mostly by men—from Plotinus through all the Catholic Schoolmen, through Hobbes, Newton, Descartes, Leibniz, Hume, Kant, Schopenhauer, Kierkegaard, and Nietzsche to Wittgenstein and Santayana—men, furthermore, who did not wed, who did not spawn, who touched the world with mind in such a way that its existence became a "problem."

Just here my critique of Jungian metaphysics has taken its aim: the paranoid effects in *practice* of the metaphysical system of the Self.[7] And just here the critiques attacking Hillman have been leveled: the inflating puer effects *in practice* of the metaphysics of archetypal *epistrophē*, leading all things to the Gods, therewith forgetting that the literal is necessary for pathologizing.[8] My point here is that metaphysics goes on in practice, and we need to see how the psychological praxis of metaphysics actually goes on.

The particular virtue of the psychological mind is its twisting of the given: seeing through, hearing echo and implication, turning back or upside down. The psychological mind makes the given imagistic, fantastic. Hence its affinity with both the pathological and the poetic, and hence, also, its distance from the programmatics of action and the formulations of the sciences. Our difference with the sciences is not that we are more faithfully phenomenological and do not abstract into more inclusive generalizations. Depth psychology abstracts all the time. The difference lies rather in the *practical effect* of abstraction. Where scientific abstractions seek to posit what is really there in the given, substitutive for it and constitutive of it, our abstractions seek to drop the bottom out of the given. That is why we so need the word "unconscious."

The trouble is that the metaphysics going on in our practice is not only methodologically negative: it is also *substantially* negative. The reduction of the given to its unconsciousness implicates our practice in a metaphysics of the negative, the "non," the "un," the by-definition unknowable and unspeakable. The method of analysis in therapy drops the bottom out of any positive statement, so our practice turns ever on its own metaphysics with its own deconstructionist tropic shiftings; our method is a uroboros, eating itself up with its own mouth, the talking-cure of its own talk.

And yet the bottomlessness into which we empty the given is in itself not negative. As Freud said, in the unconscious there is no negation. Our entire practice is filled positively with importance, "transitions of emotion"—again my reference is to Whitehead (*MT* 117). These emotions express Freud's id, a pleasure principle; or in Whitehead's terms, they are characterized by "self-enjoyment." Our entire practice is filled with *telos* ("aim" is Whitehead's word), including the deconstructive act of seeing through. And, our practice is always—because of the "un"—an adventure incurring novelty, because "the sense of process is always present" (*MT* 124).

How well what we do in our practice submits to Whitehead's metaphysical vision of life as having three essential positive characteristics: self-enjoyment, creativity or novelty, and aim (*MT* 150–54). But, should you ask what in therapy *is* the important and the novel, what *is* the purpose of the process, for the sake of *what* do you see through?—the psychological reply cannot be positively asserted. Any positive answer will itself be subject to seeing through, to twisting into fantasy. This is not a logical dilemma like the old conundrums left over from Zeno. It is not a dilemma at all, but a yoga, a *via negativa*. Not Zeno, Zen. An emptying out beyond the sheerly given to the beyond of metaphysical implications. We practice an alchemical metaphysics: "account for the unknown in terms of the more unknown." Notice here that this further unknown beyond is a *more*; at the same time that emptying is going on, so is filling. In the act of deconstruction there is constructive aim. Now what can we say about this filling? What are the constructs of this *beyond* to which the method leads and which it always implies? Beyond the verbs that carry us across—to doubt, to ask, to repeat, to twist, to echo—are there any nouns and adjectives on the farther shore?

III. Psychological Cosmology

The jottings in my folder "Cosmology" may be relevant. Bear in mind, these are merely jottings, meager and hurried. The word *cosmology* refers to the astronomical order of the heavenly bodies, and it also has a metaphysical meaning, according to Whitehead's *Process and Reality* (whose subtitle is *An Essay in Cosmology*): a scheme "of general ideas in terms of which every element of our experience can be interpreted" (*PR* 3). Now, why not keep together the two meanings, astronomical and metaphysical? Let us say that the astronomical bodies (the planets) offer metaphysical bodies (the Gods) by means of whom every element of experience can be interpreted. What is beyond in both meanings are the heavenly bodies. These afford some nouns and adjectives, some processes and some realities. The planetary persons fill the void of the beyond with the myths of their bodies and the bodies of their myths.[9] This cosmology is a psychological field—a *field* because metaphysics is placed[10] in imaginal locations; *psychological* because the planets are persons with traits, with behaviors, and in relation with one another. What the planets are and do, what goes on beyond human affairs, may be calculated astronomically and astrologically, that is, the mathematics of literal motions of actual planets. What goes on beyond can also be psychologically imagined through mythical fictions: the beyond quite literally a mythical region, even literarily a mythical region of *poiesis,* making images. Unlike other sorts of first principles that are reached through intuitions of self-evidence or through deductive or inductive reasoning, this region is accessible to imagination. More than merely accessible: mythical fictions stimulate imagination. They generate cosmological imaginings and further the soul's speculative freedom.

"Imagination finds its easiest freedom among the higher categories of eternal objects" (*PR* 115).

Myth seems to offer the only metaphysics (vision and synthesis) that I can imagine for psychology because it is imagined, it is personified, and it always presents itself as fiction. Myth negates its reality even as it presents it. Myths thus have the happy effect of forcing the mind to be psychological (as long as myths were alive we did not need depth psychology), because myth declares itself to be the supreme reality that is at the same time the supreme fiction. Twisted. Empty and full together. You *have* to see through. Myth, the poetic basis of mind imagined also to be the poetic basis of the universe. Human soul and world soul lodged in myths.

But are these stories true? So ask my jottings. Dumb question; because the answer has to be referred to the field itself, the many persons of the planets. "Truth" in terms of which planetary God's notion of truth? "Who" says this is true? Moreover, we have to inquire into truth *psychologically,* into truth as psychologically satisfying.

One characteristic of psychological truth we have already noted: it follows the way of the psychological mind, that twisting which allows the soul to make its fantasy images. Psychological truth is therefore a twisted truth, what the Renaissance called twofold truth. Psychological beauty is twisted beauty, where, as Plotinus and the Art of Memory recognized, the ugly has more immediate and memorable effect on the soul than does the harmonious (Whitehead sees discord as essential to the richer forms of beauty). And psychological goodness, the jottings say, is twisted by the shadow that falls in every intention, every action, every result, every judgment. This recognition of twistedness is what I call *psychological.*

Just here I can imagine someone arguing: "You can't start with the twisted. It requires something straight, literal, defined for it to be later twisted. Let us assert before we deform; posit first, then negate, like Hegel. The twisted cannot be the *a priori.*"

This argument views the twisted from the straight, within oppositional thinking. Actually, twistedness comes in many sizes and shapes—curves, braids, folds, labyrinths, mazes, kinks, knots, webs, waves, polyphonies—and when one views all these marvels of the twisted, the straight suddenly seems a rather narrow and naive line to hold to. I use these examples about truth and twistedness to show how difficult it is to set up a psychological metaphysics because of the ingrained prejudices against its methods, its habitual axioms, its language. I would try to do for twistedness what Whitehead did so splendidly for straightness (*AI* 216): remove it from captivity in conventional language. I will come back to language.

And so, a psychological cosmology will inevitably twist cosmology itself, reading the ancient cosmologies not merely as straight historical predecessors but also for their psychological fantasies. For instance, the pre-Socratic four elements of which the world is constituted would each become an elemental *pathe,* thereby four ways that imagination affects the soul, such as described by Gaston Bachelard.[11] And Bachelard himself would be our Aristotle, giving the concrete sensuous imagination its elemental categories. Like Aristotle, Bachelard integrates the elements of his predecessors and works them in a new way.

Another ancient cosmology: the geometric shapes of the elements in Plato's *Timaeus* would be read to mean not simply that the ground of experience is mathematical or follows deductively logical laws, but that it is shaped. The *pathe,* the sufferings of the elements, the elemental pathologizings which are the necessity of the psyche,[12] have definite limits. *Contra* Heraclitus, the soul *does have its limits*: the limiting shapes of its images. The indefinite, the infinite, and the chaos can therefore be taken not literally, but as imaginative shapes. Metaphysics, for all our attempt at a *via negativa,* cannot be other than positively formed. We may assert an absence of form, but can we imagine this absence, this formlessness? Does not imagining always make present and give shape? The world egg and eros (the generative joiner) are inherent in Chaos and Night, and even the Titans have names. The formal cause again achieves priority.

Moreover, and still in Plato's great cosmology (*Timaeus* 55c), after earth, water, air, and fire there is a fifth geometric shape, which Plato says the Dēmiourgos used for the shape of the whole. It is a dodecahedron, a twelve-sided figure, which Plato says has "a pattern of animal figures thereon." Now what in the world is this? Here is the whole, the ultimate fifth quintessentia, the overall and everything, and it has "a pattern of animal figures thereon"! A very physical sort of metaphysics here; and pluralistic, too.[13] Of course, this twelve-sided figure could refer to the astronomical cosmology of the zodiac, the animal figures of the twelve regions of the heavens. Even so, it could also be imagining the world-soul, the *anima mundi,* as a configuration of animals. Remember Plato's *Republic* 9 (589b–c), where he presents "the symbolic image of the soul," taking it from myths, as a manifold and many-headed beast, a ring of heads tame and wild?

Here is a cosmology that configures the furthest, most comprehensive beyond in animal patterns, animal faces. The soul, a multifaceted beast;[14] *anima mundi* as *animal mundi*. Here, in this twist of Plato, we are close to the ancient Egyptian idea of animals as themselves Gods, and to the idea, shared by circumpolar peoples and still alive in shamanism, that animals are divinities from whom, in direct relation, religion arises in human minds.[15] Here we can locate Santayana's "animal faith,"[16] that unmeditated trust in a continuingly living world, within an animalized cosmology that can sustain this world in the face of its extinction.

My jottings now jump to Whitehead: The movements of these animal figures affect the soul as "transitions of emotion" (in Whitehead's language). These transitions of emotion take rise in the many-headed beast, tame and wild. By means of emotions we know where, when, and how the animal patterns reveal themselves as feelings of importance or interest (again Whitehead's terms), showing us that nature is alive, as Whitehead says (*MT* chap. 8), and preventing the universe from abstracting itself into mere matters of fact (*MT* chap. 1).

At the furthest reach of the cosmological imagination stand the animals. They extend the planetary Gods beyond mythical fictions to actual presences of vigorous life, there above in the dodecahedron and here below, creeping, swimming, and flying among us. The universal in the particular, eternal repetition of form, walking archetypes. I have elaborated upon Whitehead's direction for the construction of a "systematic metaphysical cosmology" (*MT* 168), the starting point for which is: "the energetic activity considered in physics [the elemental shapes] is the emotional intensity entertained in life [the animal faces]."

This way of reconsidering Whitehead offers an animal, even ecological, sense to his notion of Importance. What gives importance? Let us derive importance from the animal shape of the soul. I am suggesting too that emotions are, as Blake said, "divine influxes," not sheerly subjective moods. If respected in this way and cared for as divinities, as living animals, tame and wild, they can maintain the cosmos as living. Recollection of and care for the animals, out there and in here, constitute the metaphysical praxis that goes hand in hand with the cosmology. The worldwide religious practice of animal sacrifice receives its psychological twist. Now it means that the survival of the world requires recognizing the sacredness of our animal souls; our animal responses bond the soul to the world in an animal faith deeper than metaphysical skepticism.

My notes twist yet another of the old cosmologies: the sun-centered universe of Copernicus. I think it is true that he never looked through a telescope, but re-imaged the world with his mind. The sun of which they spoke—Copernicus, Brahe, and Kepler—refers also to a planet of the *mundus imaginalis*. They centered the universe upon an *imagination* of the sun, which was at that time, and archetypally in all time, the yellow lion of the heart. Copernicus, Brahe, and Kepler said that the earth turns around this heart, that we circulate in the streaming light of the universal bloodstream. The source of vitality in the natural universe radiates from a solar conflagration that is a roaring animal.

According to Paracelsus, the imagination in the human heart is reciprocally related with the active imagination of the natural universe located in its heart, the sun, which endlessly radiates images, forming life with its imaging power. The Newtonian mind abstracted the rays of the solar lion into heat, light, energy, velocity, radiation, the photosynthesis of chlorophyll; but the twisted metaphysics of soul can envision chlorophyll and the *calor inclusus* of all living things to be images fulminating from the sulfuric green lion, shaping biological life into its magnanimous variety of forms. In the other words of my twisted vision, the Copernican revolution places an animal imagination of the heart in the center of the universe.

IV. Aesthetics Is
Self-Evident Common Sense

This cosmology has consequences that we cannot expand upon here, consequences for theory of knowledge and perception, theory of aesthetics and value, theory of anthropology and psychology. Some of this I have already begun in talks at Eranos: "Perception of the Unique" (1976), "The Thought of the Heart" (1979), and "The Animal Kingdom in the Human Dream" (1982).[17]

Briefly, these talks assume that all things are inherently intelligible. This intelligibility does not depend upon adducing universal physical laws or upon a coherent systematic theology; it is an intelligibility given with the shapes or physiognomy of the world which is afforded directly to our sensate imaginations, to us as animals. As animals, "we find ourselves 'accepting' a world of substantial objects, directly presented for our experience," says Whitehead (*AI* 21). Cosmology in the metaphysical sense, as the interpretation of all elements of experience, is made therefore possible by the intelligible nature of things themselves. The cosmos has a logos, it is a cosmo*logy,* which bespeaks the intelligence of the planetary persons who display themselves in the world.

Then why do we not see them? Why is the intelligibility of the world not more apparent to us? Why do we feel lost, behind a dark glass, disoriented? Is it because the Gods have withdrawn, as Rilke says? Or is it because we are fallen in sin away from them, as Christian theology asserts? No, not Luke; Locke. Our theory of perception simply does not let us see them. I do not mean "see them" in an epiphanic way, pentecostal, a deathbed vision in white light. I mean rather that our Lockean theory of perception denies qualities to things, removing intelligibility from their faces. They stand there dumb and dead, without heat, without taste, without smell, without color, without touch—*sans* everything. The physiognomy of the world has been defaced and removed all to the mind, thereby severing life from appearance, and appearance from truth and from reality.

The world had first to be abstracted for it to conform with this abstract account of it. Or maybe we should say that the loss of soul in this metaphysical position made it impossible to perceive any other way. A living sense of *world* requires a corresponding living organ of *soul* by means of which a living world can be perceived.

But Whitehead has already demolished this kind of thinking, epitomized by Locke, that removes the emotional face of things. I wish Whitehead were still around to take down structuralism and the deconstruction that follows it, because they continue this indifference to the actual occasions of the phenomenal world—this image here that is immediately presented and not some other—reducing what is as *fons et origo* to abstract structural relations or troping it transformatively into something else. Anything can be anything. Polysemous has come to mean polyethylene, polyurethane, utter plasticity—Proteus become a monster, the changeability of form become a mockery of form. All relations: a web of endless intricate relations—and no spider.

Maybe the ruling Western cosmology that cannot see the Gods in the face of things begins before Locke. Perhaps it goes back to monotheism, to the God who never showed his face, except to Moses, replacing the divine face with divine law, with abstract commandment, substituting ethics for aesthetics. But there is another way of reading that monotheism. Corbin reads the Koranic passage, "Everything shall perish except His [God's] Face," to mean: "Every thing . . . except the Face of that thing."[18]

Seeing the face of the Gods in things means noticing qualities as primary and speaking in a richly qualified language. Adjectives before nouns. During the Renaissance—in alchemy, the art of memory, and astrology—thick-crusted things, things gray and dull, wintry, or living in isolated places, belonged to Saturn, as did laconic speech, a mathematical turn of the mind, measuring tools, and so on. All "things," whether styles of mind, diseases, foods, geographies, or animals, found location according to their qualities. Everything had shelter and altar. Nothing was lost; everything belonged to a cosmos because it belonged somewhere as image to the planetary persons and their myths.

This emphasis on descriptive qualities gives back to *cosmology* its original aesthetic meaning. We have lost that first sense of the word. *Cosmos* now means empty, vast, spacey—a video game for astronomers. The Greek word meant orderly, becomingly, duly, an aesthetic arrangement. *Cosmos* once referred to the *anima mundi,* world-soul, an Aphroditic order. And our word "cosmetics," referring to the facial appearance of things, brings to light this original sense.

So, besides its astronomical and metaphysical meanings, *cosmology* implies even more fundamentally an aesthetic world whose essence is constituted in sensory images. Attempts to reduce the account of the world to the fewest coherent principles, even to mathematical formulae, have the intention of revealing by means of scientific elegance this cosmic beauty.

My Florence lecture in 1981 attempted in its very title, *"Anima Mundi*: The Return of the Soul to the World," to indicate the consequences for psychology of an aesthetic cosmology.[19] Rather than a subjective notion of human beings whose souls are privately inside and self-experienced, *anima mundi* situates human beings in a world ensouled. The human being then becomes a presentation of soul to others as much as an interior reflection to self. Jung's famous ontological phrase *esse in anima* (*CW* 6:77) states a psychology that implies this aesthetic anthropology. *Esse in anima* comes to mean not *homo faber* or *homo rationalis* but *homo aestheticus,* to coin a term: the human as a sense-enjoying, image-making creature. We are sensate creatures, animals in an ecological field that affords imagistic intelligibility. Whitehead might call this "Nature Alive,"[20] the cosmos displaying its self-enjoyment. The revolutionary theory of perception developed by J. J. Gibson and his Cornell school of direct realism advances in cogent argument and experimental analysis this aesthetic animal view of perception.[21]

Whitehead uncovers a commonsense truth about an aesthetic cosmology. It offers satisfaction to three essential metaphysical needs: the necessity of personally individual subjects, the necessity of particularly qualified objects, and the necessity of the coterminous relation. An aesthetic experience is "*my* enjoyment . . . the pleasure is mine, and the pain is mine. Aesthetic enjoyment demands an individualized universe. In the second place, there is the aesthetic object which is identified in experience as the source of the subjective feeling" (*ESP* 130). These dipolar moments, these prehensions, affirm the subject as personal—my taste, my judgment—simultaneously together with that thing there as the source of my feelings. I and it are ineluctably bound. Only an aesthetic cosmology provides this satisfaction. A physical cosmology that runs by chance, or by laws, has no necessity for the individualized experience; a logical cosmology always has trouble deducing from the mind the necessity of particular worldly occasions.

One further step: *homo aestheticus* is also *homo cordis* (or *cordialis*). The psychology entailed by this anthropology shifts the seat of consciousness from the head to the heart as the organ of the *sensus communis* and of the perception of images. Cosmology cannot become psychological—that is, given as aesthetic images to the sensate imagination and twisted by that imagination—unless the heart awakens as an imagining, sensing organ, no longer merely the organ of subjective feelings. Then "Importance" can refer to images moving in the world-soul and not only to my private proprioceptions of these motions. The practice of psychology or psychotherapy has this intention: awakening, or circumcising, the heart. Therewith the Aristotelian idea of the *sensus communis* located around the heart expands into three concurrent meanings which express the aims of therapy. The common sense as the interpenetration of all sensation and imagination (every image sensate, every sensation imaged); the common sense as ordinary animal-like reactions to the face of the world; and common sense as communal sense, what Alfred Adler said was the final aim of therapy, *Gemeinschaftsgefühl.*[22]

When the theory of perception changes, then so does theory of knowledge, epistemology. Knowledge of the world and of experiences of every sort would now mean knowledge of their relations to the Gods. Knowing would mean leading things out, *exegesis*, leading their intelligibility to their sacred home. Each Thing an E.T. calling home; *epistrophē*.[23] Knowledge becomes *gnosis* when things and experiences, by virtue of their being known, suggest their subtle bodies in the Anima Mundi. Rather than abstracting us from the world, knowing takes us more directly into its soul as aesthetic presentation. The way to see the faces of the Gods is to know the world. Practical knowledge, common sense, *Lebensphilosophie*, therefore cannot be divided from metaphysical knowledge. Knowing serves the soul's life among sense-images, dissolving that problem with which we started, metaphysics as anti-psychological. Instead, metaphysics becomes the praxis of an essentially lived life in which being, substance, method, order, and other traditional topics of metaphysics become qualities of soul.

Lest one think this path of knowledge to be utterly immanent, horizontal, as if only in the world can the Gods be known, let me refer again to Corbin. The circumcision of the heart so that it can perceive *sub specie imaginalis* is an instruction by the authority neither of philosophical learning nor of empirical testing—neither Book nor Bacon. Instead, this is initiation by the angels and daimones, the persons of the *mundus imaginalis*, who awaken the active imagination and teach the reality of their images apart from the mind that believes it imagines them. We learn their truth as witnesses and bring recitations, dramatic accounts, of what has been seen and heard.[24] After descents and flights "out of the world" by means of disciplined imagining activities—oneself the subject of an *exegesis*, being led out by an angel, the psychopompos—the world becomes transparent, the beyond *here*; and the act of seeing through into divine depth becomes not an effort of subjective analysis, but transparency appears with vision itself. Encounters with the psychopompos are the way of knowledge: an active imagination is an essential metaphysical praxis necessitated by this cosmology. This discipline is now rightly called psychotherapy.

V. Cosmic Speech

Psychological cosmology requires a specific kind of language. Its main quality is generosity, which is not merely a euphemism for empurpled indistinction. We can move beyond the old arguments of rhetoric versus reason. We need something else: the generous language of imagination.

How better to achieve "expression of what is self-evident" (*MT* 49)? The language of a cosmology may be strict and it may be abstract, but these qualities are to serve the more generous aim of fecundity—to use the term of Susanne Langer, Whitehead's pupil.

Fecundity, however, must suggest more than her transposition of *interesting,* which also needs to be led out from captivity in the subject and located with the Gods. *Interesting* evokes a Neoplatonic vision of the Gods as fertile, seminal—I have said, animal; and what makes the fiction of the Gods interesting, and thus fecund, is that they provide self-generative amplitudes, ever-emanating fountains of fantasy. Gods are inherently generous. Cosmological language responds to them in kind, and Jung's method of amplification, though diverted by a scientistic pretension, is at heart an act of ritual. Amplification responds to the amplitude of fantasy images with a correspondingly rich language.

Because cosmology satisfies the metaphysical need for a vision of invisible primary assumptions and is formed in language, cosmology cannot help but be mythical. Its language will bespeak this mythicality regardless of the very demythologizing purpose of its metaphysical intention. The language of cosmology therefore cannot submit to metaphysical analysis, because that critique too imports myth in the very words it uses. The critique of a vision itself implies a vision; metaphysics' own primary assumptions are cosmological.

The generous giftedness of the world has been stripped to the stark givenness of data. But if, like animals, we take the world as granted, then we receive this present with words of qualities that appreciate the grant proffered: not Orphic cosmology, the World as Egg, but each word an egg[25] brooding its *logos spermatikos,* a latent Easter.

The words of a cosmology are therefore not merely building blocks, buttresses for arguments, keystones in overarching concepts. They are the cosmological edifice and serve it in every part. Because cosmologies are built *in* language and not merely *of* language, the house of the soul will be a language ensouled, an Ark for the Covenant.

A psychological cosmology needs generous language because, as Whitehead says, "the notion of life implies a certain absoluteness of self-enjoyment" (*MT* 150). Why not then let this self-enjoyment, this physical celebration of what is, enter into our metaphysical interpretation of what is? The planetary Gods, the elements, the animals provide a cosmology in the noble, high style, which is what *generous* first means. Things that trace the origin of their quality to the Gods are indeed highborn, so the account of them will exhibit the pathology of the highblown. Besides, generous speech itself generates, opens out of itself. It performs a metaphysical praxis, by breaking out of operational definitions, giving generously by implication, pointing beyond in words that go beyond, twisting themselves into releasing soul as the language moves along, so that animation is going on in the construction itself. Think of the difference in language between Russell and Whitehead, between Skinner at Harvard and Santayana and James at Harvard, between Aristotle's *clarification* of the soul and Plato's *generation* of soul through his dramatic and twisting dialectic, the personifications, etymologies, ironies, scenes, and myths.

The adventure of ideas occurs already in the tongue itself in its adventure of language, that risk of speech, unpredictable diction. Who knows what is coming next? But advent is not the future as a temporal projection. It is a project of language: in the adventure of words themselves. For words are little mythical beings, popping up in jottings, fictions generating fictions, trailing their genealogies as etymology, making music and echo in phonetics, dancing their syntax, perishing and coming to be, more and more of them asking to come in, crowding forward over the exhausted heaps of wingless clichés. Words are angels.[26] Hosanna! *Hosanna* means both Save (an appeal for deliverance) and Praise (a shout of adoration). A cosmology that saves the phenomena adores them.

If a metaphysics is built to meet a paranoid need of the soul for overall meanings of spiritual certainty, jottings will always fail. From the paranoid perspective what is displayed here may seem even hysterical, characterized by theatrical exaggerations, a smiling indifference to consistency, and the *sentiment d'incomplétude*: trying to get it all in without the defense of well-prepared positions. It may so seem that the pleroma I have been proposing is *too* pleromatic, too full, too drunken, too Gods-intoxicated.[27] But the soul's need for a cosmological vision does not have to be met literally in its own terms with a paranoid metaphysical system. To elaborate upon this distinction would demand more time.

Time—time is a power, an activity, of soul. It is the soul that produces time—if we follow Plotinus—as if to say that what happens with time depends in part on our psychological condition: rushed time reveals pressed soul, the soul of the world amidst the metaphysical catastrophe that has already, in imagination, ended the world. Time belongs in any cosmology, and when that cosmology is envisioned to be filled with many different Gods, there will be different kinds of time, many times, and therefore times aplenty for each soul here to show itself. Because I have willfully omitted time from this presentation, it returns as the repressed, with a hard, dead line, bringing these jottings to a ruthless, or, perhaps, to the reader who has been so patient, a merciful, end.

15

Back of "Back to Beyond" and Creeping Dichotomism

EDWARD S. CASEY

I. Shape and an Aesthetic Cosmology

In reading "Back to Beyond: On Cosmology," we experience the rare treat of witnessing one of the most imaginative thinkers of our time as he locates himself within a domain hitherto unexplored. The position he stakes out is an anomalous and untraditional one; it is also highly revealing. Instead of metaphysical synthesis in the grand manner or metaphysical vision in the style of poets and seers, metaphysical praxis becomes the focal point of Hillman's lucubrations. For him the question is not "What does a metaphysician think?" but "What does a metaphysician *do*?" In other words, what moves does he or she make and in particular what figure does he or she cut, and what is the shape of the practice?

The more such questions are pressed, the more they move us into the imaginal background that is the proper province of archetypal psychology. Hillman's basic effort is to map metaphysics from an archetypal point of view; or, more exactly, to find forms of convergence between two such seemingly disparate enterprises. This is a bold move, especially when we realize how difficult it is to distinguish Hillman's conception of metaphysical praxis from the practice of psychology itself. Metaphysics and psychology come still closer when we speak (as Hillman plainly prefers to speak) of "cosmology." For with "cosmos" we stop short of the beyond of "meta"; it is a matter of the back *of* the beyond. Or rather, of its *front*, its face: as the ordered, immediately given aspect of the universe, the cosmic comes configured. It comes as the cosmetic, as the shaped face of the visible, its *facies* (shape, form, face).[1] To grapple with the superficies of the universe does not mean, however, to be consigned to the superficial. A particular profundity of the imaginal becomes evident in cosmology and not elsewhere—not even in psychopathology or poetry, otherwise the most congenial seedbeds for the imaginal. "The depths are on the surface," as Wittgenstein said in *Zettel*; and this is nowhere more true than in a cosmology archetypally envisioned. It is a question of getting the substance into the form, the body into the face—and thereby depth psychology into its own richly wrought surface.

Hillman and Whitehead share much in matters of cosmology: a common respect for the importance of feeling in metaphysics,[2] for the importance of the animal in human existence,[3] and for the importance of *importance* itself as a metaphysical category. One place where they begin to diverge, however, concerns precisely the role of shape in their thinking. Whereas for Hillman shape is primordial—nothing comes unshaped at any level of experience—for Whitehead shape is distinctly secondary: it supervenes on the extensive continuum, which does not possess shape *per se*. In fact, shape arises only at the aesthetic level: it is only in the phase of "aesthetic supplement" that shape "acquires dominance by reason of its loveliness" (*PR* 213). Another way of putting this same difference is to say that the aesthetic is absolutely primary for Hillman, who regards it as being at one with the cosmologically given itself: hence his notion of an "aesthetic cosmology" whose correlate is an "Aphroditic order" (see *TH*). Whitehead, despite his vast appreciation of art and the aesthetic generally (see *AI* chap. 17), cannot bring himself to regard *aesthesis* as coincidental with the most primordial substratum of human experience: as a matter of what Coleridge calls "forma formosa."[4] In Hillman's term, Whitehead's cosmology remains "physical"; it includes the aesthetic rather than being founded on it.[5]

II. Creeping Dichotomism

The matter of shape—not to be confused with the shape of matter!—is not as incidental an issue as it may appear to be at first glance. In according cosmological primacy to it, Hillman is in effect reaffirming his prior commitment to the ultimacy of the image and thus to the secondariness of all that is non-image. This is not the place to question the ultimacy of the image, which is at the very center of archetypal psychology as it has been reconceived by Hillman after Jung. But we can begin to wonder about its corollary, the diminished status of the non-imagistic. It is not only a question of being struck by the sudden and thorough demotion of whatever fails to achieve the status of image; such a demotion occurs as a matter of course whenever any entity or experience is proposed as first or last in the cosmos. Of more concern is another consequence of the image's ultimacy: what could be called "creeping dichotomism."

When shape and therefore image (we may presume that "image" is the generic term and "shape" its corporeal expression) are thrust into such prominence, it is only natural to start thinking in such bipolar terms as image *versus* concept, image *versus* word, animated *versus* de-animated, and other similar *versus*es. Soon, if this dichotomizing tendency is not checked, one's entire universe will be rent asunder into a permanently honorific region of the Image and an equally dishonorific region of the Concept, the Word, et cetera. The result would be nothing like the polyadic cosmos—or the plural *cosmoi*—which would seem to reflect most adequately Hillman's professed polytheism.[6] Rather, a diremptive universe, a model of cosmos and countercosmos, would be set in place, with all the untoward consequences about which such staunch antidualists as Blake, Bergson, and Merleau-Ponty have warned us.

In Hillman's case, the cosmological dichotomism is still only creeping and has not reached drastic, much less devastating, proportions. In fact, his thought is much more deeply akin to Blake than to Blake's bugbears Descartes and Newton. Paradoxically, it is the very *poiesis* on which Hillman lays such stress that saves him from the most costly excesses. His emphasis on *homo aestheticus*—for example, beauty, the "thought of the heart"—is precisely what helps to extricate him from what can be regarded as the outcome of an aesthetic cosmology that places shape at the origin of all things. But this is because the saving *aesthesis* is an overflowing activity, a poetic productivity, in contrast with the well-shaped economy of an aesthetic cosmology.

Likewise problematic is a twofold claim made by Hillman that the cosmos or world possesses (*a*) intelligibility and (*b*) necessity.

(*a*) Hillman writes that "all things are inherently intelligible." Moreover, this intelligibility is "given with the shape or physiognomy of the world" and is "backed by the intelligence of the planetary persons who display themselves in the world." Such statements are highly suggestive. On the one hand, "imagistic intelligibility" is imputed to the cosmos through the very notion of a primordial shapefulness. But shape can become *intelligible*—that is, amenable to intelligence or reason—only if it can be regarded as form, as *eidos*. Only the eidetic is intelligible in any strict sense. The eidetic, however, requires something beyond what sensation or the ecological field can deliver: if not a Platonic heaven of forms, then a realm of planetary gods. To secure the *logos* of cosmology, Hillman advises us to go *back* to these gods, whose intelligence backs the cosmos and gives it its intelligibility. Or must we not go *beyond* to them—to the *meta* that we thought we had left behind? Even if we need to go "back to beyond," this is still a movement that transcends the sheer immanence of face or shape. Can it be that the felt need for a backing to the image arises out of the same dichotomism identified above, only now having crept a few steps further?

(*b*) The same question arises in the instance of cosmic *necessity* in the threefold form stipulated by Whitehead and subscribed to by Hillman in these words: "the necessity of personally individual objects, the necessity of particularly qualified objects, and the necessity of their coterminous relation." Such necessity is contrasted dichotomously with chance or law;[7] and yet we are left wondering just what kind of necessity this is. It is presumably "imagistic," as in the parallel case of intelligibility. But we have just seen how the image calls forth the backing of the gods, and this by Hillman's own reckoning. At this stage the dichotomism seems to step into a slow trot. How can we prevent this from becoming a runaway situation?

III. Phenomenality

What is needed is a term that mediates between image on one side and intelligibility and necessity on the other. *Phenomenal* fills this role admirably, not as a third term between the dichotomies in question but as a term that manages to encompass both members of each dyad (image/necessity; image/intelligibility). How is this so? Here consider Kant's definition of phenomenon as a "determinate appearance." *Appearance* captures the essence of image as what appears *as* it appears—that is, in the very form or shape in which it appears. *Determinate* means inherently intelligible: such as to be comprehensible in a genuinely lawlike way. It does not matter that for Kant the lawlikeness in question is mathematical in nature; indeed the mathematical is an intrinsic part (and for Plato himself the most important part) of the eidetically known.

What does matter is that the determinacy of phenomena allows them to be at once appearances[8] and yet fully intelligible and necessary. (The necessity of phenomena is found in the fact that not only *may* they be subsumed under laws; they *must* be—in every case without exception.) It is not surprising to find Heidegger carrying forward the spirit of Kant's conception of the phenomenon in his own celebrated definition of the same term: "that which shows itself in itself."[9] For all the manifest differences between Heidegger and Hillman, here is an area of possible convergence: just as sheer showing comes together with the precise *way* of being shown in the determinacy of phenomena, so image and god, ectype and archetype, here and beyond, coalesce in the phenomenality of the manifestly given.

The same phenomenality also provides a clue to a remaining puzzle in Hillman's essay. This puzzle is located in the idea of "metaphysical praxis." It will be recalled that much was promised with this term, which was proposed as an archetypally appropriate alternative to "metaphysical vision" and "metaphysical synthesis." A close reading of Hillman's text reveals, however, that there are no less than three candidates for what constitutes metaphysical praxis: active imagination, writing (a poetic use of words), and care of animals. What could possibly connect three such disparate activities? In what could their commonality as forms of metaphysical praxis consist? The answer lies in their being different modes of achieving or specifying phenomenality. Metaphysical praxis would thus consist in picking out phenomenal forms (or more exactly, the forms of phenomena) as these present themselves in such diverse contexts as psychotherapy, poetry, and ecology, with each of these being taken in the largest sense. In active imagination one traces out the phenomenal figures first given in fantasies and dreams; in poetry one configurates images in the most fully resonant words; in ecology one follows the lead of animals in their uniquely life-enhancing phenomenality. All three instances of metaphysical praxis illustrate Whitehead's dictum that "the difficulty of philosophy is the expression of what is self-evident." For the self-evident is itself phenomenally given; but to be able to express the phenomenally given one must invoke such things as forms and laws (Plato and Kant), eternal objects (Whitehead), or archetypes and gods (Jung and Hillman). To go back to beyond is therefore not to go into *the* beyond of a meta-physics but to enter resolutely into the very back, the inherent latency, of the phenomenally manifest.

16

A Metaphysical Psychology to Un-Locke Our Ailing World

DAVID RAY GRIFFIN

James Hillman's call for a metaphysical psychotherapy is revolutionary. It can be read as a call to overcome the dualism between therapeutically oriented psychology, which in the modern world has been individualistic, and metaphysical cosmology, which in the modern world has generally regarded psyche as less than fully real, and has sought to be truthful, not therapeutic. (One modern dictum has it that "philosophy should not be edifying.") From his own side of the fence, Hillman is saying that psychotherapy, in moving beyond its previous individualism, must deal not only with the individual's family and the larger society, but also with the cosmos. If those from the philosophical side of the fence were to respond in kind, metaphysical cosmology would recover its ancient aim of *therapeia,* most obvious in Stoicism. It would seek to find and express the truth that saves. Only now it would seek to save not only the individual within the world; it would orient itself to saving the world itself.

This is indeed the context in which Hillman issues his call: the world itself is in danger of extinction. And he sees that the world's illness is psychogenic, originating in an unhealthy way of thinking: "The physical threat . . . results from a metaphysical catastrophe" (215).

Hillman rightly connects this catastrophe with the influence of John Locke. Locke was representative of that movement of thought which rejected not only Aristotelian philosophy but, even more emphatically (as recent historians have shown), the animated cosmologies arising from the Neoplatonic Renaissance beginning in Italy in the latter half of the fifteenth century. In place of both of these worldviews, Locke and Company (Galileo, Gassendi, Mersenne, Descartes, Hobbes, Boyle, the later Newton et al.) advocated a "mechanical philosophy," according to which nature was to be understood as devoid of all properties except those quantitative features necessary for mechanistic interactions. All other properties, such as color, scent, and taste, were said to be "secondary qualities" projected onto nature by the mind. And characteristics such as purpose, feeling, and enjoyment were said to be "tertiary," even further removed from the natural world.

In its seventeenth-century founders, except for Hobbes, this mechanistic view of nature was part of a dualistic worldview, in which the human soul was in effect treated as supernatural. In fact, these scientist-philosophers could remove all the nonquantitative qualities from nature precisely because they could lodge them in the soul. But in the following centuries, more and more thinkers followed Hobbes's lead and rejected dualism in favor of complete materialism. This transition was due in large part to the unintelligibility of ontological dualism: if soul and body were totally different types of substance, how could they be in constant communication with each other? The rejection of this dualism meant that not only all quality but also all soul was banished from reality. Soul was said to be epiphenomenal at most, an ineffectual by-product of purely material mechanisms which control the world.

In short, in the first stage of this movement that came to constitute the "modern" worldview, nature was disenchanted. In the second stage, the world was desouled.[1] This is the metaphysical catastrophe that lies behind the present threat of physical catastrophe.

Hillman's solution is that we need to un-Locke the world, which means to re-qualify and re-soul it. The key to this reversal lies in a "common sense" in which "animal faith" and aesthetic response are primary. Hillman rightly sees that Whitehead's philosophy, which challenges so many of the tenets of modern thought, supports his aims. I will suggest a couple of ways in which a fuller appropriation of Whitehead's postmodern philosophy would strengthen his proposals. I will conclude by discussing ways in which Whiteheadians can benefit from Hillman's insights.

Hillman recognizes that a change must be made both in our ontology—our understanding of the nature of nature—and in our epistemology and theory of perception. On the latter point, he stresses that we need to "see through" all those beliefs and features of our perception that prevent us from directly perceiving the world. Only through this direct perception will we recover the sense of the sacred depths of our souls and of the world as a whole and our bondedness to it. The purpose of "seeing through" is to drop the bottom out of what seems to be given. And yet this negative move leads to a positive end. The emptying results in a filling, for beneath the abstractions are found importance, self-enjoyment, transitions of emotion, and divine influx.

Whitehead's view involves a distinction between three modes of perception—one that is clear but superficial, one that is vague but profound, and a third that is their combination. The first he calls "perception in the mode of presentational immediacy." It can largely be equated with conscious sense-perception. For example, in visual experience, a colored shape is perceived as qualifying an external region of space. Locke part of the time, and Berkeley and Hume more consistently, took this to be our only mode of perception. This so-called empiricist doctrine of perception meant that we have no direct perception of other individual, actual things; we perceive only generic forms, such as colors and shapes. This was the basis for the metaphysical skepticism to which Hillman refers, according to which the very existence of the world becomes problematic (216, 218). This philosophy obviously could not portray our deep sense of sacred value as deriving from our perception of the values incarnate in other things, for it could not even portray us as perceiving other things! It said, in Hume's revealing expression, that all of our percepts arise from "unknown causes."

Of course, in practice we all act as if we are in a world of other things, which act upon us and suffer our acts. But philosophical theory, said Hume, could not say this. Accordingly, he introduced the fateful distinction between "theory" and "practice" which has characterized modern philosophy. We must believe all sorts of things in practice, in the marketplace, of which our theories, worked out in the ivory tower, must remain skeptical. When those things were said to include the derivation of values from other things, and even the reality of causal derivation and of other things as such, it is no wonder that the ivory tower got a bad name, and that philosophy came to be perceived as irrelevant to life.

Whitehead's solution is to point to a more primitive mode of perception, which he calls "perception in the mode of causal efficacy," or simply "prehension." A prehension is a direct grasping of another thing as causally efficacious for oneself. This causal efficacy is the transference of value. Perception at this basic level involves the "transitions of emotion" to which Hillman refers.

Whitehead associates his idea here with Santayana's "animal faith." But with one proviso: animal faith must be taken as a mode of direct perception of other things (*PR* 142, 152). This is not how Santayana meant it, as Whitehead knew, but it seems to be in harmony with Hillman's meaning, because he speaks of the heart as a "sensing organ, no longer merely the organ of subjective feelings" (227). In any case, Whitehead is a "radical empiricist" in William James's sense, as he holds that we directly perceive real things and the relations, or transitions, between them.

Human perception in its entirety is always a mixture of these two pure modes of perception. Whitehead calls it "symbolic reference," because the percepts of one mode are used symbolically to refer to those of the other mode. Usually it is the data of conscious sense-perception that are used as symbols to interpret the vague, usually barely conscious, sense of causal efficacy from the surrounding world which we feel. The mistake of the Lockean-Humean empiricists was to assume that these relatively "clear and distinct" sensory images were the most primitive data of perception. This error was due to the assumption that the essence or basis of the soul consists in consciousness and the contents it lights up.

Whitehead presupposes the basic insight of depth psychology, that conscious experience arises out of unconscious experience, and develops a corresponding epistemology, containing the following points: Consciousness illuminates only a small portion of what we perceive (prehend); a moment of experience involves both reception and complex synthetic construction; consciousness primarily illuminates the later phases of this self-constructive process; sensory data, which are among the contents most clearly illuminated by consciousness, are derivative constructs, not primitive elements.

Therefore, the fact that sensory images by themselves give us no information about other actual things, about causal efficacy, about aims, about intrinsic value (self-enjoyment), or about the communication of values—a fact about which the British empiricists were correct—is no reason to conclude that we have no direct perception of these things whatsoever. To realize this, it is best to focus not on objects exterior to our bodies, but on our experience of our bodies themselves. I have a direct, if somewhat vague, sense that my present experience is in part causally derived from my bodily parts. I directly perceive, in the sense of prehend, my body's actuality, its causal effectiveness, and the fact that this causality involves the communication of values: I feel the "transitions of emotion" from my bodily organs to my experience as a whole. Although I also directly perceive (prehend) the world beyond my body, this perception rarely rises to consciousness. When it does, we speak of "telepathy" or "clairvoyance." Otherwise, my conscious experience of the wider world is mediated through my body, especially through my sensory organs. Sensory perception should not, therefore, be taken as the basic form of perception and the paradigmatic example of the soul's relatedness to things beyond itself. Whitehead endorses the view that we have a *direct* experience of other things, and that this is an *aesthetic* perception, in which the values of other things are directly grasped. But he does not consider sensory perception to be an example of this direct perception.

Hillman is as concerned as Whitehead to overcome the isolation of experience from the world, and to recover the aliveness of the world. But his positive suggestion for doing this appeals to the direct perception of sensory images. The danger is that this will not break out of the Lockean trap. Whitehead's richer analysis of how sensory images come to be could deepen Hillman's proposal and ground it in a fuller cosmological vision.

This brings us to the question of primary and secondary qualities. From Whitehead's perspective, sense-qualities such as "red as I see it" *are* secondary, that is, products of the perceiving mind, not direct representations of qualities existing "out there." Red as I see it, by means of my visual system, cannot be thought to qualify the petals of the rose when no animal is perceiving it. The rose as a whole, or the cells in its petals, cannot be thought to be "seeing red." So in what sense is the rose red? The dualist said: in a purely quantitative sense; "red" objectively refers only to a certain frequency of light waves. The dualist then had to believe that this purely quantitative locomotion somehow gets transformed into qualitative phenomena by the perceiving mind. Whitehead gives a third alternative: "red" is *primarily* an emotion, a feeling. It is a quality, but first of all a quality *of feeling*: the cells in the rose petal feel "redly." The photons, and the cells in one's optic nerve, share this feeling, conveying it to the brain. The perceiving mind therefore need not magically turn a quantity into a quality; rather, it transmutes one kind of quality into another kind, or one mode of perceiving it into another mode. That is, what are really primary in Whitehead's universe are some of the qualities the dualists called "tertiary": feeling, emotion, and aim. This ontological and epistemological analysis lies behind his statement that what is going on most deeply in the world are "transitions of emotion."

It is on this basis that Whitehead sees the human soul as fully a part of nature, and therefore can understand all other individuals in nature in a nondualistic way, as not different in kind from the human soul. All individuals are engaged in the reception and expression of sensa, which are understood to be forms of emotion. Sense-perception is derivative from this more basic sense-*reception,* which we have in common with all creatures (*PR* 113). This sense-reception, or prehension, is hence truly a *common* sense, a sense that we have in common with all our fellow creatures. It is on this basis that Whitehead can say, in a passage quoted by Hillman (223), that "the energetic activity considered in physics is the emotional intensity entertained in life." That is, that which we characterize from an external perspective as mere matter-of-fact energy should, by analogy with our own experience, be understood to involve transitions of emotion.

Seeing all things as animated in this sense would remove the dualism that could implicitly remain as long as the "soul" or "psychic" reality of other things is based only upon their outer visage. Besides the sensory images to which our outer aspect gives rise in others, we have our own experience—"our invisible thoughts, feelings, and intentions," in Hillman's words (*S 1982*: 78). Unless we attribute *some* modicum of feeling and aim to other individuals, therefore, we will still imply an essential dualism, in which we alone have intrinsic value. Other things will still be regarded as having only instrumental value, not as things for us to care for in their own right.

Hillman has been reluctant to root images (sensory and otherwise) in some more basic *feeling,* because that could imply that images were derivative representations of inherently imageless feelings, which would lead us back to solipsistic subjectivism (*AP* 48). But it should be clear that Whitehead does not use "feeling" in this way. A feeling is a prehension. It has an objective datum, which is grasped, as well as an emotional subjective form, which is how that datum is grasped. Our final image *is* constructed; but it is constructed out of an initial form or image, which is *given.*

This idea that images have a subjective (self-created) aspect seems implicit in Hillman, because he does want to criticize some images as less appropriate than others—for example, those images that seem to be impelling us, lemming-like, to nuclear omnicide. The notion that all images are simply given to us by the soul of the world would provide no basis for these value judgments.

This point leads to a second major point on which Hillman's fuller appropriation of a Whiteheadian view would strengthen his position.

Hillman has long inveighed against all monisms in the name of the plurality of the world. Monotheism had to be replaced by polytheism. I suggested in my introduction to this volume that Whitehead's form of monotheism does not imply the mono-psychology Hillman opposes. But Hillman's recent rhetoric about the world-soul runs the risk of suggesting a pantheism in which there would be no genuine plurality. That is, after all his concern to protect the originative activity of the human soul, his recent rhetoric seems to deny it in favor of attributing all activity to the *anima mundi*. This is most pronounced in *Archetypal Psychology,* where he is speaking most literally. For example, he says that "the dreamer is in the image rather than the image in the dreamer" (*AP* 6); images come and go "at their own will . . . undetermined by personal psycho-dynamics" (*AP* 7). "It is not we who imagine but we who are imagined" (*AP* 8). This pantheism is also perhaps suggested above when Hillman says: "Myth, the poetic basis of mind imagined also to be the poetic basis of the universe" (221). Insofar as the *anima mundi* is regarded as divine, this seemingly monistic or pantheistic position not only undermines our freedom, it also leads to the conclusion that the soul of the world is no more good than evil—and then how is the return to an ensouled cosmos something in which to rejoice? Would not Hillman's program fit better within a Whiteheadian-Hartshornean pan-en-theism, according to which we all have some power of self-creation? In this view, the world-soul is still the source of new images (and ultimately the source of all images), but the images *given* to us do not completely determine the images that we use for our soul-making. These images are themselves in part the product of our own *poiesis,* our own poetic power. Accordingly, we are not just victims, passive loci for a cosmic drama being played out in us. We are partly responsible for where we are now, and we can to some extent decide the future. Also, most of the images that we inherit do not come directly from the world-soul, but derive from the past world, the past creations of previous self-creating creatures who created the images out of which they created themselves. But these inherited images were always accompanied by an image that offered a transforming possibility from the soul of the whole. Likewise, we have molded ourselves largely out of inherited images. But these are accompanied by other suggestions from the soul of the whole which can lead to transformations that can overcome the destructive aspects of the images we have inherited from our predecessors. So we cannot simply say, as Hillman has, that "the future will take care of itself." It is true that, in the future, hopeful images will always be emerging from the depths of our experience. But just how we respond to these tokens of grace will be our own doing.

This proposal involves a distinction between two possible meanings of *world-soul*. First, this term can refer to the collective soul of all sentient beings, especially human beings. This collective soul is not an individual, and as such has no experience, and exercises no initiative. Its power is the power of feelings, images, and thoughts that have been reinforced through innumerable repetitions. When I agree with Hillman that the world-soul is ill, I mean *world-soul* in this sense. The second meaning of *world-soul* is the truly divine reality, that all-encompassing soul in which we live, move, and have our being, and from which arise those novel possibilities through which we can sometimes break free from the power of the collective soul. By thus distinguishing the divine soul of the whole from the collective soul, we can affirm our own partial autonomy, and the goodness of the divine soul of the world.

I conclude with two ways in which those of us who have come to this encounter from the metaphysical side of the street should respond to Hillman's suggestions. Both of them involve overcoming the dichotomy between truth and therapy, between theory and practice.

The first concerns the nature of language. A central aspect of the Renaissance-based philosophies that was being rejected by Locke and his fellow modernists was the picture of the world as "en-thused," or filled with God. The modern, mechanical philosophy said that God moved things not by indwelling in them but by imposing laws of motion upon them from without. Therefore all "enthusiasm," based upon a sense of divine influx, whether directly or through nature, was said to be inappropriate. Religion should be sober and decorous, based upon the knowledge of deity available through historic revelation and through rational inference. Part and parcel of this rejection of enthusiasm was the development of a sober, plain, bare-bones style of writing, cultivated especially by Locke and the Royal Society in place of the poetic, flowery style of the classical stylists and the Enthusiasts.[2] No more personifications, no more ornamentation, no more pages filled with capitalizations. The literal, prosaic style of speech that Hillman finds alien to soul's imaginative essence was a deliberate program, based upon a particular theology, ontology, and epistemology, in which an absolute gap was created between object and subject, fact and value, world and divine.

Whitehead's postmodern philosophy is in many respects a recursion to the animated cosmology that Locke and his fellow modernists rejected. And to a great extent Whitehead's language is appropriate to its content. He often injected illuminating metaphors, and eminently quotable phrases, into his most technical passages. And some of his writing, such as the essay "Immortality" and the last part of *Adventures of Ideas,* is lyrical throughout, containing even the capitalizations so hated by anti-enthusiasts. But most of us Whiteheadians have continued to use the dull, prosaic style appropriate to the disenchanted world of the mechanists. The difference between Whitehead and most of us who use his thought was driven home to me by an exchange with the poet Robert Duncan, whom we had invited to a conference on Whitehead and aesthetics in 1980. A few weeks prior to the conference, the papers were mailed out to the participants. Shortly afterward, Duncan informed us that he would not be able to attend. The environment would be too alien: none of these people used language the way Whitehead did! Hillman is certainly correct in urging us to use language appropriate to an animate world and a soul that is responsive to the world's aesthetic aliveness.

But some of Hillman's formulations supportive of this appeal are unnecessarily dualistic. For example, his contrast between soul and spirit is overdrawn if it means that the *logos* of psyche and that of spirit are alien to each other, or even so independent that neither requires the other. Hillman's own work shows that this is not the case. His lucid summary of his views in *Archetypal Psychology* is written in a completely prosaic style. It is not an example of poetic, soul-building rhetoric, but a literal-as-possible account of the convictions and concepts central to this school. And it helps us respond to the mythical and metaphorical language Hillman uses elsewhere. Soul and spirit are complementary. Instead of inveighing against spirit in the name of soul, is it not better to recognize that the urge to conceptual coherence and precision which leads to science and metaphysics is as natural to psyche as the production of myth and metaphor—even though it be a later development?

Whiteheadians can also be reminded by Hillman that an occasion of experience does not proceed directly from inchoate feelings to abstract intellectual synthesis. At the heart of this process is the imagery that arises willy-nilly, involuntarily, and mainly in the unconscious. We need to remember that this is a quasi-autonomous realm, with its own "logic," as our dreams often illustrate. If we took this aspect of our own theory seriously, it would surely have a great impact not only upon the content of our reflections but also upon our style. We need to un-Locke our language. It is noteworthy that insofar as this un-Lockeing is taking place among Whiteheadians, the writers are primarily women (such as Catherine Keller herein).

The second point concerns the relation between theory and practice. Whitehead's philosophy has already overcome the modern divorce between them in one sense. Whereas modernists from Hume to Santayana have said that theory needs to be *supplemented* by practice (or faith), Whitehead said that practice should be the final *test* of all theory. He stressed this over and over:

> Metaphysics is nothing but the description of the generalities which apply to all the details of practice. (*PR* 13)

> Philosophy's ultimate appeal is to the general consciousness of what in practice we experience. (*PR* 17)

> [T]he metaphysical rule of evidence [is] that we must bow to those presumptions which, in despite of criticism, we still employ for the regulation of our lives. Such presumptions are imperative in experience. Rationalism is the search for the coherence of such presumptions. (*PR* 151)

On the basis of this view, that a theory is no good unless it coordinates all those "commonsense" notions which we inevitably hold in practice, Whitehead could not be content with a philosophy that rejected our knowledge of an outer world, of causal relations, and of objective values. Again there is an agreement with Hillman. Theory must be grounded in practice, in particular those "commonsense" responses to the world which we share with the other animals. And our theory should be such as to renew our confidence in those responses, in which every sense of "importance" is finally rooted.

But there is a second sense of the unity of theory and practice in Hillman. This is the sense that our theorizing needs to be carried out with the major problems of the day explicitly in view. Hillman has rightly concluded that today this means that psychotherapy must be done in the context of the possibility of nuclear holocaust! Because we are all in this cosmos together, and because the collective soul enters into each of us, there can be no health of the parts when the whole is ill. Because this illness is ultimately due to bad metaphysics, psychotherapy must include a metaphysical dimension, in which the sources of this illness are redressed.

I suggest that psychotherapy and Whiteheadian metaphysics must be joined from the metaphysical side as well. Those of us who are primarily engaged in metaphysical cosmology today need to see our activity as therapy, as part of our practice to save the world from our own worst images. We need to bring out, much more explicitly than did Whitehead himself, and with all the rhetorical soul-transforming power we can muster, those features of this cosmology that can replace modernity's deadening images of the world with the enlivening images suggested by this postmodern metaphysics, and that can help our souls experience that mutual sacredness and bondedness which alone can reverse the current trajectory of death.

17

Responses

JAMES HILLMAN

Response to Edward Casey

Regarding Ed Casey's delightful phrase "creeping dichotomism," I would like to remove discussion of it from a philosophical to a psychological perspective. Then, the first question becomes: what else is going on in Hillman's dichotomies such as underworld and dayworld, image and concept, peaks and vales, and now a seemingly unseemly dichotomy between psychology and philosophy? Let us ask not only with Casey what the philosophical consequences of dichotomizing are, but what its psychological value could be.

The *philosophical* consequences are probably clear to all: a creeping crevasse between pairs that grows to a split between opposites, a chasm between contradictories, coming ineluctably to rest in that Great Fault— Dualism! I think that in our culture we live under the law of contradiction; contradiction is culturally innate to our minds: if soul, then not spirit; if image, then not concept. To think of "unlikes" and "differents" simply as such is not our habit, and so we forget that an innate law of contradiction sets up problems in this oppositional fashion, problems that are not there until we pick them up with this two-pronged tool. I tried to show in *Re-Visioning Psychology* (141) that our ideational tools form our notions. The tool we use for solving a problem has already constructed the problem into the shape that the tool is supposed to solve. Jung's transcendent function, for instance, is the necessary consequent of his thinking in opposites to begin with.

So, let us now ask about the psychological value of dichotomizing. Perhaps this value lies precisely in its aesthetic (not logical or ontolog-

ical) pragmatism. It is fecund for specific "poetic" purposes. It helps
soul-making. Here I follow Patricia Berry, who sees in oppositions an
artful way of making tensions, of limning this against that, of contrasting to bring forth salience. Casey understands these moves because he
is a painter himself. A good dichotomy, like a strong black line in a
painting, makes a hard edge, says Berry. It has pragmatic value as a
move that helps the painting. Only if one takes a philosopher's stance,
looking with the law of contradiction in mind, will one read the black
line as a creeping dichotomy, splitting the picture and leading to an
ontological disaster.

Casey also asks about "imagistic necessity." What sort of necessity
is this, especially when it is contrasted with chance on the one hand
and law on the other? What I mean is this: an image is what is there,
"that which shows itself in itself," using Casey's quote from Heidegger.
As such it is in the realm of the necessary and not the realm of the
possible, because "it could not be otherwise," which is the definition
philosophers frequently give to necessity—*quod non potest non esse* or
nicht-anders-sein-können. I would enjoy being strict here, saying that
the image that is there is all that there is and is therefore all there (there
is no more to the image than what it shows), and that even its hidden
dimensions are there (all depth is on display). I would like to be strict,
again for psychological reasons, because we always wish an image to
be otherwise. Freud placed this wish for otherwise at the very root of
psychic motivation, and he deeply understood this trait of human nature.
We each would escape the necessity of the image, whether it be dreams,
fantasies, or the images in which we find ourselves behaving.

Imagistic necessity, however, need not be taken literally, as a kind
of *kismet,* as if fantasies were implacable forces and dream images
determined fate. Rather, "it could not be otherwise" is a psychological
rule of thumb, saying that one works with what is given and only with
that, and even if insufficient it is necessary and cannot be wished into
something other than it is, either by explanation, by reduction, or by
association. Yet, an image can be amplified (made to sound richer),
clarified (led out of its opaqueness by exegesis), and brought to reverberate (echo in daily consciousness) and to propagate further images.

Second, imagistic necessity refers to the inescapability of images.
"If the psyche consists essentially of images" (Jung), then ensouled
being is essentially subject to the imagination. We are always behaving
with imagination and always within the borders of an image.

Third, imagistic necessity refers to the claim that images make upon the subject. I have called this a "moral claim" and, if the editor allows, I shall incorporate a long passage from *Healing Fiction* (61–62) that describes the moral aspect of imagistic necessity more adequately than I could recapitulate afresh.

> The question of ethical relativity which raises its head whenever one speaks of a . . . plurality of Gods is answered by the dedication which the images demand. It is they—not we—who demand meticulous crafting into jewelled idols; they, who call for ritualized devotions, who insist they be consulted before we act. Images are the compelling source of morality and religion as well as the conscientiousness of art. And, as we do not make them up, so we do not make up our response to them, but are "taught" this response by them as moral instances. It is when we lose the images that we become moralistic, as if the morality contained within the images becomes a dissociated, free-floating guilt, a conscience without a face.
>
> When an image is realized—fully imagined as a living being other than myself—then it becomes a psychopompos, a guide with a soul having its own inherent limitation and necessity. It is this image, and no other, so that the conceptual questions of moral pluralism and relativism fade in front of the actual engagement with the image. The supposed . . . teeming imagination is limited to its phenomenal appearance in a particular image, that specific one which has come to me pregnant with significance and intention, a necessary angel as it appears here and now and which teaches the hand to represent it, the ear to hear, and the heart how to respond. There is thus revealed through this engagement a *morality of the image*. . . . The ego is no longer the place where morality resides. . . . Instead, it is the daimon who is our preceptor, our *spiritus rector.*

Casey's third question is about "metaphysical praxis." Here I caused a confusion: I should have distinguished further between "metaphysical" and "cosmological" with regard to praxis. The first kind of praxis is in part the practice of psychologizing the metaphysical assumptions tacitly at work in the soul. For example, if dichotomizing is not brought to awareness, then it will unconsciously rule psychological life. We not only will experience opposites all over the place but will also tend to assert a metaphysics of opposites. Or, if an unexamined metaphysics of time determines our *Weltbild,* we will tend to take history and development literally. A great deal of Whitehead's examination of the empiricist's theory of perception exemplifies a brilliantly skillful metaphysical praxis because it shows *the psychological effects of theory.* I do want to stress, however, that metaphysical praxis is more than an operation of sheer thinking. It can occur through frowns, quizzical looks, and grunts, which check and sophisticate behavior, bringing it to aesthetic sensitivity about the moves and modes of thought (or unthoughtfulness).

"Cosmological praxis" would be the better term for connecting the three seemingly arbitrary examples that Casey asks about: active imagination, poetic language, and care for animals (not merely 'of' animals or animal husbandry), by which I mean extending care (*caritas, Sorge*) to all affairs one calls "animal"—from the Id of Freud, to the theriomorphic Gods, to actual ecology.

Here I have circumscribed the initial steps of this praxis to images, words, and animals. No mention of persons and things! This because our present sense of person would first have to be delivered from its Christian subjectivism, sentimental personalism, and horizontal (explanatory) humanism, a task I have elsewhere called "dehumanizing." And, as the focus on persons reinforces subjectivism, so focus on things keeps us in an inanimate and anaesthetized objectivism, at least until the eye of the heart has been opened. So we must start in a place between subjectivism and objectivism, in the *metaxy* of animated autonomies or the world of the *daimonia,* an area that psychology has recently rediscovered and baptized anew as the realm of "transitional objects."

The connection between personified images, words, and animals lies in their relative autonomy: words as angels that we struggle to get the better of; animals as sacred presences, the foundational Gods of religions the world over; the figures and voices of our invisible psychic life as other than ourselves, doing and saying surprising things. As Jung learned from his encounters with these imaginal figures: "figures of my fantasies brought home to me the crucial insight that there are things in the psyche which I do not produce, but which produce themselves and have their own life."

In each of the three instances—imagined figures, words, animals— what at first seems in my control, as a cluster of objects to be dealt with as I please, soon awakens my respect for its autonomy as Other. This peculiarly paradoxical engagement, starting as bewildered curiosity, leading on to inquiry and then to empathy, myself as immersed in *its* realm—whether as one imaginal figure among these Others, or as an inhabitant of language that simply comes on its own, or as a creature of animal nature—un-Lockes the human person from his or her egocentric predicament (and metaphysical catastrophe), and so constitutes the first steps of practice in accord with the cosmology I sketched.

Response to David Griffin

David Griffin has put his sure finger on the weakest link in my jottings: the failure to connect Gibsonian direct perception with the notion of image. We do indeed need Whitehead's more subtly complex theory of perception rather than what appears to be my naive realism.

On the one hand, I do hold for direct perception (Whitehead's "presentational immediacy"), the animal common sense both as basic to *homo aestheticus* and as the base for *Gemeinschaftsgefühl*: what we each sense is common to all. We sense a world in common. On the other hand, every perception is shaded by an image, having its underworld dimension, so that we see both more and less than what we naively see. I wanted to suggest that what is actually prehended are the "affordances" (as Gibson calls these kinds of sense-meanings) inherent in the world of things. These, as Griffin says, reveal values, aims, and their aesthetic relations (the perceptual field). A thing displays itself both to the senses and to the imagination, at once. An actual occasion is simultaneously also an image.

By introducing the term *image* into the theory of perception, I am stressing the imaginative factor that is always at work, not merely in my mind (or feelings) as a mental image or merely in the act of prehension. The image is there in the thing and as the thing—I would even like to say, *is* the thing—giving it its inherent intelligibility, its commonality, and its potential for animation (that a thing presents itself in display). Although I cannot identify my notion of image with Whitehead's "causal efficacy," I appreciate that causal efficacy brings to presentational immediacy a depth and a past, let us say, an archetypal background.

Articulating the relations between sensation and imagination calls for a philosopher's adroit hand, and I wish Griffin would take up the task in service to psychology. Psychology of soul desperately needs a re-visioned theory of vision. Our modern cosmos of vision (subjective eyeballs looking at dead objects providing sense-data) contributes to the metaphysical catastrophe that our modern souls suffer. We must remember the overpowering part that optics played at the expense of "vision" in the establishment of the modern myth of perception. New-ton, Leibniz, Descartes, Spinoza, and Berkeley all wrote on optics. What they left us is the fiction of "seeing red." (When I follow their line of thought, I too "see red.")

They posit a world out there that is thoroughly different from the human soul, and so perception theory is rife with problems. They can never figure out how things out there make sense to us in here. If, however, the world in which we are embedded is itself an embodiment of the *anima mundi* and fundamentally aesthetic (and seeing red is primarily an aesthetic moment), then what we see is that-red-thing-there. Perception shows it to be a specific tonality of red, shaped by the actual thing that is red, itself remembering and reflecting absent other reds and absent other things, contrasting itself with not-reds, in a specific locus and nexus, transitional with moods, pregnant with meanings, and enfolded with names, that-red-thing-there in a context, as a text; in short: each thing an image. And, *contra* Whitehead, the red is in the thing and not in my feeling—unless we understand feeling to be given by the *anima mundi,* and not 'mine' in the restrictively personal sense.

Actual things exist in a medium between sensation and imagination, and consist in both. The Greeks, in their theories of perception, were always concerned with the nature of the medium, which the post-New-tonian mind has interpreted to mean *physical* media, thereby making the Greeks sound naive and archaic. No, the medium is the soul in which perceptible things have their being as images.

So, as Griffin says, what are called sense-data are not actually given to the senses. Color, smell, taste, sound, size, mass, and motion are secondary, derivative constructs (not even actual qualities), yielding no knowledge of actual things. Yet this lie that they *are* given lies at the base of our Western way of viewing things and of the usual empirical notion of truth. The so-called empiricists' insistence on turning to sense-data to establish truth is delusional. For what they turn to are not the actual aesthetic data of the senses, but abstractions formulated by that abstract tool *par excellence,* numbers.

Psychologically we need to see through this empirical fiction. We need to see what it has done to our culture's psyche. Of course, it has an-aesthetized the world, but it has also reinforced subjectivism and the ego. (All aesthetic qualities are personal sensations and feelings, says Hume's empiricism.) Our egocentric predicament and our dead world, and therefore the patient's anomie ("connect, only connect," said E. M. Forster), derive in part from an untruthful theory of perception. And the therapy of this condition requires the re-visioned metaphysics of Whitehead (whom Hopper quotes above): "The metaphysical doctrine, here expounded, finds the foundations of the world in the aesthetic experience, rather than . . . in the cognitive and conceptive experience. All order is therefore aesthetic order" (*RM* 101).

Though *anima mundi* needs more conceptual clarification, I have trouble with Griffin's twofold distinction: on the one hand, a collective soul of humans that "has no experience, and exercises no initiative" and may be ill, and, on the other hand, a world-soul as "divine reality," which is good, creative, and all-encompassing. Does this approach not set the notion of *anima mundi* back into the moral ontology of our culture: human nature as locus of the pathological and sinful, while God is good and creative?

A focus upon freedom (moral agency) versus determinacy ("we are not just victims, passive loci for a cosmic drama") and Griffin's concern for responsibility and decision moves discussion of *anima mundi* into the psychology of will and the relation of conation with imagination.

I tend to think of will adverbially, as "willingly," as a style of the heart in complying with, and thus enjoying, necessities, rather than as a verb on its own requiring a subject who pushes it along. There is so little attention paid to conation (will, ego, hero, conflict, choice, et cetera) all through my writing and therapy because an aesthetic cosmos requires receptivity more than agency. To notice the world with the senses and hear the echoes of imagining means a perfection of the will (Augustine) by teaching it to sit still willingly, senses opened. This is another reason for learning to dream.

I prefer to imagine myself a vehicle, like a jitney, picking up and discharging passengers *en transit* rather than an agent at the driver's wheel. The driver must keep his eyes on the road and his foot on the pedal, whereas the vehicle bumps along allowing conversations among persons with different destinations.

Griffin's concern with agency seems to be a case of spirit running away from soul, for will is not free of archetypal fantasies, and to treat it so is to take the notion of "free" literally. Questions of will can be located in a material imagination of sulfur in an alchemical cosmology (e.g., Jung, *CW* 14) or of earth in an elemental cosmology (e.g., Gaston Bachelard's *La Terre et la Volonté*), or in the heroic myths of creative self-determinacy. From the viewpoint of soul we are obliged to ask what compelling images in the *anima mundi* are at work in the imagination when we consider ourselves as agents "breaking free from the power of the collective soul."

These remarks regarding will also serve to amplify a bit Griffin's very fine understanding of seeing-through as an emptying that is a filling. Yes, seeing-through intends "to drop the bottom out of what seems to be given"—in this case, moral agency and free will. (Compare above Stanley Hopper's "We must break through the bottom of the pail, as the Zen people say.") But the entire work of negative metaphysical praxis, such as I characterized it in the first part of my paper, also includes the positive filling of the pail with fresh imaginings (sulfur, earth, heroism). Filling drops the bottom, because mythical fantasies of the imagination are not substantial fillings but more like empty conceits. "Myth negates its reality even as it presents it," as I said in my essay. We are satisfied and dissatisfied at the same moment, an erotic moment, and Eros is the child of emptiness and fullness conjoined. Thereby negation can maintain its two senses: privative and absentive. If emptying out were the only function of seeing-through, we would be using negation only literally, in its privative sense, whereas negation is also a move of process, of opening by absenting: not nihilism, but *śunyatta.*

Griffin is right for challenging me to spend more time on the mutual interplay of soul and spirit, instead of so much on their distinction. Yes, they require each other; but first things first. As the alchemists are said to have said: "Only separated things can be conjoined." Distinctions thus seem crucial because they can provide a polemical way of generating interplay, so long as we do not literalize distinctions into oppositions. Coleridge cautioned that distinctions in mind are not necessarily separations in actuality. I stress "polemical" because *polemos,* said Heraclitus, is the Father of all, and is itself a phenomenon of spirit. A polemical psychology reflects the inspirited psyche. So I agree with Griffin that soul-tending without logos or pneuma would be mindless. Soul requires spirit to mind the storehouse of her images.

Response to Catherine Keller

Catherine Keller puts me in the dock on two major counts, felonies even. First, matriphobia; second, patriarchalist rape.

To the first charge I plead guilty, and beg the court to widen the accusation to more serious, serial crimes: hero-phobia, ego-phobia, and paedo-phobia—that entire cluster of straw-enemies whom I perceive as the divinities dominating depth psychology and whom I scald and flay in most of my writings just because they rule our theory, norms, ideals, and practice.

Breasts, orality, infancy, nurturing, sucking and biting, envy and desire, good mothers, bad mothers, and adequate, good-enough mothers fill the pages of our journals, the hours of our therapy, the longings of patients for cure, and the research grants of the entrepreneurs out to realize those cures. Childhood is the focus, and strong, independent, heroic egohood the goal. This myth is called Developmental Psychology. Mother is the ground, the first cause, the enemy, and the cure.

If attempting to slay this vision of the soul's disorder and cure is matricide, then so be it. What other culture would lay in the lap of the mother the reasons we get sick, go mad, lose our souls? Spells, demons, broken taboos, ancestral hauntings, failed rites, evil spirits, planets, foods, waters, places—these are the causes of my craziness. Never, never would I turn to my childhood or blame my mother.

The mother whose bounty I entreat and who I hope finds entry into my consulting room is probably little different from Catherine Keller's. I see this mother like Hathor, who brings an ever-shifting moon between her sharp horns, like Isis, who restores and revives, like a cow in an Indian bazaar, slowing the world, munching amid the hustle, an everyday reminder of omnipresent animal warmth, a galactic power given with life itself, obtrusively here and now (not back in childhood where she should have been different, better, wiser, kinder, for that is not a cow but a dragon who blocks or a chimera who deludes us from the wide open baskets of the bazaar).

Keller's second charge asserts that I am the-rapist. I refuse to defend against a position that she borrows from Mary Daly and then cloa[c]ks me in. Even if she summons noble experts like Susan Griffin and Adrienne Rich and has social justice legitimately on her side, her mythical imagination is faulted. The central female mystery of antiquity cannot be forced, without raping it, into the contemporary feminine mystique. Worse: this approach is boring; and if Winnecott is right that the way to recognize a sick patient is that he or she is boring, then this approach to Eleusis is also sick. Why boring? Because it is not fecund but formulaic: nothing sparkling or nourishing can come from myths, because myths come from a patriarchal rapist culture.

Like Freudian, Marxist, and seventeenth-century Jesuit modes of retelling the myths, that shibboleth "patriarchy" (coupled with the fantasy of an earlier, and therefore better and truer, "matriarchy") allegorizes the mysteries so that they serve ulterior interests, in this case those of contemporary feminism. Even if Greek society was as horridly male-dominated as we, thousands of years later, insist, why did they honor all those marvelously differentiated Goddesses, grant them such power, celebrate their rites? What else may have been going on that our right and righteous urge for social justice prevents us from seeing? And myths, let us not forget, do prevent us from seeing even as they allow re-visioning.

Keller and I, even as we clarify, are ourselves caught and partially blinded by the myth we are discussing so that some of our contention is due to it. While I feel the deep sorrow of Demeter and the anger over loss in Catherine Keller's words, mine are aggresively out to win her away from what I perceive as naturalism in favor of the shady mystifications of Hades to which I retreat when cornered.

For an example of the blinding effect of myth, I turn to one of Keller's own positions. I claimed that materialism and personalism are corollaries of the archetypal perspective of the mother. Keller herself brings evidence for my claim in the presentation of her charges, thereby showing that the topos we enter—in this instance, defense of the mother—involves us willy-nilly in a rhetoric that is personalistic and materialistic. Keller finds me guilty of "the assumption that the realm of the mother, of nature, and of life is metaphorically less conducive to soul-making, to depth, than that of wife." (As if Persephone were Hera's daughter!) To me it seems that Keller, despite the token and free-hanging adverb "metaphorically," here commits the naturalistic fallacy by reading mythical realities in terms of actual marriages in which she sees actual women submitting to actual males.

To transcend biology or first naïveté, indeed to descend, as she says, demands *not,* as she says, subordination of the female to the male sphere in life, in nature, in the realm of matter and persons, but rather surrender to the invisibility of psychic truths which often violate the perspective of that green consciousness without seizures or raptures, where depth and life intermingle harmoniously, idealized. The mysteries at Eleusis are saying that things must go very, very wrong before the naturalistic fallacy can be left and mothering protection shown to be barren. If getting married (actually becoming a wife) is the way to this experience, then so be it. The point, however, is not marriage but soul-making through surrender.

The basic question remains, as it has done for thousands of years: Why did Persephone want to stay below? (She was not *only* a captive.) Surely not because wifeyness was so satisfying, the loss of maiden-flower to the dark violator so thrilling, or the queenly power over all things that die so alluring, as to hold her in that ghostly realm. Truth is, we do not know the reason for her not wanting to return above. The secret has been kept all these centuries because it is a mystery. And, this desire for Hades' mystery was shared also by Aphrodite and Psyche. There is a desire, and a resistance, to be held in bondage to what is below (just as there are other desires and resistances—to ride free as an Amazon, to run free with Artemis, or to dance free with the Mae-nads). Some inner body, some psychic figure, desires to be uprooted and carried down to Plutonic nights of ruin, shame, loss, and sexualized disordering of the dayworld senses. This descent, as Keller says, does indeed make life more fecund—not only-natural life as such, but life as soul, psychic life.

To equate (which to me means to reduce) the Hades-Persephone mythologem with the rape and abuse perpetrated outrageously upon women in our civilization is another instance of the personalism and materialism of the mother archetype. "The rape of Persephone is cer-tainly [*not*] a metaphor for all the literal rapes of all women." First, today's word "rape" narrows the connotations of the Greek and Latin originals; second, as Keller herself says, there are endless captures and violations in an innumerable variety of styles in tales of the Gods and Goddesses. Each has a specific meaning within each narrative and needs examination in terms of its eachness. Moreover, and finally, it is just the purpose of the Hades-Persephone-Demeter myth, as enacted at Eleusis, to dissolve the very misapprehensions that Keller and I are now victims of and to release us from a distanced consciousness about the myth by luring us to surrender to its sublime beauty.

Response to James Heisig

I thank James Heisig for the generous understanding of things he brings to my work, for his perspicacity in seeing through to its basic assumptions, and also for so well exposing a major fault to which I again plead guilty as charged. Yes, I do make "allusions to myths as arguments to bolster logical connections." I have no remorse about this and shall probably perpetrate this very crime in this response to him. And yes, "[regarding] the relationship between therapy and mythology, we are left wondering what to do with the conceptions . . . without any clear logical archeology behind them." Yes, I do "tend to slip away from the demands of a rational frame."

In Heisig's ballpark, built by Aristotle, reconstructed by Saint Thomas, and reinforced by every philosopher of rationalism since, I can hit only foul balls. Heisig has a penchant for high flies and solid grounders. The demand that I ground my positions ontologically repeats again the hubris of the spirit that it is superior to soul. Soul must be based, anchored, framed in a greater whole of theology, ontology, metaphysics. So, I cannot contend with Heisig because I do not want to set foot in his ballpark, called Ontological Ground. Nor should I argue with him, because the psyche does not argue; it imagines, mythifies, and it does indeed try ever and again to slip away from the demands of a rational frame. Pathologizing, personifying, fantasying, loving and suffering, dreaming of beauties and running from terrors—these too escape the demands of a rational frame. Eros, Hermes, Pan, Artemis, Dionysos, Hades—the figures invoked in my texts resist capture; puer wants to keep his wings. Yet if anything "archeological" goes on in my writings, it is precisely this rhetorical turn to the Gods and Goddesses. By alluding to them in great detail I have shown structures in those deep experiences we feel are soulful.

Here I have tried to enter the lineup with some powerful sluggers from Aeschylus through Shakespeare to Yeats and Stevens who present the soul's demands in the language of "poetic truth," as Vico called this manner of speaking. Why can't psychology be allowed an aesthetic language that makes its statements rhetorically, aiming to persuade through the magic of language, by appealing to the precision of imaginative thinking rather than the logic of conceptual thinking?

Heisig's resolution of the illogic of my vision is for me to confess to the pantheism of a unifying God underneath (ground of being) my panpsychism (all things are full of soul). But I am trying to maintain eachness in the face of philosophies obsessed with allness, wholeness, and unity. As witness I again call on William James, who insisted that eachness and "unwholesomeness" were preferable to, maybe "truer" than, wholeness. Heisig wants it all to hang together, but I have spent thirty years at dismemberment. The pearls rather than the rope. Dionysos the Loosener. Things do fall apart: it's not logical, yet it's true.

Philosophy will grant me the right to describe psychic events phenomenally as discrete eaches without a string to the pearls, but philosophy insists that, as soon as I append logos to psyche and write *psychology,* then its logos must comply with the logos of philosophical convention. I have tried rather to work within a method that does not succumb to the strictures of the spirit but instead is more in tune with the way psyche appears in dream, fantasy, emotion, humor, love, conversation, and illness. Hence my reversion to illogic, to juxtapositions rather than connections, to figments and fragments. Let Hermes make the connections; the unseen ones are anyway the best, as Heraclitus said.

As for my God-term "soul," discourse has to beg some starting point or it cannot make moves, and I beg the term "soul." I do not, however, beg the question or use the word to mystify, because I have given as full and loud amplification of its necessities, its nature, and its complaints (against philosophy) as any other champion of anima since the Romantics (see *RVP* x). I want here to recall that, whenever possible, I have tried to keep clear of speaking of soul as a substance, preferring to imagine soul instead as a perspective toward events. Adverbs and adjectives, which qualify and value, more aptly speak soul than do nouns, which objectify.

The usual history of thought claims that logos drove out mythos. I don't believe it. I think mythos just went to Hell, into the realm of Hades, and from there gives a deeper, hidden sense, a *hyponoia,* right within rational discourse. I try to exhume bodies from concepts by allusions to myths; philosophy keeps myths mummified in concepts such as Ontological Ground, Rational Frame, Logical Connections, Psychic Circle. Most psychology does the same with its hypostases: Ego, Transitional Object, and the like. Jung said, the Gods have become diseases. I would add that they have also become diseases of speech, that is, concepts drained of *ichor,* that divine blood replenished by the aesthetic sweetness of ambrosia. We need to sweeten our speech not only to keep the Gods alive, but also for the sake of our souls. So, I can accept Heisig's request that I admit pantheism below my panpsychism only if it invokes Pan fleshed out as a force and an image, together with his intertwined mythical associates who differentiate this world into so many particular energies that *pan* could never be translated as *all*.

Response to Stanley Hopper

For Stanley Hopper's careful reading, that loving attention he brings to the texts, I am bashfully grateful. I stand informed by his spirit and instructed by his lucid, concise critique of my carelessness regarding "metaphor." Still, I stand by "image"—although not as still as he suggests when saying that my preference for image implicates my thought in stasis.

The important issue seems to be less to determine which is the *via regia,* "image," "metaphor," or "anecdote," and to be more our common interest in keeping that *via regia* open, vital, and in motion. For motion is an ancient hallmark of soul. Hopper speaks well for anecdote; perhaps I need to say another thing or two about images—although I believe it is how we see them rather than what they are that is the bone between us.

From my perspective an image does have the primary function of arresting movement. It stops the natural, unconsidered flow, acts as an *opus contra naturam,* brings us up short, releases an ah! as gasp (not an aha!-*erlebnis* of recognition or understanding of meaning). But arrest is not stasis. This is because "the Image is more than an Idea. It is a vortex or cluster of fused ideas and is endowed with energy . . . a Vortex, from which and through which and into which, ideas are constantly rushing" (Pound). Or, as I have said elsewhere: "To conceive images as static is to forget that they are numens that move." Charles Olson put it this way: ". . . always, always one perception must move instanter on another" (see *ET* 50–51 for references).

The image's movement arrests mine. Its ceaseless activity, its instigation of anecdotal tellings about itself, is as potentially endless as the soul's own depth. Hence, image is psyche, as Jung said.

Despite these assertions, Hopper is right about the iconic, static aspect of images. What shuts them down and turns them off is symbolization—reading the image with a symbolic eye, attempting to get a dominant anecdote from it so that its numen can be left behind in favor of its "meaning." The snarling black dog, baring its teeth and yanking on its chain, becomes my leashed sexual hunger, my violent hatred, my touchiness when anything comes too near my proprium,

Hekate's wrath, Cerebros whom I must brave, my mother's or father's restrained fury—all anecdotal meanings that too soon leave that ferocious image with its movement toward bottomless possibilities of emotion, memory, and fantasy. As Hopper says: "Mythic figures and images must remain fluent; otherwise they become impediments and interfere with the psyche's descents." Symbolization impedes the psyche's descents, closes off the *via regia*.

I also still stand as a *bricoleur*, hoping to achieve in lucky moments precisely what Hopper asks for: "juxtapositions of images which, while retaining their own integrity, nevertheless impel new meanings to emerge." Less new meanings, however, than "images that yet / Fresh images beget" (Yeats) until there is that drop through to recognition that the mind imagining is itself being imagined. Below the tension of the lyre, which gives structure and the *harmonia* of Apollo and Orpheus, roils the gong-tormented sea, the mermaids calling, ancestral voices and shades of the underworld, those figured dreams of misty wishes, and each little concrete thing of this world chanced upon anywhere, each thing its cosmos, each thing ensouled, even Zen nothingness and emptiness and bottomless, images.

NOTES ON CONTRIBUTORS

EDWARD S. CASEY is the author of *Imagining* (1976), *Remembering* (1987), and *Getting Back into Place* (1990), the editor of *Explorations in Phenomenology* (1974) and *The Life of the Transcendental Ego* (1986), and has translated two books by Mikel Dufrenne. He teaches in the Department of Philosophy at the State University of New York at Stony Brook.

JOHN B. COBB, JR., is the author of *The Structure of Christian Existence* (1967), *Christ in a Pluralistic Age* (1975), *Theology and Pastoral Care* (1977), *Beyond Dialogue: Towards a Mutual Transformation of Christianity and Buddhism* (1982), and (with Charles Birch) *The Liberation of Life* (1982). He is Ingraham professor of theology at the School of Theology at Claremont, Avery professor of religion at Claremont Graduate School, and director of the Center for Process Studies.

DAVID RAY GRIFFIN is the author of *God, Power, and Evil* (1976), *Process Theology* (1976, with John B. Cobb, Jr.), *God and Religion in the Postmodern World* (1988), *Varieties of Postmodern Theology* (1989, with William Beardslee and Joe Holland), *Primordial Truth and Postmodern Theology* (1989, with Huston Smith), and editor of *The Reenchantment of Science: Postmodern Proposals* (1988) and *Spirituality and Society: Postmodern Visions* (1988). He is professor of philosophy of religion at the School of Theology at Claremont and Claremont Graduate School, and executive director of the Center for Process Studies.

JAMES W. HEISIG is the author of *Imago Dei: A Study of C. G. Jung's Psychology of Religion* (1979), translator of Yoshinori Takeuchi, *The Heart of Buddhism* (1983), and General Editor of *Nanzan Studies in Religion and Culture*. He is Permanent Fellow of the Nanzan Institute for Religion and Culture and a professor in the faculty of arts and letters at Nanzan University.

JAMES HILLMAN is a writer, teacher, and Jungian analyst. Previously the director of studies at the C. G. Jung Institute in Zurich (1959–69), he now resides in Connecticut. His most recent book is *A Blue Fire: Selected Writings* (1989). Many of his other writings are listed at the front of the book.

STANLEY ROMAINE HOPPER is the author of *Metaphor and Beyond: The Bucket As It Is* (1979) and *Why Persimmons and Other Poems* (1986), and the editor of *Spiritual Problems in Contemporary Literature* (1952) and

Interpretation: The Poetry of Meaning (1967, with David L. Miller). He is professor of religion emeritus at Syracuse University.

CATHERINE KELLER is the author of *From a Broken Web: Separation, Sexism, and Self* (1986) and is currently working on a feminist eschatology as the first volume of a constructive theological project. She teaches theology at The Theological School, Drew University.

ROBERT L. MOORE is the author of *John Wesley and Authority: A Psychological Perspective* (1979), co-author of *The Cult Experience: Responding to the New Religious Pluralism* (1982), and co-editor of *Anthropology and the Study of Religion* (1984). An analyst in private practice, he is a Diplomate of the Alfred Adler Institute in Chicago and has also studied extensively at the C. G. Jung Institute of Chicago. He is professor of psychology and religion at Chicago Theological Seminary.

J'NAN MORSE SELLERY is the author of *Elizabeth Bowen: A Biography* (1981), co-editor of *Faust, Part I* (1969) and *Scapegoat: Ritual and Literature* (1972), and, as senior editor of *Psychological Perspectives*, editor of special issues on *Women's Voices* (1986) and *Gender Relations* (1990). She is coordinator of Women's Studies at the Claremont Colleges and teaches English at Harvey Mudd College and Claremont Graduate School.

GERALD H. SLUSSER is the author of seven books on religious education, the New Testament, cultural commentary, the environmental crisis, and other topics. His most recent book is *From Jung to Jesus: Myth and Consciousness* (1986). He is professor emeritus of theology and education of Eden Theological Seminary in St. Louis, and currently lectures at United States International University in San Diego.

CHARLES E. WINQUIST is the author of *The Transcendental Imagination* (1972), *Homecoming: Interpretation, Transformation and Individuation* (1978), and *Epiphanies of Darkness: Deconstruction in Theology* (1986), and editor of *The Archaeology of the Imagination* (1981) and *Text and Textuality* (1987). He is Thomas J. Watson professor of religion, Syracuse University.

NOTES

Chapter 1

1. James W. Heisig, *Imago Dei: A Study of C. G. Jung's Psychology of Religion* (Lewisburg, Pa: Bucknell University Press; London: Associated University Presses, 1979), 1.

2. James W. Heisig, "Jung and Theology: A Bibliographical Essay," *S 1973*: 204–55, esp. 232.

3. James W. Heisig, "Whitehead and the Jungian Archetypes," unpubl. ms., available from the Center for Process Studies, 1325 North College, Claremont, Ca. 91711.

4. See my *God and Religion in the Postmodern World* (Albany: State University of New York Press, 1989), my contributions to *Varieties of Postmodern Theology*, co-authored with William A. Beardslee and Joe Holland (1989), my introductions to *The Reenchantment of Science: Postmodern Proposals* (1988) and *Spirituality and Society: Postmodern Visions* (1988), and the "Series Introduction" to these or any of the other volumes in the SUNY Series in Constructive Postmodern Thought.

5. Peter Homans, "C. G. Jung: Christian or Post-Christian Psychologist?" in *Essays on Jung and the Study of Religion*, ed. Luther H. Martin and James Goss (Lanham, Md.: University Press of America, 1985), 26–44, esp. 44. This passage is also contained, with slightly different wording, in Homans's book *Jung in Context: Modernity and the Making of a Psychology* (Chicago: University of Chicago Press, 1979), 204, where it appears as a summary statement of Homans's argument that a response to modernity constituted one of the three core dimensions of Jung's thought. Although psychological and religious factors are equally important, the "sociological key" to the formation of Jung's psychology is "an attempt to integrate traditional and modern orientations to life" (140). Whereas the "persona" of modern persons embodies modernity, and "the archetypes of the collective unconscious . . . constitute the essence of tradition," the concept of "individuation" represented Jung's attempt "to synthesize or integrate the outstanding features of both modernity and tradition into one unified, consistent process" (142; see also 150–56, 178–81, 186, 201–4).

6. Ibid., 37–38.

7. Besides the references in n. 4, see my "Charles Hartshorne's Postmodern Philosophy," in *Hartshorne, Process Philosophy and Theology*, ed. Robert Kane and Stephen H. Phillips (Albany: State University of New York Press, 1989).

8. Heisig, *Imago Dei*, 26, 28.

9. Demaris S. Wehr, in *Jung and Feminism: Liberating Archetypes* (Boston: Beacon Press, 1987), points out that Jung's psychology is "in some ways a theology and an ontology" and "a worldview" (xi, xii); she also discusses his epistemology (77).

10. K. M. Abenheimer, "The Ego as Subject," in *The Reality of the Psyche*, ed. Joseph B. Wheelwright (New York: B. P. Putnam's Sons, 1968), 61–73.

11. Ibid., 61–64.

12. C. A. Meier, "A Jungian Approach to Psychosomatic Medicine," *Journal of Analytic Psychology* 8/2 (1963).

13. Michael Fordham, "Jungian Views of the Body-Mind Relationship," *S 1974*: 166–78, esp. 172.

14. Besides the evidence I cite in the text, see James Hillman, "Some Early Background to Jung's Ideas: Notes on C. G. Jung's Medium by Stefanie Zumstein-Preiswork," *S 1976*: 123–36; Henri F. Ellenberger, *The Discovery of the Unconscious: The History and Evolution of Dynamic Psychiatry* (New York: Basic Books, 1970), 663–723; and J. Marvin Spiegelman, "Psychology and the Occult," *S 1976*: 104–22.

15. The best single collection for an overview is *Handbook of Parapsychology*, ed. B. B. Wolman (New York: Van Nostrand Reinhold, 1977). *Psychic Exploration: A Challenge for Science*, ed. John White and Edgar Mitchell (New York: G. P. Putnam's Sons, 1974), also contains many good studies. The definitive overview of the field is *Foundations of Parapsychology: Exploring the Boundaries of Human Capability*, by Hoyt L. Edge, Robert L. Morris, John Palmer, and Joseph H. Rush (Boston and London: Routledge & Kegan Paul, 1986). An excellent series is *Advances in Parapsychological Research* (3 vols.), ed. Stanley Krippner (New York: Plenum Press, 1977, 1978, 1982). For other references, see nn. 7–22 to chap. 6 of my *God and Religion in the Postmodern World*.

16. I therefore strongly disagree with Marie-Louise von Franz, who says: "Through his investigations into the principle of synchronicity Jung prepared the way for an eventual alliance between depth psychology and microphysics, and therewith for the use of his ideas by contemporary natural science" (*C. G. Jung: His Myth in Our Time* [New York: C. G. Jung Foundation, 1975], 253).

17. See Anthony Storr's editor's introduction to *The Essential Jung* (Princeton: Princeton University Press, 1983), esp. 24, 26.

18. Heisig, *Imago Dei*, 156 n. 107.

19. See William Roll, *The Poltergeist* (Metuchen, N.J.: Scarecrow Press, 1976); A. R. G. Owen, *Can We Explain the Poltergeist?* (New York: Garrett, 1964); Hans Bender, "Modern Poltergeist Research," *New Directions in Parapsychology*, ed. John Beloff (London: Elek Science, 1974).

20. See ibid.; and *Foundations of Parapsychology*, 25, 61–63.

21. The first extensive version of this interpretation was given by Angelos Tanagras in a book translated as *Psychophysical Elements in Parapsychological Traditions* (New York: Parapsychology Foundation, 1967). A more recent account, which is both psychologically and philosophically sophisticated, has been given by Jule Eisenbud; see his *Parapsychology and the Unconscious* (Berkeley: North Atlantic Books, 1983), 44–46, 143–44, and his philosophical reflections at the end of his fascinating account, *The World of Ted Serios: "Thoughtographic" Studies of an Extraordinary Mind* (1967; New York: Pocket Books, 1968). This interpretation has more recently been endorsed by Stephen Braude in a chapter entitled "Precognition without Retrocausation" in his *The Limits of Influence: Psychokinesis and the Philosophy of Science* (London: Routledge &

Kegan Paul, 1986), a very good and important book both for parapsychology and for the philosophy of science in general. I have supported this interpretation as an explanation for some so-called precognitive experiences in the midst of a defense of the irreversibility of time and causality in the introduction to David Ray Griffin, ed., *Physics and the Ultimate Significance of Time: Bohm, Prigogine, and Process Philosophy* (Albany: State University of New York Press, 1986), 1–48, esp. 30–31.

22. Andrew Samuels, *Jung and the Post-Jungians* (London: Routledge & Kegan Paul, 1985), 26.

23. See Wehr, *Jung and Feminism*, 51, 92, 94; and Samuels, *Jung and the Post-Jungians*, 25, for discussion of this issue.

24. Samuels, *Jung and the Post-Jungians*, 37–38.

25. Ibid., 25.

26. See Rupert Sheldrake, *A New Science of Life: The Hypothesis of Formative Causation* (London: Blond & Briggs, 1981, 1985), and my review of it in *Process Studies* 12/1 (1982): 34–40. See also Sheldrake's *The Presence of the Past: Morphic Resonance and the Habits of Nature* (New York: Times Books, 1988).

27. Heisig supports this view (*Imago Dei*, 137).

28. Jung's belief that only his idea of God was in harmony with "reality" is reflected in the dogmatic fashion with which his idea is defended by some of his followers. For example, Marie-Louise von Franz, in commenting on the fact that many people are offended by the dark side of Jung's God, says: "Evidently our infantile side is reluctant to give up the idea of a 'loving God' who graciously watches over us, even though the reality is so completely at variance with such a picture" (*C. G. Jung: His Myth in Our Time*, 171). It evidently did not occur to her that there is more than one way to make belief in God consistent with reality—meaning the reality of evil. Jung modified the traditional idea of divine goodness while retaining the traditional idea of divine omnipotence. But one can instead modify the traditional idea of divine omnipotence while retaining the traditional notion of divine goodness. Neither position is necessarily more "infantile" than the other. Our preference for one strategy or the other will be influenced, of course, by our psychological makeup, but the issue between the two positions is a legitimate philosophical and theological one, and should be discussed on this level, not in terms of psychologizing putdowns.

29. See my chapters on these theologians in *God, Power, and Evil: A Process Theodicy* (Philadelphia: Westminster Press, 1976).

30. Demaris S. Wehr, "Religious and Social Dimensions of Jung's Concept of the Archetype: A Feminist Perspective," in *Feminist Archetypal Theory: Interdisciplinary Re-Visions of Jungian Thought,* ed. Estella Lauter and Carol Schreier Rupprecht (Knoxville: University of Tennessee Press, 1985), 23–45, esp. 37.

31. Ibid., 241 n. 30.

32. Ibid., 27.

33. Ibid., 44. The thesis of the book by Lauter and Rupprecht (see n. 30) is that "feminist archetypal theory" is not a contradiction in terms, and that the Jungian tradition should not be totally rejected because of its corruption by patriarchal theories, but should instead be re-visioned (3–6, 220, 223).

34. Ibid., 23. On these points, see also Wehr's *Jung and Feminism: Liberating*

Archetypes, which is devoted to liberating the archetypes "from their static and eternal associations" (xi, cf. 14), and from the idea that they "are divinely ordained" and therefore "stand on sacred ground" (90).

35. I have discussed these ideas in the final chapter of *God, Power, and Evil*; in chap. 4 of *Process Theology: An Introductory Exposition* (Philadelphia: Westminster Press, 1976), coauthored with John B. Cobb, Jr.; in my contribution to *Encountering Evil: Live Options in Theodicy*, ed. Stephen Davis (Atlanta: John Knox, 1981); and in *Evil Revisited* (forthcoming).

36. Wehr, "Religious and Social Dimensions," 32.

37. Ibid.

38. See Ira Chernus, *Dr. Strangegod: On the Symbolic Meaning of Nuclear Weapons* (Columbia: University of South Carolina Press, 1986).

39. Regarding the objective psyche, meaning the collective unconscious, Jung writes in his reply to Buber: "For me its reality is amply attested by the truly diabolical deeds of our time: the six million murdered Jews, the uncounted victims of the slave labour camps in Russia, as well as the invention of the atom bomb, to name but a few examples of the darker side. But I have also seen the other side which can be expressed by the words beauty, goodness, wisdom, grace" (*CW* 18:1505). In this same essay he says that one's felt relationship to a divine Thou "is primarily to an autonomous psychic content" (*CW* 18:1507). At the close of this essay he makes the statement, cited earlier, that the God of Job and of the 89th Psalm, which fits well with the God-image in the unconscious, is "a bit closer to reality" than the orthodox concept of God with its purity (*CW* 18:1511). There is no doubt, therefore, that he blames the Jewish holocaust on God.

40. Edward Whitmont, "Prefatory Remarks to Jung's 'Reply to Buber,' " *S 1973*: 188–95, esp. 189.

41. Heisig, *Imago Dei*, 110, 111.

42. Ibid., 131.

43. Demaris Wehr comments that Jung's theological critics are "taking him to task for what they see as his opportunistic recourse to Kantian epistemology—his use of Kant when it suits him to 'justify' his psychology philosophically and his disregard of the boundaries of philosophy on the whole" (*Jung and Feminism*, 77).

44. Samuels, *Jung and the Post-Jungians*, 243.

45. Naomi R. Goldenberg, *Change of the Gods: Feminism and the End of Traditional Religions* (Boston: Beacon Press, 1979), 125.

46. Kathleen Raine, "Response to Hillman's 'Psychology: Monotheistic or Polytheistic,' " *S 1971*: 216–19.

47. Jacques Monod, *Chance and Necessity: An Essay on the Natural Philosophy of Modern Biology* (New York: Vintage Books, 1972), 21, 165, 170–71.

48. Gilbert Durand, "Psyche's View," *S 1981*: 1–19, esp. 6.

49. Hillman was strongly critical of deconstructive postmodernism in a speech delivered at Yale University, one of its strongholds.

50. In an interesting piece called "The Autonomous Psyche: A Communication to Goodheart from the BiPersonal Field of Paul Kugler and James Hillman" (*S 1985*: 141–85), Hillman says: "What is centrally at stake in this discussion is the idea, and

my faith in it, of the autonomous psyche, the self-moving, self-forming activity of the soul" (146). In response to Kugler, who had spoken of the recent view that "autonomous structures have a certain degree of independence from the environmental influences . . . [and thus] are freed from the causal arguments of a strict Newtonian interactionalism," Hillman says: "What you're saying delights my puer love for the idea of spontaneous events" (159).

51. Besides Hopper's essay herein, see his "Whitehead: Redivivus? or Absconditus?" in *America and the Future of Theology,* ed. William A. Beardslee (Philadelphia: Westminster Press, 1967), 112–26, in which he has elaborated his claim about the aesthetic nature of Whitehead's philosophy at considerable length.

52. If God be only a conservative force, the question arises, for those who allow it, as to how novel forms enter the world—which they must if the evolutionary picture, which Jung accepted, is in the main true. This is a question, as Samuels reports (*Jung and the Post-Jungians,* 34), that has been raised about Jung's position. Whitehead's answer is that God is the source of novelty as well as of order (*PR* 88, 108, 247), so that "the pure conservative is fighting against the essence of the universe" (*AI* 274).

Chapter 2

1. Aniela Jaffe, *The Myth of Meaning* (New York: Penguin Books, 1975), 1.

2. Ibid., 2.

3. M.-L. von Franz, *C. G. Jung: His Myth in Our Time* (Boston: Little, Brown & Co., 1975), 82.

4. Ervin Laszlo, *A Strategy for the Future: The Systems Approach to World Order* (New York: George Braziller, 1974), 3.

5. Ibid., 8.

6. Ibid., 7.

7. Joseph Campbell, *The Masks of God: Creative Mythology* (New York: Viking Press, 1968), 609.

8. Ibid., 611.

9. Ibid., 4.

10. Ibid., 6.

11. Ibid., 624.

12. Ibid., 6.

13. Von Franz, *C. G. Jung,* vii.

14. Quoted in ibid., 91.

15. Donald W. Sherburne, *A Key to Whitehead's Process and Reality* (Bloomington: Indiana University Press, 1975), 28. It was necessary to insert the term "initial" into the quotation from Sherburne for the sake of accuracy and of avoiding any suggestion of divine determinism. A subject's "subjective aim" is, as the term suggests, ultimately determined by the subject itself. It is only the initial phase of this subjective aim, generally called by Whitehead the "initial subjective aim," or simply the "initial aim," that is derived from God.

16. Ibid., 245.

17. James Hillman, "On the Necessity of Abnormal Psychology," *Eranos 43*: 1974, quoted in Robert Avens, *Imagination Is Reality: Western Nirvana in Jung, Hillman, Barfield, and Cassirer* (Irving, Tex.: Spring Publications, 1980), 29.

18. Sherburne, *A Key*, 226.

19. Avens, *Imagination*, 43.

20. Ibid., 95.

21. Ibid., 99.

22. Ibid., 100, quoting John White, *The Highest State of Consciousness* (Garden City, N.Y.: Anchor Books, 1972), xii.

Chapter 3

1. Unless otherwise noted, all page numbers inserted parenthetically in the text refer to Slusser's essay, above.

2. George S. Lensing and Ronald Moran, *Four Poets and the Emotive Imagination: Robert Bly, James Wright, Louis Simpson, and William Stafford* (Baton Rouge: Louisiana State University Press, 1976), 71.

3. Wallace Stevens, *Opus Posthumous: Poems, Plays, Prose*, ed. Samuel French Morse (New York: Alfred A. Knopf, 1966), 161.

4. Wallace Stevens, *The Palm at the End of the Mind: Selected Poems and a Play*, ed. Holly Stevens (New York: Alfred A. Knopf, 1971), 367.

5. Kathleen Raine, "The Poetic Symbol," *The Southern Review* 1/2 (April 1965): 243–58, esp. 246.

6. Joseph Campbell, *The Masks of God: Creative Mythology* (New York: Viking Press, 1968), 6.

7. To Jung, myths offer "archetypal dramas of the soul," so myth and archetype may be perceived as deriving from a similar domain if one takes "unconscious" as a noun (referring to a place). In ego psychology, the word "unconscious" becomes an adjective; in the psychology of the self, an adverb: "so and so acts unconsciously." The core of the complex is the archetype which, when translated into poetic language, comes forward in narrative, which is perceived as fiction rather than as myth. James Hillman says: "As truths are fictions of the rational, so fictions are truths of the imaginal." As collective individuals in contemporary society, we have often lost an individual inner connection. Mythic gods have, as in television, been denigrated into mere "soaps" or "sci-fi" tales of old, and society has idealized the concept of originality in prose fiction. Writers too often think of themselves as gods. Fiction encompasses myth when it refers to the narrator's depiction of his or her vision of the other world and this one. It is a conjunction of the descent or the imaginative and the world we live in. See Stevens's poem "Notes Toward a Supreme Fiction," in which the speaker says to a friend:

> Begin, ephebe, by perceiving the idea
> Of this invention, this invented world,
> The inconceivable idea of the sun.

In literature, the world has lost its center, and poets are holding on to the last remnant (language), hoping Coleridge's albatross won't land on their ship in the sea and leave them the last "Ancient Mariner." Often, poets speaking in the concrete have lost touch with the values expressed by Jung and Whitehead. Because Jung deals with myth and self from the perspective of the experiencing subject, he realizes the need to personify the images in the dream, to make them into narrative, to create a fiction, to actively imagine and hence to broaden and deepen the introjected experiences. This amplification is critical to move from having myth live you, to living your own myth.

8. Campbell, *Masks,* 6–7.

9. Harold Bloom in a chapter on Poetic Misprision explains a strong writer's misreading: "Poetic Influence—when it involves two strong, authentic poets—always proceeds by a misreading of the prior poet, an act of creative correction that is actually and necessarily a misinterpretation. The history of fruitful, poetic influence, which is to say the main tradition of Western poetry since the Renaissance, is a history of anxiety and self-saving caricature, of distortion, of perverse, wilful revisionism without which modern poetry as such could not exist" (*The Anxiety of Influence: A Theory of Poetry* [New York: Oxford University Press, (1973) 1981], 30).

10. Kathleen Raine, *The Lost Country* (London: Dolmen Press, 1971), 40.

11. Joseph Campbell, "The Historical Development of Mythology," in *Myth and Mythmaking,* ed. Henry Alexander Murray (New York: Braziller, 1960).

12. Iris Murdoch, *The Fire and the Sun: Why Plato Banished the Artists* (Oxford: Oxford University Press, 1977), 65.

13. Kathleen Raine, *The Land Unknown* (New York: George Braziller, 1975), 105.

14. Edwin Muir, *The Estate of Poetry,* with a foreword by Archibald MacLeish (London: Hogarth Press, 1962), 25.

15. Raine, *Land Unknown,* 203.

16. Raine, "The Poetic Symbol," 248.

17. Northrop Frye, *Creation and Recreation* (Toronto: University of Toronto Press, 1980), 54.

18. Ibid., 67.

19. Ibid.

20. Frye, *Creation and Recreation,* 5.

21. Harold Bloom, "The Breaking of Form," in *Deconstruction and Criticism* (New York: Seabury Press, 1979), 1.

Chapter 5

1. Paul Weiss, "Recollections of Alfred North Whitehead" (an interview with Lewis Ford), *Process Studies* 10/1–2 (Spring-Summer 1980): 44–56.

2. William James, *A Pluralistic Universe* (New York: Longmans, Green, & Co., 1916), 87.

3. Charles Olson, *Maximus Poems IV, V, VI* (London: Cape Goliard Press, 1968), 75 [79].

4. I have documented this aesthetic emphasis of Whitehead at length in "Whitehead: Redivivus? or Absconditus?" in *America and the Future of Theology,* ed. William A. Beardslee (Philadelphia: Westminster Press, 1967), 112–26.

5. David Bohm, *Wholeness and the Implicate Order* (Boston: Routledge & Kegan Paul, 1980), 48.

6. Ibid., 49.

7. Ibid., 64.

8. Ibid., 210.

9. Ibid., 212–13.

10. Gary Zukav, *The Dancing Wu Li Masters* (New York: William Morrow & Company, 1979), 56.

11. Ibid.

12. Ibid.

13. "Introduction," *The Portable Jung*, ed. Joseph Campbell (New York: Viking Press, 1971), xxxi.

14. Robert Bridges, *The Testament of Beauty* (New York: Oxford University Press, 1930), lines 6–7.

15. Claude Lévi-Strauss, *The Savage Mind* (Chicago: University of Chicago Press, 1968), 17, 21.

16. Philip Wheelwright, *Metaphor and Reality* (Bloomington: Indiana University Press, 1962), 70–71.

17. Ezra Pound, *Drafts and Fragments of Cantos CX–CXVII* (New York: New Directions, 1968), 11.

18. Wheelwright, *Metaphor and Reality*, 91.

19. D. T. Suzuki, *Zen and Japanese Culture*, Bollingen Series, vol. 64 (New York: Pantheon, 1959), 353.

20. Friedrich Nietzsche, *Beyond Good and Evil*, in *The Philosophy of Nietzsche*, The Modern Library (New York: Random House), no. 289.

21. Wallace Stevens, *The Collected Poems of Wallace Stevens* (New York: Alfred A. Knopf, 1954), 437.

22. Ibid., 383.

23. In Thomas Merton, *The Way of Chuang-Tzu* (New York: New Directions, 1965), 74.

24. Robert S. Avens, "Heidegger and Archetypal Psychology," *International Philosophical Quarterly* 22 (June 1982): 183–202, esp. 183.

25. Ezra Pound, *The Cantos of Ezra Pound* (New York: New Directions, 1948), Canto 74.

Chapter 7

1. David Bohm, *Wholeness and the Implicate Order* (Boston: Routledge & Kegan Paul, 1980), 63.

2. Karl Jaspers, *Truth and Symbol*, trans. Jean T. Wilde, William Kluback, and William Kimmel (New York: Twayne, 1959), 14, 35.

3. Ibid., 41.

4. Friedrich Nietzsche, *Thus Spake Zarathustra*, trans. Thomas Common, The Modern Library (New York: Boni & Liveright, n.d.), xii, 62.

Chapter 8

1. Susan Griffin, *Pornography and Silence* (New York: Harper & Row, 1981), 258.

2. Apuleius, *The Golden Ass*, trans. Adlington (New York: Collier, 1962), 145.

3. Griffin, *Pornography*, 258.

4. if from time to time I long to turn

like the Eleusinian hierophant
holding up a simple ear of grain

for return to the concrete and everlasting world
what in fact I keep choosing

are these words, these whispers, conversations
from which time after time the truth breaks moist and green.

Adrienne Rich, "Cartographies of Silence," *The Dream of a Common Language* (New York: W. W. Norton, 1978), 20.

5. Mary Daly, *Gyn/Ecology* (Boston: Beacon Press, 1978), 8. Such reversals have their truth within an unbroken culture of patriarchal consciousness—the sunlit daily hell for women; and so we revert to the image of pre- and post-patriarchal underworld goddess, suggested by, for example (1) her close friendship with old Hecate, with whom she and her mother had formed a triune Great Goddess; (2) the more ancient (albeit already patriarchal) Sumerian figure of Erishkegal, the underworld goddess, with whom Perera has done such suggestive psychological work. See Sylvia Brinton Perera, *Descent to the Goddess* (Toronto: Inner City Books, 1981). Thus her rape may display the violation of the underworld in its connection to the upperworld, performed by the invading and usurping latecomer, brother and shadow of heroic Zeus.

6. Catherine Keller, *From a Broken Web: Separation, Sexism, and Self* (Boston: Beacon Press, 1986).

7. See Cobb's *Is It Too Late? A Theology of Ecology* (New York: Bruce Publ. Co., 1972), *Christ in a Pluralistic Age* (Philadelphia: Westminster Press, 1975), *Process Theology as Political Theology* (Philadephia: Westminster Press, 1982), and (with Charles Birch) *The Liberation of Life: From the Cell to the Community* (Cambridge: Cambridge University Press, 1981).

8. Mary Daly, *Beyond God the Father* (Boston: Beacon Press, 1973).

9. C. J. Jung and C. Kerenyi, *Essays on a Science of Mythology* (Princeton: Princeton University Press, 1949), 138.

10. Martin P. Nilsson, *The Mycenean Origin of Greek Mythology* (Berkeley: University of California Press, 1972), 175.

11. Susan Griffin, *Rape and the Power of Consciousness* (New York: Harper & Row, 1979), 43.

12. Daly, *Gyn/Ecology*, 254.

13. Christine Downing, *The Goddess: Mythological Image of the Feminine* (New York: Crossroads, 1981), 45.

14. See Jung and Kerenyi, *Essays*, 137.

15. Naomi Goldenberg, *Changing of the Gods* (Boston: Beacon Press, 1979), 124.

16. Adrienne Rich, *Of Woman Born* (New York: W. W. Norton, 1976), 239.

17. Plato, *Cratylus 404d (The Collected Dialogues of Plato)*, ed. E. Hamilton and Huntington Cairns (Princeton, N.J.: Princeton University Press, 1961), 441.

18. Griffin, *Pornography*, 260.

Chapter 9

1. See Victor W. Turner, *The Ritual Process* (Chicago: Aldine Publishing Co., 1969) and *The Drums of Affliction* (New York: Oxford University Press, 1968).

2. Carol Gilligan, *In a Different Voice: Psychological Theory and Women's Development* (Cambridge, Mass.: Harvard University Press, 1982).

Chapter 10

1. I have discussed this issue in "Toward a Postpatriarchal Postmodernity," in *Spirituality and Society: Postmodern Visions*, ed. David Ray Griffin (Albany: State University of New York Press, 1988), 63–80.

2. See, for example, Charlene Spretnak, ed., *The Politics of Women's Spirituality: Essays on the Rise of Spiritual Power within the Feminist Movement* (Garden City, N.Y.: Anchor Press/Doubleday, 1982).

3. Nancy Chodorow, *The Reproduction of Mothering: Psychoanalysis and the Sociology of Gender* (Berkeley: University of California Press, 1978).

Chapter 11

1. Cf. E. R. Dodds, *The Greeks and the Irrational* (Los Angeles: University of California Press, 1951).

2. Jean-Jacques Rousseau, *On the Origin of Inequality*, Great Books of the Western World, vol. 38 (Chicago: Encylopaedia Britannica, 1952), 336.

3. Nikos Kazantzakis, *Report to Greco* (New York: Bantam Books, 1966), 180.

4. C. Lévi-Strauss, *Tristes Tropiques* (Paris, 1955), 284, 353. F. Engels, *Anti-Dühring* (Paris, 1950), 170–71.

5. Cited in my Translator's Introduction to Y. Takeuchi, *The Heart of Buddhism: In Search of the Timeless Spirit of Primitive Buddhism* (New York: Crossroads Publishing Co., 1983).

6. Thomas Berry, "Classical Western Spirituality and the American Experience," *Cross Currents* (Winter 1981–82): 388–99.

7. Berry, "Future Forms of Religious Experience," *Riverdale Papers 1* (New York: Riverdale Center for Religious Research, n.d. [privately circulated]).

8. Wilfred Cantwell Smith, *Towards a World Theology* (Philadelphia: Westminster Press, 1981), 18.

9. I do not mean to imply that important basic ethical principles might not be argued from the premises of Whitehead's thought, only that he himself did not deal systematically with the questions that moral theory considers foundational.

10. *SMW*, chap. 13. The ideas presented in this chapter are not directly linked by Whitehead to the issue of religion, which is treated in an earlier chapter by itself. Moreover, it is curious that he did not come back to many of these insights later, except in more abstract form.

11. Ernst Cassirer, *An Essay on Man* (New Haven, Conn.: Yale University Press, 1944), 44.

12. I have ruthlessly smothered this simple argument with documentation in an earlier, rambling, unpublished account of comparisons between Whitehead and Jung, "Whitehead and the Jungian Archetypes," available at the Center for Process Studies (abstract in *Process Studies* 8/2 [September 1978]: 137–38).

13. A confusion arises in the writings of Jung due to his failure always to honor the distinction he draws between consciousness and self-consciousness or ego-consciousness. Even though Hillman has proposed that we depose the empirical ego from its imperial post and restore it to the status of a commoner in a democracy of conscious centers—a sort of *nos*-consciousness in place of ego-consciousness—the distinction between conscious experience and the reflex into reason we are calling self-consciousness should not be dismissed. When Hillman writes, in a Jungian vein, that "direct experience . . . generates consciousness" (*SS* 166), he is pointing to this sort of tautology. The problem here is more than linguistic, however, because it slides readily into the naive realism that both were so firm to reject. There is a very definite sense in which the realm of conscious experience can be viewed itself as arational, and can thus be spoken of as an empirical ground; but this same claim cannot be made for self-consciousness. In their eagerness to disassociate themselves from ungrounded rationalism flying free of facts, Jung and Hillman appeal to "consciousness" at times when in fact they mean "self-consciousness" or the very rationality they are using to make the judgment.

14. Jung's comments appear in unpublished material.

15. "Psychic existence is the only category of existence of which we have *immediate* knowledge, since nothing can be known unless it first appears as a psychic image" (*CW* 11:769).

16. See, for example, *PR* chap. 5; *CW* 6:354–56, 387–88; *JT* 85–86.

17. Hillman seems to me to be confusing frames of reference, therefore, when he writes: *"For psychology, the ontological basis of polarity is ego-consciousness; the quality of the polarity, ranging from conflicting antithesis to harmonious cooperation, depends upon the psychological relation between ego-consciousness and the unconscious"* (*PP* 12). He has no intention of offering an argument on ontology, but only of forestalling one.

18. *CW* 6:398–401, 453; *AI* 295; *MT* 48–50. It seems to me that Jung distinguished intuition as an "irrational" function and feeling as a "rational" function for reasons not unlike our attempt here to delimit the rational frame in terms of the irrational workings of mind. Although insisting on the irrationality of perception independent of sense-perception, he recognized the danger of inflation this carries when the ego is cut off from all critical, rational controls; and in spite of the common bias toward feeling as irrational, he wished to insist on the basic similarities it shows to the functions of thought that we normally associate with rationality (*CW* 6:600). My shift of terminology indicates only a shift of emphasis, not a basic disagreement. Likewise, Whitehead speaks of "feeling" as including that "positive prehension" by which all actual entities establish a bond with the items of the universe as subjects feeling their objects, whether this take place in the narrow world of conscious cognition or in the broader world of unconscious relations, including of course the unconscious of human experience. When he notes a sense in which this notion of feeling is an extension of Bergson's notion of "intuition" (*PR* 41), Whitehead is not, I think, basically aiming at anything different—

at least not on the level of rationality—from what I am aiming at in referring to intuition and feeling as irrational.

19. See Jung's letter to W. Corti dated 30 April 1929.

20. Cited in W. Barrett, *The Illusion of Technique* (New York: Doubleday, 1979), 17.

21. We owe the isolation of this genre of the *double-entendre* as the key to psychotherapy's hermeneutic to Paul Ricoeur, who introduced it in his 1961 Terry Lectures, later expanded in book form (*Freud and Philosophy* [New Haven, Conn.: Yale University Press, 1970]). Hillman refers to it in his own Terry Lectures (*RVP* 152–53).

22. *RVP* chap. 2. Originally Hillman used the term "pathological" in its accepted sense of a self-poisoning of the psyche which it was the task of therapy to supply with antidotes (*I* 32), only later developing the richer connotations we are alluding to here. He speaks of the deviations of abnormal psychology as "irrationalities" grounded in the complex and comprising a "creative principle" working jointly though in tension with reason. A quotation from E. R. Dodds on Plato's notion of an "inferior soul" reconfirms his definition of the irrational in terms of its relationship to the establishment of norms for rationality (*FG* 14–15, 29).

23. "Not life but *light is the healer's true God*. The healer represents consciousness" (*SS* 121). The apparent esotericism of the analytic experience and its independence of outside evaluation (*SS* chap. 11) make this *more* important, not less.

24. What Whitehead has said of Plato, that he had written up most of the heresies of his own doctrines (*AI* 105), could as well be applied to Jung and Hillman's departures from him, nearly all of which can be documented with ideas expressed but not developed by Jung himself.

25. When Hillman speaks of the transpersonal, one should not think merely of helpful, healing, good forces, but should always keep in mind the qualification he implies when he asks: "Are there not gradations of transcendence, so that all that lies on the other side of my ego's borders, all that transcends it, need not be called ultimate and divine?" (*I* 80). The *numinosum* remains amoral. Moreover, when Hillman states that each archetype or God "works upon the feeling function in general by both compelling it and inhibiting it with awe of the numinous," he is clearly confirming his aversion to locating such experience merely within the "rational" function of feeling (*JT* 127).

26. It is not only the one who plays the role of therapist in an analytical setting but all of us who qualify here as "psychologists." See n. 29 below.

27. I am playing here on an idea that, to my knowledge, was first expressed by George Wald in his introduction to the 25th edition of J. Henderson's *The Fitness of the Environment* (New York: Macmillan, 1958): "It would be a poor thing to be an atom in a universe without physicists. And physicists are made of atoms. A physicist is the atom's way of knowing about atoms." See Hillman's remark about the *lumen naturae* as the individual's "giving back to the Gods what it has stolen from them" (*PP* 49).

28. Here Hillman speaks of an "upward pull" of spirit and a "downward pull" of matter lying behind our approach to reason as speculation and measurement respectively, each of them a sign of an "archetypal orientation" from the viewpoint of the imagining soul that stands midway between them (*LE* 134–35). His longtime preoccupation with the myth of the *puer aeternus* as the image that opens us to an awareness

of the "transcendent spiritual powers" of the psyche attests further to the reverence Hillman pays reason (see *PP* 23).

29. Note the qualifications introduced by Hillman: "Therapy, or analysis, is not only something that analysts do to patients; it is a process that goes on intermittently in our individual soul-searching, our attempts at understanding our complexities, the critical attacks, prescriptions, and encouragements that we give ourselves." And again: "Not just any ideas are passionately important, not just any ideas are worthwhile to the soul; the kind for which I make this claim are psychological ideas, for it is by means of them that the psyche reflects upon itself and furthers soul-making" (*RVP* xii, 117). Finally: "*The gift of meaning is not the result of interpretation. . . .* The analyst brings meaning out in two ways: by laying bare and cutting through to essentials, and by swelling events into pregnancy through amplification" (*SS* 148–49).

30. This seems to be behind Hillman's inclusion of polytheism, pathologizing, and the "images of the soul in the soul" among the "fundamental qualities of soul-making in distinction to spirit disciplines" (*SS* 69).

31. I include here Hillman's description of Jung's psychic functions as "archetypally given" and therefore "necessary and sufficient" (*JT* 76), a clear confusion of frames of expression.

Chapter 14

1. "De la certitude mythique," *Cadmos* 17/18 (Geneva, 1982): 29–51.

2. The proceedings have been published as *Science et Conscience* (Paris: Ed. Stock et France Culture, 1980).

3. See Henry Corbin's papers in English translation in *S 1972, S 1975,* and *S 1980*; also his *Temple and Contemplation* (London: KPI Ltd., 1986); *Creative Imagination in the Sufism of Ibn Arabi* (Princeton: Princeton University Press, 1969); and his *Avicenna and the Visionary Recital,* 2nd ed. (Dallas: Spring Publications, 1980).

4. See my "Alchemical Blue and the *Unio Mentalis*" in *Sulfur* 1 (Pasadena: California Institute of Technology, 1981): 33–50.

5. See Gilbert Durand, "The Image of Man in Western Occult Tradition," *S 1976:* 81–103, for an excellent account of the "metaphysical catastrophes" in the history of Western thought; also, Henry Corbin, "The *Imago Templi* and Secular Norms," *S 1975:* 163–85.

6. Stephen C. Pepper, *World Hypotheses: A Study in Evidence* (Berkeley: University of California Press, 1942). I am told that Pepper later expressed a more favorable view of Whitehead in "Whitehead's 'Actual Occasion'," *Tulane Studies in Philosophy* 10 (1961): 71–88.

7. See my *On Paranoia,* Eranos Lecture Series No. 8 (Dallas: Spring Publications, 1988).

8. See *RVP* chap. 2, "Pathologizing." Rather than grounding pathologizing in literalism (which only returns blame for the pathological to the ego who has fallen away from the metaphorical vision), we do better to ground the literal in the more fundamental need of the soul for pathologizing. Then we can say the soul itself demands literalisms, so that it can suffer delusions, projections (and other defense mechanisms), and be-

haviors that seem to be sheerly what they are—without depth, without echo. It is the soul's need to undergo pathologizing, by which it is opened beyond its identification with subjectivity and forced to see through, that necessitates literalism and its advocate, the heroic ego. The ego derives from pathologizing; it is a product of psychopathology and necessary for it. See David L. Miller, "On Literalism," *S 1984*: 151–61.

9. For an elaboration of these ideas about myth, see *RVP* chap. 1, "Personifying," and chap. 3, "An Excursion on Fictions"; see also *DU* 191–202.

10. On the metaphysical importance of *placing*, see Edward S. Casey, "Getting Placed, Soul in Space," *S 1982*: 1–25.

11. For a good introductory collection of passages demonstrating Bachelard's method and the nature of the four elemental realms, see Colette Gaudin, ed., *On Poetic Imagination and Reverie* (1971; Dallas: Spring Publications, 1987).

12. See my "On the Necessity of Abnormal Psychology," in *Eranos Yearbook* 43—1974 (Leiden: E. J. Brill, 1977).

13. Immediately following the "pattern of animal figures," as Cornford observes, "Plato interrupts his argument to reopen the question, whether there is more than one 'cosmos'. . . . This passage (55D) is extremely puzzling. There is nothing in the previous context to suggest a plurality of worlds" (F. M. Cornford, *Plato's Cosmology* [London: Routledge, 1937], 219–20). Puzzling as it may be to Cornford, the pluralistic (polytheistic) possibility is evidently suggested to Plato by the pattern of animal figures.

14. See Patricia Cox, "Origin and the Bestial Soul: A Poetics of Nature," *Vigilia Christianae* 36 (1982): 115–40. In an amazing passage defining the soul, Whitehead writes: "Each animal body is . . . a living society which may include in itself a dominant 'personal' society of occasions. This 'personal' society is composed of occasions enjoying the individual experiences of the animals. It is the soul of man" (*AI* 211).

15. See my "The Animal Kingdom in the Human Dream," *Eranos Yearbook* 51— 1982. See also Whitehead's statement: "There are thus millions upon millions of centres of life in each animal body. So what needs to be explained is not dissociation of personality but unifying control" (*PR* 108).

16. The reference is to George Santayana, *Scepticism and Animal Faith*.

17. *ET*; *TH*; and "The Animal Kingdom in the Human Dream."

18. Corbin, *Creative Imagination in the Sufism of Ibn Arabi*, 244 & note; *Man of Light in Iranian Sufism* (Boulder and London: Shambhala, 1978), 112–13.

19. The lecture, which is published in *S 1982*: 71–94, attempted to redesign psychology from a Ficinian Renaissance perspective.

20. "Nature Alive" is the title of chap. 8 of Whitehead's *MT*.

21. See J. J. Gibson, *The Ecological Approach to Visual Perception* (Boston: Houghton Mifflin, 1979); *The Senses Considered as Perceptual Systems* (Boston: Houghton Mifflin, 1966); C. F. Michaels and Claudia Carello, *Direct Perception* (Englewood Cliffs, N.J.: Prentice-Hall, 1981); Charles Boer and Peter Kugler, "Archetypal Psychology Is Mythical Realism," in *S 1977*: 131–52; R. E. Shaw and J. Bransford, eds., *Perceiving, Acting and Knowing: Toward an Ecological Psychology* (Hillsdale, N.J.: Erlbaum, 1977).

22. See Part 3 of my *HF*.

23. ". . . *ta' wil*, which etymologically means 'to bring back' the data to their origin, to their archetype, to their donor" (Henry Corbin, *Spiritual Body and Celestial*

Earth [Princeton: Princeton University Press, 1977], 53). Cf. Corbin, *Avicenna and the Visionary Recital*, on *"Ta' wil* as Exegesis of the Soul." For a *psychological* understanding of *epistrophē (ta' wil)* in Corbin and Neoplatonism, see my *DU* 4 and chap. 2.

24. "By substituting a dramaturgy for cosmology, the recitals guarantee the genuineness of the universe; it is veritably the place of a personally lived adventure" (Corbin, *Avicenna and the Visionary Recital,* 4).

25. See Russell Lockhart, *Words as Eggs* (Dallas: Spring Publications, 1982).

26. See H. Corbin, "Nécessité de l'angélologie," in *L'Ange et l'homme* (Paris: Albin Michel, 1978), 15–79. "Words are angels" refers not only to the Greek meaning of *angelos,* "message-bearer"; the assumption expressed above (224–25) that "all things are inherently intelligible" requires an imaginal ground of intelligence that communicates through things, making the world a message-bearing world or an angelic cosmology.

27. See David L. Miller, "Rhythms of Silenos in a Poetics of Christ," *Eranos Jahrbuch* 47—1978: 67–121, on *pleroma. full. drunkenness.*

Chapter 15

1. For further treatment of the cosmic/cosmetic in the context of archetypal psychology, see the excellent essay by Catherine Keller herein.

2. Hillman's first book is entitled *Emotion: A Comprehensive Phenomenology of Theories and Their Meanings for Therapy* (London: Routledge & Kegan Paul, 1960).

3. See Whitehead, *PR* 64: "The animal body is nothing more than the most intimately relevant part of the antecedent settled world." See also Hillman's "The Animal Kingdom in the Human Dream," *Eranos Yearbook* 51—1982.

4. "When the whole and the parts are seen at once, as mutually producing and explaining each other, as unity in multaity, there results shapeliness—*forma formosa"* (Samuel Taylor Coleridge, *Letters, Conversations and Recollections* [London: Farrah, 1964], 106).

5. It is of interest that F. S. C. Northrop's idea of an "aesthetic continuum" expressly combines the two directions of thought; see his *The Meeting of East and West* (Woodbridge, Conn.: Oxbow Press, 1979).

6. See especially "Psychology: Monotheistic or Polytheistic?" *S 1971*: 193–208; reprinted in expanded form in David L. Miller, *The New Polytheism* (Dallas: Spring Publications, 1981).

7. "A physical cosmology that runs by chance, or by laws, has no necessity for the individualized experience" (227).

8. Though not *"mere* appearances," which are precisely indeterminate in status.

9. Martin Heidegger, *Being and Time,* trans. John Macquarrie and Edward Robinson (New York: Harper, 1962), 51.

Chapter 16

1. I have told this story of the two stages of the modern worldview at greater length, and with documentation, in the introduction to *The Reenchantment of Science: Postmodern Proposals* (Albany: State University of New York Press, 1988), and in

several of the chapters, from various perspectives, in *God and Religion in the Postmodern World* (Albany: State University of New York Press, 1989).

2. See Frank Manuel, *A Portrait of Isaac Newton* (Cambridge, Mass.: The Belknap Press of Harvard University Press, 1968), 78–83.

INDEX

Page numbers in italics indicate passages that contain definitions or that are otherwise especially significant.